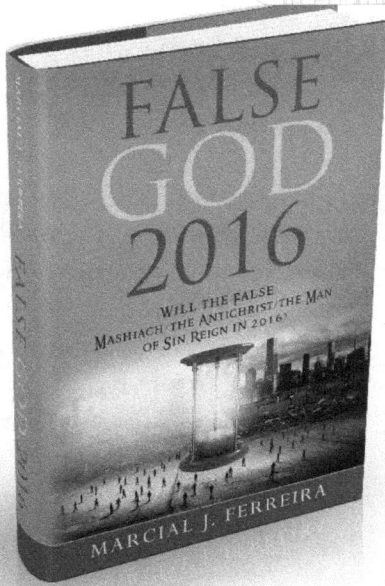

FALSE
GOD
2016

WILL THE FALSE
MASHIACH, THE ANTICHRIST/THE MAN
OF SIN REIGN IN 2016?

MARCIAL J. FERREIRA

This is a complete true story and a revelation for a world in need of truth—evidence has been found.

# CONTENTS

# THE OMEGA
## THE BOOK: A REVELATION, A STORY, AND THE TRUTH

# Acknowledgements

The list is endless, but I'd like to begin with the homeless and those suffering much throughout the whole world; these men, women, and children fed me daily. And without them, this work would have been much more difficult—perhaps impossible. Also, I wish to acknowledge the following people for their true companionship, relentless effort, and amazing inspiration throughout this marathon:

- ❖ My divinely-given wife, Bianka Ferreira; my sons, Brandon and Jonah Ferreira
- ❖ My mother and father, Pura Amarilys Peña and Marcial Eloy Ferreira
- ❖ My brothers: Miguel Ferreira, Angel Ferreira, Alfred Ureña, and Marcos Galvis
- ❖ My entire family in The Dominican Republic and in Puerto Rico
- ❖ My mother-in-law, Mrs. Juana Acosta (*Doña Juana*) and her family
- ❖ Dodanin Castillo and family
- ❖ Ana (*Yosi*) Taveras and family
- ❖ Eddy and Liliana Moreno and family
- ❖ Coach Noah Wilbanks, from *Fellowship of Christian Athletes*
- ❖ Coach David Silveira and family
- ❖ Coach Pete Monzon
- ❖ Coach Jerry Beverly from *The University of Miami*
- ❖ Coach/Pastor/Professor Andre Mooney and family—from *Grand Canyon University*
- ❖ Coach Guido Trinidad from *Peak360 Fitness*.
- ❖ Bryan S. Vasquez from *The University of Miami* IT Dept.
- ❖ Pastor John Perdew and family, and the people from *Point of Grace Church* in Pembroke Park, Florida

- ❖ Pastor Bob Hamilton and *Community Bible Church* in Bottineau, North Dakota
- ❖ Brother Jason Raymond Pollidore
- ❖ Roderick C. Meredith and the people of *Tomorrowsworld.org*
- ❖ Tyrone and Synthia McBride from Miami, Florida
- ❖ Randy Velazquez, Jesse Maldonado, and the people of *Cusano's Bakery*
- ❖ Authors: David Montaigne, Jonathan Cahn, and Thomas Horn
- ❖ Youtube Channels: Jason A, DAHBOO77, David Vose, Renee M, FreedomFighter2127, The Alex Jones Channel, Professor Doom 1, Ron Paul Liberty Report...
- ❖ Ardell Lund and family from Bottineau, North Dakota
- ❖ Lazaro (Lazarito) Istiraneopulus and the staff of *Almavision Radio*
- ❖ Rev. Deborah J. Burger-Peery from Bottineau, North Dakota
- ❖ Tim and Patricia Bryantt from Bottineau, North Dakota
- ❖ Pablo F. Boza and Karina E. Perez from Miami, Florida
- ❖ Dr. Gary Albrightson, my English college professor
- ❖ The wonderful people from the town of Bottineau in North Dakota
- ❖ Dr. Ken Grosz and the wonderful people of *The Dakota College at Bottineau*...

If I forgot your name, please forgive me. Above all, I thank You, Yeshua Ha Mashiach, for carrying me and all of us in this journey.

*What good fortune for governments that the people do not think.*
—Adolf Hitler

*If you tell a big enough lie and tell it frequently enough, it will be believed.*
—Adolf Hitler

*My people are destroyed for lack of knowledge.*
—Hosea 4:6, NKJV

*For nothing is secret that will not be revealed, nor anything hidden that will not be known and come to light.*
—Luke 8:17, NKJV

*But concerning the times and the seasons, brethren, you have no need that I should write to you. For you yourselves know perfectly that the day of the Lord so comes as a thief in the night.* **For when they say, "Peace and safety!"** *then sudden destruction comes upon them, as labor pains upon a pregnant woman. And they shall not escape.* **But you, brethren, are not in darkness, so that this Day should overtake you as a thief.**—1 Thessalonians 5:1-4, NKJV

*Whatever we once were—we are no longer a Christian Nation...*
—Barack Hussein Obama

*So teach us to number our days,*
*That we may gain a heart of wisdom.*
—Psalm 90:12, NKJV

*How much better it is to get wisdom than gold!*
*And to get understanding is to be chosen above silver.*
—King Solomon, the wealthiest man to ever live,
(Proverbs 16:16, NASB)

*And Jesus came up and spoke to them, saying, "All authority has been*
*given to Me in heaven and on earth.*
—The Alpha and the Omega, The Savior of the world, after His
resurrection, (Matthew 28:18, NASB)

**My sheep hear My voice**, *and I know them, and they follow Me.*
—The King of the Jews, (John 10:27, NKJV)

Brandon and Jonah, run my sons as the True Shepherd writes. Bianka, my divinely given wife, let the music of the Spirit of Truth define you. For life is a book written by the distinctive and unidentified blood of your hearts.

# Introduction

*The most horrific era that mankind will ever experience is about to begin.*

*The revelations you are about to read may not make any sense in the beginning, but when you finish this journey, you will see the truth, the biblical evidence, and much more. You will have an idea of why so much had to be revealed, and why I finally decided to lay my life down for my friends, my loved ones, and for you.*

The visions continued daily, and I knew I was held responsible for them. I had to speak; I had to blow the trumpets somehow. It all birthed when The Voice began to speak to me. Then, most things shifted when it led me to overwhelming signs—supernatural signs. These signs and visions were geographical, mathematical, linguistic, scientific, spiritual... the categories remained limitless. I struggled daily because I felt the pressure intensifying as time passed. I was trained to change multiple habits rapidly, and it was hard to keep up, but not impossible through The Voice. I also learned that this message was much more essential than anything else in the entire world because of one factor: time. But there was a problem: I had to share my personal life experiences that jeopardize my future and the future of many, including, the future of my very own family. "This is too much! I can't do it!" I often complained to The Voice of Truth. But He consistently responded, "Millions of lives; millions of lives, My son." Still, I fought back with all my strength, but this only took me so far. "How about we make this a fiction book and hold the meaning of the story?" I asked continuously. "No, My son, you write as I speak," He responded. For months, I struggled with this and didn't know how to overcome it. Slowly, I realized that this was no longer about me, and instead, about millions of deceived lives living in a soon-to-decease Era. "Why me?" I asked consistently, but silence just hovered around the surface during the beginning stages. "Just allow me to share the facts, but not my story?" I always complained, attempting to negotiate with The King of the Jews. "Millions of lives at stake; the children, the women, the men—My son," He responded regularly. And I just desired to live a normal life with my precious wife and lovely kids. Every single day the visions came without permission, and I could not escape. I couldn't run fast enough or jump high enough—the visions remained, and The Voice continuously whispered.

One day, I fought back spiritually and said, "I'll move; I'll speak. Ok, I'll blow the trumpets wherever, however, and whenever—even in Israel or at the White House. But I need evidence, the whole truth, the real deal, and not just these visions that most won't comprehend or even believe."

"Begin with the visions, My son, and I'll meet you with the evidence in due season."

"The visions?"

"Yes, write about the journey you had to experience to find the evidence, and then reveal the truth as I show you in My Word."

"What I had to go through?"

"Yes, and do not fear!"

"But this is risking it all and many will persecute me!"

[18] "If the world hates you, you know that it hated Me before *it hated you*. [19] If you were of the world, the world would love its own. Yet because you are not of the world, but I chose you out of the world, therefore the world hates you. [20] Remember the word that I said to you, 'A servant is not greater than his master.' If they persecuted Me, they will also persecute you. If they kept My word, they will keep yours also. [21] But all these things they will do to you for My name's sake, because they do not know Him who sent Me. [22] If I had not come and spoken to them, they would have no sin, but now they have no excuse for their sin. [23] He who hates Me hates My Father also. [24] If I had not done among them the works which no one else did, they would have no sin; but now they have seen and also hated both Me and My Father. [25] But *this*

*happened* that the word might be fulfilled which is written in their law, 'They hated Me without a cause'" (John 15:18-25).

"Will they really persecute me?"

"Yes, and do not fear; for I AM is with you."

"But Thomas Horn wrote about this in *Zenith 2016* and David Montaigne wrote about this in *Antichrist 2016*. Why should I write my story?"

"Because it is a story and not just evidence: this is the difference. Your story began to unfold before you were born, you received a glimpse of it when you were 12 years of age, you received the revelation and understood when you were in college in 2010..."

"What's this all about?"

"Only two books have been published about the rise of a false god in 2016—the rise of the Antichrist."

"And?"

"And not one book has been written about this topic in the way you will reveal this to the world."

"And?"

"Don't you think that My little children deserve to know the truth about the most horrific era that mankind will ever experience?"

"I don't know; You tell me."

"You're running out of time, My son."

"Is this You?"

"Keep listening.

"Your story and what I have revealed to you will help validate, even more, the truth found in *Zenith 2016* by Thomas Horn, in *Antichrist 2016* by David Montaigne, in *The Harbinger* and in *The Mystery of the Shemitah* by Jonathan Cahn, and most importantly, in My Word—in the Bible."

"How's this?"

"It will reveal what was happening and what The Spirit of Truth was doing many years before these books were published, and how all things are pointing to late 2015, 2016 and beyond."

"But how?"

"Your story is the answer."

"But this isn't about me?"

"You are correct, but it is about the countless lives that remain waiting for your story and the Truth."

"Do You really want me to do this?"

"Do not fear, My son."

"No fiction?"

"Truth shall spring out of the earth,

And righteousness shall look down from heaven" (Psalm 85:11-13).

"Truth?"

"Yes, and tell the reader to be patient; they will comprehend in the end once the dots are connected."

I struggled much because of this message you are about to read. I still don't fully comprehend why I had to be the chosen one to live this and now reveal it. I continuously asked, "Why not share this in another method?" but The Voice never changed the message and its directions.

Be careful of what you ask because you may receive just that and much more.

The Voice of Truth begins...

# THE

# ALPHA

*A TRUE STORY*

*AND*

*REVELATIONS*

# Chapter 1
# *The Voice of Truth*

## First True Story

I was beginning to hear something as the sun set and the moon shouted. And as "the voice" was becoming clearer and clearer—my bedtime drew nearer and nearer. The voice was speaking and speaking, and it seemed not to desire to depart from me. It was growing and growing like a virus inside of me. It was beginning to catch my attention, simultaneously, concerning me because I was extremely disciplined about my two-a-day training. The football season was approaching soon, and I fully comprehended that I had to rest enough to recover from the procedures I put my mind, body, and soul through—each day. I truly needed to rest. I was tired.

As I followed along through a dialog with "the voice," I began to ask the voice to leave my presence, politely. I noticed that my efforts were not working as it usually worked when I trained: I wasn't taken to the place of my heart's desires—my bed. I asked once! Twice! But the voice remained consistent, and instead of leaving, it grew intensely inside of me—desperately. It was like a world-boxing-championship match happening inside of me. The voice and my mind were the fighters, and my body was the boxing ring. As this dilemma continued, the ropes of my body began to wear and tear, rapidly. I was running out of resistance from all the bouncing-pushing-punching-spitting and jabbing happening in this ring. It was starting to feel like one of these warriors had broken his left wrist from endless jabbing to its opponent. At this point, even the boxing ring longed desperately for the final bell, the referee decided to take a nap:

"Let us go home! It's over! It's over! No more!" said the audience in agony.

"Ok! Ok! Just tell me what to do, and I'll do it!" said the wounded warrior.

All of the sudden, the boxing ring received strength from an unknown source, the wounded warrior encountered a healing miracle, and the 'undefeated World-Champ of all times' said, "It is 'I.'"

"What do you mean—'I'?" I thought.

"It is 'I AM,'" the World's Champ said.

And, as I began to think about the meaning of 'I AM,' suddenly, the remarkable sound encountered my presence:

"It is 'I,' The Voice of Truth."

Rapidly, I noticed a complete spiritual alteration and preparation approaching me—just as if I was being prepared to fight for a world championship against Rocky Marciano in his prime.

"Death or Jail time," I heard suddenly—a message from the same voice. I paused. And somehow—in the midst of my fatigue—I automatically became focused in the most incredible and unrecognizable tranquil way. I waited and waited...and waited. I was nervous. Anxious! A moment passes...

Unexpectedly:

"Go to your brother's residence, now! Or someone will die or go to jail tonight," once again, The Voice of Truth whispered.

"Death or jail, death or jail," kept calling and it continued—on and on and on..."Death or jail," the only words my set of ears firmly acknowledged.

It was almost 11pm, and I was supposed to be in bed by 9pm. I was ready to go to bed, but at the same time, I understood that this message was life-changing—perhaps life-saving—and that I could not just fall asleep. Getting up by 4:15am to train was no longer a possibility.

"Are you ok?" I text messaged, my brother, "Is everything alright?"

"I'm ok," he replied.

"Are you sure? Are you really sure? Please tell me the truth. Is everything ok between you and Natalie?"

"I'm fine," he said. But through The Voice of Truth I knew he was discouraged.

"Are you sure?" I asked desperately.

"Sure, everything's fine. I just...I just..."

"I just what? What happened?"

"No...no, I'm alright."

"It doesn't appear to be," I continued, "please be honest and don't hold back a thing."

"I'll call you."

"No...no, wait," still through text messaging, I replied, "please tell me what's going on?"

Then, I called him and we conversed for some time, but the conversation ceased, suddenly, when he responded, "I have to let you go," rapidly.

I texted him biblical scriptures. I attempted to guide him along the best path. Desperately, I tried to explain to him my recent experience with The Voice of Truth. And he seemed to be reading my text messages because he was also responding. By then I was truly sensing that this was far more important than just getting my training done, in time, before sunrise. Rapidly, I began to realize that someone might truly die or go to jail as "The Voice" had confirmed. And, as I sat there thinking, once again, The Voice came to me and stated, explicitly:

"He will not reply to this last text message that you just sent to him— leave now! Now!" once again, "now! Now!" I heard intensely in my heart. And the word 'now' just kept on trembling through my whole being.

"I have to leave rapidly," I immediately told my girlfriend, Bianka, who lived with me. I could tell she thought I was losing it by her facial expressions, but I also felt she comprehended somehow. So, I ran to my uninsured car, I quickly opened up the front gate of my mother's house—saying goodbye to Champ, my red nose pit-bull—and I drove off quickly.

By then, I was concerned intensely and hearing The Voice as I was driving, simultaneously. I was speeding, and thank God it was nighttime, and there was not much traffic. I was having difficulties controlling my emotions... I headed northbound on US1 and as I approached the traffic light:

"It will turn red, but you must take it," The Voice said.

"No! You will break the law!" responded my finite human instincts—along with all the evil forces working behind the scenes.

"If you do not take this light immediately, someone will indeed break the law," The Voice of Truth spoke even louder.

Of course, at that point I was convinced that it was certainly a life or death scenario; therefore, in a split of a second, I took the red light.

"Death or jail, death or jail...death or jail...," it's all I could hear as I drove my uninsured NAS-CAR. And suddenly, I was on the Florida's Turnpike trying to speed faster than the evil spirits working behind the scenes. I remembered that during prior nights, on my way home—as I drove by this same highway exit that leads me to my brother's apartment—the highway exit was under construction. And I quickly thought about all the alternatives.

"Exit before or after your brother's exit," my mind whispered. But The Voice of Truth said, "Do not exit before or after." And it continued, "For I have opened the highway exit that leads you directly to your brother's apartment," and more intensely, "Hurry! Hurry!"

And I listened and flew through the turnpike, no longer sleepy or tired, but instead wide awake—as if I was seeing The True Messiah face-to-face. I was getting closer and closer to the exit. As I glanced from few hundred yards away, I received a confirmation from my very own view. The highway exit was wide open—no longer under construction as it had been for the past few weeks. I exited, mentally prepared to take another red light, but this time, The Voice of Truth allowed me to be an honored citizen by following man-made laws—the green light was His choice. I was almost there. I could smell his apartment and the environment in it, somehow. I could almost taste the "jail time" or even the "blood of death." Thank God—I arrived... I was there. Finally. Well, not really. I searched for my brother's car, but could not seem to find it.

"You see, you're going crazy...no one is here," evil forces dictated. But the Voice of Truth immediately said, "Jump out! Hurry! Run! You're running out of time!" So I jumped out of my car and ran toward the main gate that leads me to his apartment. I broke the Olympic long-jump record of all times when I jumped toward the main gate to open it. And as I landed at the gate and opened it, in that very instant, I saw, in the natural and unnatural realms, the definition of 'jail time or death'—when I saw my brother being pushed away by his girlfriend as she pointed a gun at him; when I saw her—in The Spirit of Truth— being pushed away by my brother even before it happened. They both froze, of course; who wouldn't?—when they heard the sound of the main gate. It probably sounded like the gates of heaven. Who knows?

Soon after, they were both staring at me as if I was God-in-the-flesh visiting them, and a never before experienced silence hovered over the divinely protected surface as this human triangle stood there staring at each corner. I saw everything unfold: she shooting him, or he snatching the gun away from her. Thankfully, the reality was dissimilar. And the presence of God was palpable, even to them, as we stood in awe of this life-changing, life-filling, life-saving moment. I couldn't utter a word; my brother and his girlfriend remained speechless as well. Suddenly, I saw my brother walking toward me— almost as if we were both directed by the same Voice of Truth. And we mutually walked away from his apartment toward the parking lot— speechless as we walked for a moment. We were trying to initiate a conversation, but we both remained in a silent state of confusion. The Voice directed us to his car, he carried the keys for some reason, and we sat in it, and we poured out our hearts to each other. I felt his disappointment, in his relationship, just by the look in his eyes as he spoke to me—I recognized his look, clearly. His appearance and avalanche of emotions, alone, were enough for me to know the main reason for this, for what almost led them both, for what could have been a 'death or jail time scenario.'

"She is being unfaithful to me," in the midst of an outpouring of emotions he said, "I know! I know!" speaking through pain he continued.

I thought, "I know. I know," just by the look in his eyes. I truly wanted to share my personal experiences with him, but I was still recovering from my low blow. I wanted to share with him how I felt about his delicate situation, wholeheartedly, but I was not courageous enough to do it. I wanted to tell him: "I know, I've been through this before, with my very own wife, and this is how I'm dealing with it." But I was embarrassed to think even of the idea.

It was not the appointed time for me to unfold this truth. It just wasn't the time for me to share how I had been a victim, and how I had also committed adultery many times—before I truly knew The Voice of Truth. But at least, in the midst of the storm, I delicately shared with him my recent personal life experiences—how this moment came to be. How it could have been much easier just to stay at home and to have chosen to enjoy my sleep. I shared with him how it all began with the Voice of Truth—how this Voice continued to escalate inside of me, and how it directed me throughout this whole path. And how it asked me to drive like a NASCAR driver, to take a red light, to long-jump Olympic style, to run like a low testosterone athlete, and to listen to each and every single mandate—just to ensure that I would arrive at his apartment on time. My brother, eagerly listened, a moment of silence encountered us, and we began to cry like little children. We hugged and hugged each other some more, and he said to me:

"In that instant, when you opened the main gate, when I heard the sound of the gate, in that very instant, I was going to attempt to take the gun away from Natalie." And he continued as tears dropped by bunches, "But you came, you interfered. I don't know what it was, but I was stopped by the 'sound of the gate.'"

"Like the Gates of Heaven?"

"Yeah, yeah...something like that."

"Wow!"

We hugged each other, more and more, as all kinds of emotions flowed through us, filling us both. Unpredictably, I began to feel The Voice of Truth once again. I felt the pressure, the weight:

"Tell him how much I love him," I heard it again, "tell him how much I've always loved him."

So I was filled with The Spirit of Truth: The Spirit of the Living God came upon me, and it used me as a conduit to share God's unconditional love. And I proclaimed to him something like, "Brother do you know that God loves you? Do you know that He sent me tonight—one of His servants—to save you or your girlfriend from jail time, death, or a lifetime-culture of lamentations? I am not God, brother, but it was God's Spirit who kept me awake because He knew this moment prior to its existence."

We both began to cry in an undreamed-of way: "Don't stop!" The Spirit of God told me. "Keep on! Tell him! Tell him!"

"Brother, look around you," I said, "come on, get out of the car. I need you to take a close look at these apartment buildings surrounding you—your neighbors." And I continued speaking:

"Unfortunately, they are too many individuals borrowing beds from married women or men in this very instant—in their hearts, they believe that they are having fun. Their promiscuity may seem like an adventure for a moment, and the truth is that it is 'almost' just that: an 'evil' adventure for a brief moment. Just as this Voice of Truth guided me along this path, at this time of the night, to interfere in this life-changing moment, also, The Voice of Lies whispered to your girlfriend, leading her to follow a path of self-destruction—when she decided to engage in this satanic adventure. You and I both know that the same Voice of Lies has led you and me, and the whole world, to follow a perishable path.

"Just read here," I said as I flipped through the pages of The Bible:

"So the great dragon was cast out, that serpent of old, called the Devil and Satan, who deceives the whole world; he was cast to the earth, and his angels were cast out with him" (Revelation 12:9).

"Is this true?"

"The whole world, brother."

By then, I could see his brokenness, his desire to be loved, his in-the-happening change of character, and for some reason, I was completely broken and touched by this unbelievable phenomenon. At this point, I was overwhelmed by his unusual unpretentiousness. And without even thinking about it, my lips uttered:

"Bother, God loves you. He loves Natalie, He loves me, He loves those sharing their beds in this very moment...He loves those you are probably beginning to hate by now, and He loves His Perfect Creation—us, Mankind—His children! He even created us in His image!

"Just read here:

"So God created man in His own image; in the image of God He created him; male and female He created them" (Genesis 1:27).

"That means that He created you and me in His image."

"How can this be?"

"How can we not praise Him for this; for what He just did?"

I was feeling his readiness to receive The Voice of Truth. I could almost see him screaming loudly, "Give me this God of Love! Please give me this God of truth!" But I did not allow him to say anything—it was not God's perfect time yet. Instead, I continued and shared with him the message of love from The One that is Love.

"Just read here," I said as I skimmed through the Bible.

"He who does not love does not know God, for God is love" (1 John 4:8).

"But how can this be?" my brother asked.

"He loves you," I replied passionately and continued, "and this Voice of Truth that used me to deliver you and your girlfriend from a potential disaster—wants to speak to you directly and personally. The Voice of God longs to share real intimate moments with you and Natalie, with those comforting themselves with temporary satisfaction in borrowed beds all over these apartment buildings."

"How can this be?" he asked searching for truth. And holding on to The Voice of Truth I continued, "He wants to give all of us true-everlasting-life because He loves us—He is truly the definition of love. He longs to give each and every one of us our own sacred bed—to share with our true and faithful partner. Brother, the truth is that this same Voice that saved you and your girlfriend from this catastrophe happened to be the same One who willingly chose to die for you, (John 3:16). This Voice came to this world and became a man just like you and me (John 1:14). He walked and shared His divine love and purpose with mankind."

"Which is?"

"Read here."

"Where?"

"Look."

"Jesus said to him, "'You shall love the Lord your God with all your heart, with all your soul, and with all your mind.' This is the first and great commandment. And the second is like it: 'You shall love your neighbor as yourself.' On these two commandments hang all the Law and the Prophets" (Matthew 22:37-40).

"The Law and the Prophets?"

"There's more brother."

"Tell me."

"He was persecuted instead of persecuting those like you and me (John 5:16). He was betrayed by His so-called friends (Luke 22:48, Mark 14:66-72). He was repeatedly tortured in preparation for another heartless torture. He was hung, till life fled, like a sacrificial lamb (John 1:29). And as unbelievable as it sounds, He allowed it all—including His inhuman death—willingly (John 10:17, 18)."

"All this?"

"Even in the midst of this disloyalty, He still managed to pray willingly for those performing His historic murder."

"How did He pray? What did He say?"

"...Father, forgive them, for they do not know what they do" (Luke 23:34).

"Forgive the murderers?"

"And the whole world, also."

"But I don't quite comprehend?"

"He died for you and all mankind, and after three days, He resurrected from the grave."

I looked into my brother's eyes, and I saw a heart of repentance, so the Voice of Truth gave me the legitimate non-traffic green light:

"Will you follow The One who died for you and now lives in all of us that have allowed Him to become Lord of our entire lives—through this Voice of Truth?" I asked my hurting brother—hoping with all my being that he would respond with a 'yes.' And I continued, "Will you exchange this emptiness, deception, and confusion for the fullness of truth and clarity? Brother, will you embrace the unconditional love of your Savior—Yeshua—instead of embracing those women at the nightclub?"

His eyes remained lubricated with tears, his t-shirt had become a towel:

"It hurts! It hurts!" voices of pain from his mouth.

"I know! I know!" an answer embarked by pain as I encountered a flashback.

"Brother," I said attempting to provide counsel for him, as I desperately needed the Real Counselor to heal my personal pain. "If you are truly convinced that this is not a coincidence, and that you must follow The One that has given you true life, then, just let me know, at this very moment, if it is in your heart's desires to trust your whole life in His Hands?"

He slowly agreed with me and His Creator even before I finished with the question by bobbling his head. And as we were both filled with a combination of emotions, I said to him, "Just repeat this simple prayer, wholeheartedly, if you're truly ready, and if you're ready to mean it." I felt that he had acknowledged the Voice of Truth in his heart even prior to verbalizing a prayer—he followed along in true humility, and repeated:

"My Father in Heaven, thank you for giving me life. Thank you, for sending Your only Begotten Son to this world to die and resurrect for me. Oh, Father, I thank you for saving me from this mess," and suddenly, crying terribly he paused, then I paused. I looked into his eyes, and somehow I felt his pain even more. A brief and unique moment passed: "Should we continue?" I asked. And he asked me to proceed through the voices of his body language.

"Forgive me! Forgive me! for disobeying you. I have sinned against you. Please come into my heart right now, and from this moment forward, I'll follow You. Thank you, Yeshua—thank you for never giving up on me. In your Holy Name, I pray. Amen."

Drowned in tears, and our hearts filled with the love of The Spirit of Truth, we both stood behind his apartment building desiring that that moment never flee from us. I honestly couldn't believe how a simple act of obedience, and finally listening to this Voice had—physically and spiritually—saved my brother's life. And perhaps, his girlfriend's life, and my relationship with the Perfect Navigation System—The Voice of Truth. I remember when I squeezed my brother with all my heart, with all my strength, and with all my joy. I believe these emotions were mutual. All of it moved me radically. I couldn't fully comprehend how the same Voice that once spoke to me—through Coach Noah Wilbanks—when I repented of my wrongdoings, happened to be the same Voice that decided to guide us along this incredible life-saving journey.

I looked into my brother's eyes and said to him, "I will be a world-boxing-champion one day." But only his body and emotions replied. We cried and hugged each other as tough men do, but there was only One True Fan watching the super bowl—The Voice of Truth.

## Second True Story

Midnight was approaching, and I was still tossing and turning all over my bed: 1 a.m. and the same actions remained. I was beginning to recognize the Voice of truth as my body began to give up on me: "Get up and go for a jog," suddenly—at around 1:15am, I heard.

"But I just ran five plus miles, today; why do I need to run again?" I thought.

"Get up and go for a jog, now," The Voice of Truth repeated with preciseness.

By now, I was becoming a little bit more cooperative. I had learned from previous experiences to act quickly, and I was not willing to miss a moment with The Voice of Truth—an amazing opportunity. Thus, I rose immediately and told my wife, "I have to go for a jog," as I reached for a pair of sweat pants rapidly. She stared at me like Bruce Lee, and to calm her tension, I rapidly said, "I have to train hard, you know!"

"Do you know where we live?"

"Of course, in an efficiency!"

She gave me the Bruce Lee look again: "This is West Park, Florida! It is 1:40 a.m. Are you ok?"

By now, I knew that the timing was essential, as it has been always: "I must go; I know The Voice," I said to her, running out the back door—the only door. As I ran by the Chinese Catholic Church, I was prepared mentally to fight anyone if necessary. And I was not entirely sure—100% convinced—if this was the Voice of Lies or the Voice of Truth. As I kept on jogging, I began to comprehend that this was certainly The Voice of Truth.

"Don't stop, keep on..."

"What is it? I asked, "please tell me, it's almost 2am, and here I am running and not knowing where to go. Please tell me: what is it?" I asked The Voice of Truth. I ran southbound toward Miami Gardens Drive—the nearest traffic light remained located about 3/4 of a mile away. And as I began to approach the light, "Make a left; turn at the traffic light," The Voice of Truth said. Thus, I made the left, and as I jogged, I began to think all kinds of things, like:

"Ok! Where am I going? What do you want me to do, Voice of Truth? I guess you want me to run another five plus miles at two in the morning.

"You will speak to someone, soon," The Voice answered.

I was running and thinking about the recent announcement of The Voice of Truth. All of the sudden, I saw from about a football field away, a group of people sitting on the bus-stop bench. I began to feel this heaviness in my heart signaling me to stop, but not due to fatigue, but because of compassion. In my mind, I had not received the complete signal yet. But before I could think again, "Speak to my people sitting on the bus-stop bench," the signal from the Voice of Truth, again.

Soon, I became confused because I thought this was a set up from the Voice of Lies. I thought that I was going to speak to someone, not a group of four homeless men and one woman drinking beer on the bus-stop bench. Rapidly and desperately, I began to ask The Voice, all sorts of questions, as I was approaching the bench. I wanted to know with certainty that these were indeed the people The Voice had been referring about as it spoke to me while I ran. I knew, I could not afford to miss the assignment ordered by The Voice of Truth. So, I asked from about fifty yards away as I approached the bench, "Do I stop now or do I continue?"

"Now!" From about seven yards away, The Voice shouted within me. And I stopped immediately, and I remember thinking: "Ok! Now, what?" Suddenly, I discerned an overwhelming presence holding me in place as I stood in front of these men and woman. And I decided to do the natural thing, "Hello! How are you all doing this evening?"

The old lady, with a can of beer in her hand, said: "Wow, you must be a boxer or something, look at those abs! How do you get them like that; you probably eat lettuce all day?"

"I just exercise a little," and I continued as The Voice led me, "I've been sent by a Voice, a Voice I recognize and speaks to me often. You see, it is past 2am, and I'm out here jogging."

"I can see," said the old lady firmly gripping her can of beer.

"This is not a coincidence," they all agreed with their heads as I spoke, "that I'm out here running without a shirt as I always wear one."

"Oh, honey, you made the perfect choice by not wearing one," the old lady again.

"You see, your True Father sent me," I replied staring at them, "He led me through His Voice to simply meet you all here—to share some time with you. What do you think?"

Holding on to his beer joyfully, "Oh yes! Thank you for coming!" one of the old men replied and continued speaking, "We need some company out here. I don't know what's wrong with people, nowadays, they don't even greet you anymore. I'm telling you this world is ending."

As I listened to their opinions, the Voice of Truth stirred up in my heart, and it whispered: "These are my people, they just need real guidance, and you are their guide. They have been let down over and over, discouraged, betrayed, and they've lost many loved ones."

"What do you want me to do?" I asked the True Voice as I stood facing them all.

"Just use the tools given."

Somehow, I understood that the tools were the message; that it was too late just to be out here running for nothing, and that something important had to happen. Led by The Voice of Truth, I began to speak, gazing unknowingly at the youngest man of the group (in his 50's, I assumed). And I said, "Brother, do you know that God loves you all and that He wants you all to follow Him?"

They all agreed and began to say so many wonderful things about God at first, but soon after, one of them changed his heart's desires. He said with emotions fueled by pain:

"Why did God take my family? Why did He take my wife? My kids? My house? Why did He take it all? I guess He was nice enough to leave me with my father, right? And he paused for a moment of relief, but couldn't contain himself and suddenly shouted: Why!?"

His father—sitting next to him—tapped his back attempting to calm him, but his son violently increased more and more the tone of his voice:

"Why did God kill my family? Why did I have to be in jail when they killed my family? Why?" he continued, filled with sadness in his countenance and devastated. And as he furiously shouted all kinds of evil—fueled by anger, hopelessness, disappointment, and alcohol—I began to beg for help in silence as I simultaneously prepared to defend myself if necessary.

He got up from the bench, the others attempted to hold him back, and he faced me filled by fury: "Why did He? Didn't His Voice send you? Why? He shouted as he stumbled in all directions.

He was trembling, and his friends were attempting to calm the alcoholic storm. I was trying to calm the storm within me, and simultaneously, I was asking the 'Perfect Storm Calmer' to deliver all of us from a soon-to-come disaster. The Voice of Truth visited my presence again, and it spoke through me—while he was all in my face about to vomit:

"You've never done anything wrong?" I asked with tough love.

"Everyone has! I'm not the only one," he replied as he danced in the boxing ring.

"You've never hurt anyone?"

"Of course, who hasn't?" he said, "I just hit that M* F* in jail..."

During this moment, I had probably prevented myself from applying multiple jabs and body shots to this homeless brother in need—by delicately listening to The Voice of Truth. His character was shifting from anger to a desire for hope.

"That number on your shirt," I said.

"What number?"

"That one!" as I pointed it.

"Oh, no! This is my number for life. This was my riding number, my street number. They call me Tony—Tony the 13...this is my number."

"Get rid of it," The Voice of Truth through me said.

"No way! I had this number all my life! I'm keeping it!"

While I was waiting for a response from The Voice of Truth, I noticed that the others were staring at the show, and suddenly, The Voice came:

"Just like him, they are many people holding on to too many possessions: mental possessions, money-oriented possessions, habits...The whole truth is that these possessions rob us our true life. It removes us from the vital comprehension of time and the purpose for a true everlasting life. These possessions come with an invisible veil that ultimately creates blindness to its possessors. Son, unfortunately, too much of My creation remains veiled by this invisible curtain. But don't worry, My grace and truth remain active. Just tell him that, although he has been through much, I desire to restore his life. Tell him that I long to receive him in My arms—that I love him, unconditionally, above all."

Placing my arm on his shoulders:

"Tony, although you've been through much, God desires to restore your life, and He longs to receive you in His arms—He loves you unconditionally, above all, brother."

I can begin to feel his transformation while we're still standing on the sidewalk, and his friends remained speechless as we interacted in this amazingly prearranged event. And all of the sudden:
"You see, I know God!" falling on his knees Tony stated. "Pray for me!" with his arms wide open he shouted, "look, I carry Him on my chain," and he pointed to the cross of his necklace. Almost as if he had just regretted his words, he exclaimed with tremendous disappointment: "Why did He take them away from me?"

"It's ok, son; it's ok," his father Cornelius said multiple times as he rubbed his back compassionately.

"Now! Now is the time for praying!" The Voice said. And, I fell on my knees, along with Tony and said, "Repeat after me," as I stared into his eyes confidently.

"Ok," Tony shouted as he simultaneously drank some beer.

"My Father in Heaven; O Father of Mercy and Love. Please deliver us from all evil. Let your unconditional love fall upon us—this very moment."

Unexpectedly, in that very moment that the word "moment" was uttered out of Tony's mouth, the God of Love, released an unexplainable peace. Tony, his father, and I hugged as if we had known each other for a lifetime. All his friends followed along and joined us for the homeless/alcoholic hug—filled with compassion and the unfading peace of Yeshua.

"I'm Cornelius, and these are my real friends," said his father.

"You know, I use to believe in Catholicism," said the old lady who prefers me without a shirt, "but I stopped going to church because I saw too many things."

"Wow," said the other old man, out of the blue—almost as if he had just woken up—while he held on to his beer also, and just stared at us in awe. And by then, it was almost 4am, and I was trying to make sense of the experience. Part of me wanted to stay with them, wanted to bring them food, wanted to buy them a house, and maybe throw away all the beer cans. And the other part of me, just wanted to go home to rest. As I walked away from the bus stop:

"Never forget this moment, I love you all!" I shouted, and I walked home—holding onto this unforgettable moment in my heart. I kept thinking and marveling:

"If I would have stayed at home? Or, if, I had not made the choice of stopping at the bus stop to fellowship with the old, drunk, and homeless people, and Tony (motorcycle 13)? Or, if I had just backed down when Tony turned aggressive while sipping on his canned beer? Or if I would have listened to the fear of my wife before leaving the house: What would have been the outcome of that evening?

Those of you who have a wife or a husband: listen to them always. But most importantly, follow The Voice of Truth till the very end—and you shall find the perfect will of your Creator, delivering you to a discovery of true personal identity.

## Third True Story

For some reason, I was beginning to feel that time was flying by. I was dressed and ready to go to work, and I had enjoyed a God given meal. It was early, only 1pm, and I had nothing else to do before leaving for work. For the most part, I tend to make it right on time, but rarely, half an hour early.

"Leave now!" The Voice of Truth stated as I was waiting for direction. But I remained seated on the living room couch—thinking about how much better it may be just to spend time with my family. If I could just...

"Leave now!" again boldly.

Not fully comprehending the reason for leaving for work early, but fully understanding the order given, I reacted quickly and left. Now, I was driving northbound on 441. And as soon as I passed the *Pollo Tropical*, where I met my wife on Father's Day, I noticed a broken down car, and a dark skin lady standing next to it—about as old as my mother. I began to pray as I drove by her—unknowingly leaving her with the unsolved problem. The image of the popped hood, the wide open driver's door, and the helpless lady standing played back and forth in my memory cassette.

"Go back and help," The Voice of Truth penetrated and interfered the prayer.

"I can't; I'm going to be late," I thought.

"No, you're not, remember? You left early today because I sent you to help this lady."

"Wow, ok," and I made a U-turn.

And as I drove into the parking lot, I saw the fear or confusion in her eyes. Perhaps she thought I was a thief instead of a helper—being led by The Helper. After all, we were in a rough neighborhood.

"Hello, I see you are having some problems; by the way I'm Marcial. Have you checked it carefully?" I asked from a distance hoping she would allow me to help her.

"Yeah, I did," discouraged she replied.

"May I check it? I'm not a mechanic, nor do I know much about cars, but I do know when something is wrong with a car."

"Sure, but listen: my son is on his way right now, and he will take care of it," with disappointment in her eyes she said. "Oh God! I just spent over $1100 fixing it recently."

As I walked toward the driver's side to sit inside the car and check the possible issue: "Ask her if it's ok to pray," The Voice of Truth declared.

"Is it ok to pray?"

"Please."

I immediately placed my arm on her shoulders and bowed my head to ask for help through these words:

"My Father in Heaven, I thank you for this opportunity. Only You know the outcome of this situation." And in the midst of the prayer I sensed a direction by The Voice of Truth, and I continued, "Please help this lady as if she is my mother, deliver us from all evil and let Your will be done on earth as it is in heaven. I ask You in the name of Yeshua. Amen."

As soon as I finished praying, we both lifted our heads, stared at each other into our eyes, and I hugged her as if she was my very own mother.

"God loves you," uttered out of my lips with tears of joy and pain. I felt that I was speaking to my very own mother for some reason. I knew she had accepted my help although the car remained in the same condition.

"Listen, I'm a sales manager for *Florida Fine Cars*—the huge car dealership on 441 and Countyline Road," and I continued, "I can exchange this car for a newer one. You need not fix it, nor do you need to tow it there—I can simply call one of our towing trucks to have your car delivered. Only if it's ok with you and your son of course."

"Oh, no, I'm just not ready for something like that yet, you know, it is just not the best time."

"Listen, I fully comprehend. May I, at least, take you to the dealership where you may sit and wait for your son? I think it's much safer there."

"No, no...that's ok, I'm just going to wait here," she responded with indecisiveness in her voice and in her body language.

"Ok, I comprehend; here is my business card—just in case you decide to stop by one day. And on the back, I wrote the radio station show's information, where I share the Good News of The Kingdom to-soon-come; please tune in. And remember, God loves always," driving away I voiced these words—feeling as if I was speaking to my mother. I quickly glanced at the dashboard clock and noticed that I was just on time for work.

When I arrived at work, I truly couldn't get this lady off my mind. The images of the current event just kept on playing over and over on my mind. I proceeded with my daily responsibilities, but I just could not stop thinking about the sweet lady and her situation. I tried praying, but I felt obligated to help...I left her there alone. Five to six hours passed by, and my good co-worker and friend, Lionel Ben-David, approached me, and began to share with me his current struggles and desires to earn a car deal. He said:

"Brother, you know, I come here every single day, work hard, and follow up with my clients. I'm nice to people, I speak five languages, and for some reason, I never get leads from the Business Development Department. I'm tired of this unfairness, I'm a great salesman, and you know this, brother."

Lionel appears to be a great human being in my eyes; we cried together a few times—in the midst of our frustrations—at work. We understood each other. I always wanted to help him because he comprehended fairness.

"Lionel, don't worry," I replied to my brother, "you know well that God always provides in the midst of this unfair world system." He shook his head various times agreeing, and I continued, "You know that, by the end of the month, you'll have the required numbers." And once again, he nodded his head agreeing, and I continued, "Brother let us hope and believe that, today, you will make it happen!" Proudly he got up and gave me a polar bear hug, and then replied, "Let's do this, brother!"

I just wanted to give a bone with meat (a deal) to Lionel, but, unfortunately, it just doesn't function that way. I was closing deals after deals for different sales consultants, but Lionel's deal seemed not to arrive yet. Suddenly, I received a call and the caller voices:

"Hi, I'm the son of the lady you helped today—on 441. Firstly, I'd like to thank you for going out of your way to help my mother, today. She said many great things about you, and to be sincere, for this reason only, I'm calling you."

"Thank you for calling, I'm glad to meet you, sir."

"Same here, sir.

"You see, I never buy from car dealerships because I've been robbed many times," he continued, "but *something told me* to call you and to stop by your store. And frankly, I still don't understand, but I think I'm doing the right thing."

"Feel free to stop by at any time, I'll be here till close—In fact, I close the store, so feel free to come in whenever."

"Ok, thanks a lot. I'll be there soon," hanging up he said.

I didn't think much about it until he showed—a couple of hours later—with his mother. Out of the thirty-plus sales consultants, Lionel was the one that greeted them. He brought them to me, to the sales desk with a smile on his face, and said, "Hey brother, you got these wonderful people looking for you."

"Hello, how are you, ma'am? Long time no see! I'm glad your son brought you in today!" happily I replied, and continued, "come on, follow me to Lionel's desk to comprehend better your primary goal for today."

I asked them a few questions, and I found out she desired to have a new car, but she just wasn't so sure. Her son wanted to help her, and sincerely, I wanted to help her. And, therefore, I asked Lionel to assist them. One thing led to another, and my new friend signed on the dotted line.

"I can't believe that my payments are less than $200!" happily she said and continued in excitement, "I guess God still works through miracles. Look at me! Hours ago I was in the middle of 441 with a broken down car. And now, I'm about to drive away from this car lot with a new car! Thank you so much for stopping to help me. I can't believe this is happening."

Lionel appeared to be blown away by the client's statement as he stood in front of me. He wanted to say something, but he held it. He seemed shocked, but he was attempting to hide it. Suddenly, the client drove out happily, and we were all excited about the outcome. And as soon as they drove off the lot:

"Brother, did you really stopped to help this lady today?" said Lionel. And I looked at him with a smile on my face, filled with joy, and before I knew it, I had the Israeli bear hugging me again.

It was time to go home, to close the store and to finally rest—thank God. And as I was driving toward the house, where I momentarily live, I began to think about the miracles that had just occurred throughout the day. I thought about the significance of just listening to The Voice of Truth as I drove to work. I couldn't fully comprehend the perfection of these miracles, but I knew that the origin of these miracles had originated from the True Originator. Being thankful, as I was driving, for the fantastic opportunity to serve The Almighty God, suddenly, I received a phone call from The Dominican Republic. It was my mother! It rarely happened. I guess that day was an unusual day. And as usual, we dialogued in Spanish:

"*Bendición mami* (blessings mother)" answering the call, I said.

"*Que Dios te bendiga mi hijo* (God bless you, my son)." It is a Dominican tradition. We conversed about many issues, and one thing led to another, and unexpectedly she said:

"Son, I was stranded today for hours in the middle of nowhere. I was thirsty, hungry, and no one seemed to be around to help me. Oh, but thank God I was able to find assistance at some point."

I listened to her voice and concerns from hundreds of miles away through this technological invention, and swiftly, The Voice of Truth came to me and said:

"Today, I asked you to help my daughter when her car broke on 441; to make a U-turn when you passed the scene; to pray for her to help alleviate her pain; to help her, and her son, with the purchase of a new car, and all of this and more you also did for your mother." And The Voice continued, "While all this was happening, your mother was being helped as I saw your actions when I entrusted you with My orders."

Shaken, I began to think about the moment when I hugged the lady and felt as if I was hugging my very own mother. I couldn't fully comprehend such precision and unconditional love, simultaneously. I was feeling high on something, and it wasn't marijuana: I was feeling filled by something, and it wasn't seafood. In the midst of it all, I heard The Voice shouting within me, "Son when you were hugging the lady and crying, you were hugging and crying with your mother."

I remained speechless, and didn't know what to respond to The Voice of Truth, or my mother, as she held on to her high-tech device. Suddenly, I began to cry out loudly, but just in my heart without voicing a word—out of joy and confusion. Joyful because of the perfection of The Perfect One, and confused because in my human nature, I wanted to be the one helping my mother physically...And being unable to continue a conversation with my mother, I informed her,

"Mother, we'll speak again tomorrow, God willing," and the technological device rested.

The Voice of Truth replied again in the midst of my triple-feeling of confusion, loneliness, and joyfulness:

"Son, just trust in 'I AM.'"

## Chapter 2
# My Childhood

I feel obligated to share a portion of my childhood—for you to better comprehend the essential message of this book for humanity.

### 1996

It was Thursday around 3pm, and suddenly, my father said, "Son, hurry up! Julito and the driver are waiting for you downstairs to drive around town. Hurry! You need to make sure that they announce tomorrow's event, loudly, remember? It'll be Friday tomorrow, and we need to pack the nightclub!"

"Ok, father. I'm going! I'm going! I'll make sure we cover the entire *City of La Romana*," I responded, "I hope that the truck has loud speakers."

Here I was, riding in the back of the "advertising company"—a 1970's *Toyota* pickup truck with multiple trumpet speakers—advertising for Friday's event. And, I was having fun with Julito—the night club manager. The words of Friday's event consistently blasted over and over in my ears—by then, I knew the entire message. Finally! It was time to go home. The whole city should know about the event, already—as the sun set. I was tired, hungry, and I was glad we arrived at home.

"How was it, son?" my father asked, smiling.

"It was fun, father."

"Go to *el colmado* (the mini market) and buy a case of malt with condensed milk so that we may drink it with our supper. What do you think?"

"Great! Thank you, father!" I answered and walked away joyfully. I enjoyed the rest of the evening with my father as we bonded at the kitchen table, and as he shared much wisdom every evening. Till this day—though it has been over a decade since his earthly body fell asleep temporarily—I treasure those moments, daily.

It's getting late,

"Son, get some rest," my father said, "I'm going downstairs to check up on the club. Get some rest, son. I love you—I'll never leave you nor forsake you." And he sported his night club robe and headed downstairs. I, on the other hand, decided to lay down on my bedroom floor—to listen to the echoes of some *merengue, bachata*, and Michael Jackson's songs. I remember falling asleep on my bedroom floor with the frequency of these sounds most nights. And also, thinking about my mother and brothers living in Miami. At times, I missed them; at times, I didn't comprehend. But above all, the love residing in my heart for them would never disintegrate.

## Sports

As a 12-year young boy, I was a member of a club called: *Casa de Puerto Rico*, in *La Romana, Dominican Republic*—where I was born. There, many sports programs were available like swimming, basketball, table tennis, billiard...and I rode my bike there every day after school—to participate in all sports for the rest of the day. One day, I decided to jump into the deeper side of the pool to swim across by faith—I had never jumped into a pool prior to this. I jumped, for the first time, and fought and wrestled my way through until I made it to the final destination—five to seven meters away. Unknowingly, the club's swimming coach happened to be standing there watching the whole drama. He approached me immediately and asked, "Would you like to join the swimming team?"

"Is it free?" amazed by the offer, I asked.

"Of course—for you!" pointing his hands toward me he replied, "I want you on my team."

"Fine. But I have to speak with my father first." From that day on, I made the decision of showing up every day, and becoming a champion as well. I practiced every day for two to three hours, and swimming became like walking. Within a few months, I was already competing in that very same club, and in another club in *El Central Romana*—where aunt, Mati, works. And soon after, a few months into time, I received additional news by my coach:

"We're going to the nationals!"

To me, it wasn't really a big deal because I did not fully understand the importance of these games. I didn't even know that all the best swimmers, all the best athletes in The Dominican Republic, were all uniting at *The Olympic Center,* in *Santo Domingo*, and in *The City of Mao*. I slowly noticed the importance of this event when my coach sat down with my father and carefully explained to him my potential, and when he asked him to allow me to attend. I saw the importance of this when my team and I were given a brand new 2-piece sweat suit, swimwear and goggles, and a huge carnet "with our picture in it"—as soon as we arrived at The Olympic Center. For the first time in my life, I constantly remained surrounded by countless athletes. I observed that some of these girls did not just come to compete, but to check out my tiny six-pack as well.

"It's time to do what we came for!" said *Coach Orlando,* suddenly. The whole team stared at him in panic. And I was still rubbing my hamstring and gluteus muscles due to the pain caused by diving—from the 10 meter platform into the diving pool (it was my first time jumping, and it was a bet also). We began to prepare ourselves for this competition. Unexpectedly, my turn to compete arrived—my time! It was my first time swimming in an Olympic size pool. And I guess I was ready for the experience. My coach stared at me holding on to my shoulders and shouted, "Son! You got this!" And I took his words with me and walked away to my platform and lane. I was ready. I looked to my right, and I saw seven other competitors ready to race me. I was fine, focused, determined, and with "a whole" six months of experience. Everyone was ready. I was ready...I thought. And it was time to jump off. Three, two, one, and the race commenced.

I was racing against the top seven swimmers in The Dominican Republic. I was swimming as fast as I could, and I glanced quickly to my left and I saw my coach and team cheering,

"You're first! Save your gas!" they kept shouting, but I couldn't hear much. Swimming as fast as I could, I glanced to my right this time, and I realized that I was really ahead of everyone else. First 50 meters, I was ahead. On the way back, I was still winning, but toward the end of the third lap something shifted—I ran out of gas. I was exhausted and did not know why: I was behind and did not know how. In a blink of an eye, the race was over—yes, over. I was the last one to make it to the final destination—8th! I couldn't believe it. I did not comprehend how I was winning, but then I lost. I was very disappointed, discouraged, and suddenly, "You did great, son," said my coach as he tried to encourage me. But I was still wondering how it all happened. I was used to winning every single cycling and roller-skating race sponsored by the local bike shop—I had never lost for two consecutive years. Losing was never on my agenda.

"Son, you are ranked eighth in the nation!" coach said attempting to remove pain from me, "remember, you're only twelve." And still discouraged, I sat on the bench, and just mentally allowed my current reality.

## More Sports

I continued to play all kinds of sports in 1997, and 1998. And, while continuing in swimming, I joined teams in baseball because my father wanted to, in basketball because it was my favorite sport, and in soccer because it was right across from the baseball field. And I kept on winning the roller-skating and bicycling races every week. I rarely watched TV, rarely played a video game—besides killing the ducks in *Nintendo*. And I always played and played, and played sports. I played so much basketball that my father eventually made me a miniature basketball court, from the flooring to the rim—from scratch. It was a big deal in *La Romana, DR*, as most nearby kids would fight their way through poverty. It was there, where I practiced more and more each day. My neighbors and best friends—Francisco and Eddy— periodically came to play with me, and to help me improve my skills. By the time I was thirteen, I was hanging on to the rim at 5' 2" short; I was having 14-15 steals per basketball game; throwing 88-89 mph from the outfield in baseball; winning every swimming race I attended; running 16 laps around the track to warm up for soccer, and I attended to all these events pedaling in my champion bike—a 20" *BMX* bike. All of this, while helping my father supervise his nightclub while attending to school, and while assisting him as we visited different places—to give free medicine and to treat many hurting people.

## My Father

One of the scenes remaining in my imagination is when a lady visited us in our apartment home, and she said, "Dr. Ferreira, I came from a very distant place because I heard that you help people for free. Is it true?

"Yes, please come right in!" with a smile on his face my father responded, "Tell me; what's the issue?"

"Well sir, the situation is that I have not been able to defecate for over a month now, and I just hope you can help me, please."

My father asked her a few more questions and then said, "Wait here; I'll be right back," once determining the main issue. And as I sat there, the lady bowed her head instantly and began to pray while my father searched through his medicine cabinet. A few minutes passed, and my father returned, and as he handed to her a bottle, he said, "Just drink this now, and you'll be fine—God willing." She opened it right away and consumed the liquid entirely.

"What else must I do, sir?"

"Nothing, just wait."

Two to three minutes vanished, and suddenly, the lady said—with multiple facial expressions, "Oh, what's happening to me? Oh! Uh! Oooh! Where's the toilet?" she whispered in her struggle as my father pointed toward the nearest restroom—my restroom. And then, we were both in the living room waiting for the nice lady. And suddenly:

"She'll be fine," whispered my father.

"I don't know what to do first," she walked out and said to us soon after.

"I don't comprehend," my father responded.

"I don't know if I should thank you for helping me, or if I should ask for forgiveness for messing up your toilet."

"Oh, don't worry at all; I'm glad you're ok now," he responded with joy.

"May I borrow some bleach and a bucket to clean the restroom, please," she insisted.

"No, it's unnecessary; please enjoy the rest of the day."

She walked away thanking us so much. And rapidly, "Take care of your responsibility," my father said to me. I knew he was referring to the "toilet situation." Thus, I visited my personal restroom with a visitor's mindset, and as I walked in, I noticed the human waste floating in the toilet—it was filled with it. I didn't know whether to clean it or to ask my father to see it first, simply. So, to avoid any dilemma with my father, I just dealt with it.

When it was all done, I thought about the essentiality of helping others—how someone, just willing to help one person at a time, can change significantly the daily lives of many in need.

## Chapter 3
# *The Voice of Truth Whispers*

The truth is that The Voice of Truth just whispered again. Today—as I'm writing—it's Wednesday, October the 1st, 2014. And I just arrived at *Hotel Adamanay* in *La Romana*—from Hollywood, Florida. And I'm sitting here attempting to write this book. But I keep hearing the sound of some Olympic boxers as they shadow box downstairs in the parking lot—from the $18.00 a day hotel room. These are different times now—I'm thirty years young—and I'm still trying to figure out how I am going to unfold this message God has placed in my heart for mankind.

The Voice of Truth said,

"Son, don't you worry; I will tell you what to write. And stop allowing The Father of Lies to tempt you with the boxers downstairs," He continued, "all you have to do is to share your story, and those who desire wisdom—for times as such—will remain in this journey with you."

"I guess this won't be that hard for THE LORD OF HOSTS," I'm thinking, "but I'm still trying to grasp His full message to deliver perfection according to His Will for Humanity."

Allow me to go back to 1998—when my mother snatched me away from my father.

"Son, I'm going to Miami, Florida," my father said, "to take care of some things. Here are your documents. Inside this book, I'm leaving you money for any emergencies—only emergencies. And if you have a problem with Lilian (his wife after he divorced my mother) we'll solve it when I get back.

Understood?"

"Yes, sir!" I responded with my 110 pounds of strength.

The next day he departed as my mother was simultaneously coming to *La Romana*, from the same place he was on his way to. I remembered seeing my mother for the first time in about 2-3 years.

How I felt as I hugged her while I simultaneously thought about my father's landing in Miami. I was already missing him, but even more, my heart melted when I was with her. We hugged, kissed, and suddenly I said, "Mom!"

"What is it, son?"

"When am I going to live with you again? I miss you much." And with a smile on her face she said, "Do you know where your passport is?"

"Yeah!" I said as I ran up the stairs to grab it, "Here mom; here's the passport!"

"Would you want to come with me?"

"Yes!" I shouted with joy, but simultaneously with a soundless alarm pounding inside of me because of my father.

"Let's go now."

"Ok."

We spent a couple of days together, and soon after we departed to Miami.

Then we were in the airplane in destination to the same state where my father was visiting. And suddenly, something very important crossed my mind, "I forgot to ask my father for permission." I had just realized that soon he was going to return to *La Romana*, and I wasn't; that, yes, I was going to see my brothers, once again, but that I was separating myself from my loving father; that although I was going to enjoy life with my mother and brothers, that now, I was practically forced to see him no longer. It was too late; we were landing at the Miami International Airport already. And all the lights were shining in the midst of darkness—everything seemed so different. All I remember from this place is an image of my brother, Angel—riding his electrical four-wheeler from when we lived near the elementary school—when I was in Kindergarten. The image reminded me of my trip to *La Romana*, for first grade, when I attended to *El Collegio Sinai (El Sinai School)* at the Santa Rosa Avenue (*La Avenida Santa Rosa*); it reminded me of the time when my mother took me and my brothers, Miguel and Angel, to live in Corona Queens, New York for a year—to attend P.S 13; it reminded me of the time when we moved to *Villa Carolina and El Verde,* Puerto Rico, and I liked some twin girls from school. These shining lights really took me back to the times when my brothers and I were living in *La Romana* for my fourth, fifth, sixth, and seventh grade years in school—with my aunts as my mother worked in the states.

I was having a flashback from when I played for the basketball team for *El Collegio Inmasculado de Corazon de Maria*, (a Catholic School) and reality came back to haunt me: I didn't tell my father. I was disappointed, and simultaneously filled with joy—kind of like a lukewarm Christian. I don't even know what I was feeling. All I know is that I got what I asked for.

## The Voice of Truth Whispers

I'm still here at the hotel room no longer listening to the shadow boxing sound effects of the Olympic boxers from Puerto Rico. Instead, I hear the sound effects of the *moto-conchos* (motorcycle-taxis*).* My fleshly desires still long to go back to the boxing gym, but The Voice of Truth keeps me in the 'Ultimate fight.' Rapidly, The Voice of Truth said:

"Tell them about your life. Otherwise, most people won't fully believe or comprehend the message behind **this soon-to-come worldwide event that will affect all Mankind.** I need all people to know the deep mystery hiding in plain sight. Keep telling them—all creatures must know."

## Arriving at Miami

Once I got to my step father's house, Angel Bravo, I felt different—it was a new feeling. Within a week or so my mother enrolled me in West Miami Middle School. Then my stepfather signed me up for baseball again, and I tried my best to apply every word and act of discipline that I acquired from my parents—in all areas of my life. I remember receiving a certificate from some sort of achievement every other week. I also received a certificate from Bill Clinton with his signature on it to find out later it was a stamp—it still filled me with joy somehow.

And for some reason, my mother worked continuously, and as most marriages, arguments would escalate periodically at home. I remember thinking about a solution to these multiple predicaments but never finding one. Playing basketball and flag football with my brothers, and my friend Rolle at Banyan Elementary remained as an escape. Lifting weights became one of my hobbies as my older brother Miguel inspired me. The "Backyard Cement Gym" membership was only "free-99" a month. With an eco-friendly tanning bed and an opened air steam room—I truly had all I needed. Then my brother Alfred came from New York to live with us again, and finally, all five of us were living together: Miguel, Angel, Alfred, Marcos, and I.

Then we moved to West Miami closer to my school, but my mother forgot her husband, or maybe, he forgot to ask her to take him with her. Few months passed by, and it was time to move once again to my new step father's house, Guillermo. There, my brothers and I found a new brother, Willy, Guillermo's son. Willy and I attended Southwest Senior High School together, as my brother Miguel, attended Coral Park Senior High—and I continued in this roller coaster, but it was normal to me.

## Chapter 4
# *High School, Steroids,*
# *And Sports*

The boxers have been training downstairs since about 5am, or before. And I'm being tempted by the shadow boxing sounds—I'll explain later.

## October 2, 2014. Day 2 at the Hotel in
### *La Romana, Dominican Republic*

For some reason, I did not have The Voice of Truth activated within me throughout all these years. Well, to be more precise, I heard a voice once when I was 12, but that's for another chapter. At this point, I was 14 years young and a freshman, and I was showing up to class each day, but no longer focusing much. I met, Rodney, my first high school friend, and all things appeared ok then. I noticed that weight-training was my favorite class, and I trained at home and at the school. Thus, I was pushing 24/45 lbs. plates on the leg press machine, I was scoring in all the P.E flag football games, and quickly, Coach Rodriguez, the Head Football Coach, saw me as I was performing, and said, "Son, why don't you try out for our football team?"

"Well, the problem is that my mother doesn't let me. She needs me to work and help her and our family."

He looked at me and said, "Keep asking, you got something in you, son—use it!"

I walked away in hope of a positive answer from my mother, but when I asked again, the same accurate answer was received. I was discouraged, not knowing what to do, wanting to join the football team, basketball, track and field, and even baseball; To who do I turn? Nothing completely happened until the Spring Football Season—when I would tell my mother that I had a detention every single day just to attend to practice. It didn't last long, as she embarrassed me when she showed up to the weight room one day, and said: "*¿Que tu hace aqui,*

*José?* (What are you doing here, Jose?)" in front of all my teammates (She always called me by my middle name). Coach Rodriguez attempted to save me by attempting to speak with her. But this didn't go far as my mother rejected him when she said, *"No tengo nada que hablar con usted"* (We have nothing to discuss).

As I walked away in disappointment, I could see clearly the mutual feeling in Coach Rodriquez' face. Sad and discouraged, and not wanting to disobey any longer my mother's decision, I had to accept my reality...

## My First Job

Today, I can say that I have worked in over 30 different industries so far: from cleaning toilet—while in high school for my step father's cleaning company (*Arcade Building Services*)—to laboring in the construction sites prior to attending to college (*El Camino College*) for the first time; to laboring in various dry cleaners and laundries (*Dry Clean USA, Intercontinental Hotel* in Downtown Miami, *Big Daddies Cleaners, Crest Quality Cleaners*, etc.); to owning two dry cleaners with a custom-made business plan (unique among all others); to working for multi-million dollar car companies (as *AutoNation, Kendall Toyota, South Motors BMW,* and *Florida Fine Cars*). And moving from Sales Consultant to Internet Sales Manager, to Sales Manager...But it all started when I began pedaling my way to my uncle's concentrated juice factory called, *La Chichi Products,* in *La Romana*—when I was 12 years young. We used to remove the old beer and rum bottle labels—to later wash them thoroughly and re-label them with *La Chichi's* product labels. Then we prepared concentrated juices, or dark or clear vanilla—to later hand-bottle them one-by-one. All for *100 pesos* a week (2.5 U.S dollars). I enjoyed doing it, and today, I believe this created a foundation for a soon to experience personal journey.

## Back to High School

...I finally got a chance to play high school football. I just had to attend to school from 7:30am-2:30pm; then practice till about 5pm; then clean toilets, polish floors, shampoo carpets—for my stepfather's cleaning company—in a Downtown Brickell edifice, from 6pm-10pm, and everything would be just fine. I remember driving back home one day in my passed down—from my mother to my brother to me—1989 *Ford Aerostar* minivan, and running out of fuel by *The University of Miami* (as I drove south on USı). I could see myself gazing at the prestigious Institution and wondering if I could ever be a part of it. Suddenly: "Do you need help young man?" the UM security guard said.

"Sure, sir," I replied, "I just ran out of fuel, and I just need to get my van to the gas station," as I tiredly pushed my van toward the gas station.

"Wait a minute; I have a container," he replied as he drove away in his golf car, "here, just use it. And bring it back when you're finished."

"Thanks a lot, sir."

## High School Football & Steroids

I was already practicing with the football team, thank God, and the lift-a-ton came around. I was excited, thrilled, and ready to compete. But there was a problem I see today, but did not see then. What was it? Steroids.

I bought a bottle of *NORTEK*, which was sold over the counter at your local supplement store, and took them as multi-vitamins. I was innocent about the truth behind this product, but today, I know the truth—it was an over-the-counter steroid. Not being so innocent about the *ANABOLEX* pills I bought in *La Romana* once during a time when I visited my family—I combined them both. It was kind of like a steroid cycle, and I just did not find any harm in this process. I was not sensitive to The Voice of Truth since I had unknowingly chosen to not follow Him—the One that freely gives—by simply choosing to follow anything I desired. "He who is not with Me is against Me, and he who does not gather with Me scatters abroad" (Matthew 12:30). The truth is that I was never able to grasp the message of The Truth, fully, since it was never thoroughly explained to me in a way I fully comprehended. Also, I was not fully prepared to accept the information given to me about The Truth as my heart remained unprepared to attain the fullness of it.

I noticed a drastic increase in muscle mass and strength as the lift-a-ton approached. It was time to shine in the midst of my unknown darkness. It was my turn to choose from the 315 lbs. or 225 lbs. from the squat rack. I choose the heavy set. And after the thirty-third or thirty-fourth repetition, Coach Rodriguez shouted, "Stop!"

The second place surpassed just over twenty repetitions. And I believe he was taking *DIANABOL* pills since he used to sell them in school. Those pills contain ten times more of the amount of *ANABOLEX* as it was the same steroid with a different name—with amounts of 30mg per pill instead of 3mg per pill. *ANABOLEX* is used in The Dominican Republic for kids with a low appetite—they used to sell them over the counter; perhaps, they still do today.

At the time, I probably could have been as strong, perhaps weaker or even stronger, as I was already leg pressing over one thousand pounds as a freshman without steroids. Plus, my joints seemed to remain stronger without steroids as I used to dunk without a problem and felt no limits in them. Today, I know that taking these steroids was, perhaps, one of my worst decisions in life. And as odd as it sounds, that decision could be one of the greatest things that have happened to me because of my current reality. And because of this decision that seemed so innocent over the surface—as The Father of Lies accommodates through the Voice of Lies—unfortunately and, fortunately, today, I cannot provide for my wife's conjugal needs. Why, fortunately? I will explain soon. In other words, as I try my best to encourage you, and to warn Mankind of the soon to come worldwide events, today, as I write this book, I remain as a 1 minute man for over a year now, at the age of thirty. I had no impotence issues whatsoever prior to embracing steroids. In fact, I was supernaturally strong and very agile. Of course, these side effects did not kick in right away, where it became recognizable through my personal "detectable system." But they surely appeared clearly in the same landscape four to five years later, and progressively when I was about 26 years-of-age. Fortunately, there is a good side of this story that I will explain later on. And, I also believe that when this book publishes, I will receive healing soon after—The Voice of Truth keeps telling me.

# Chapter 5

# Events After
# High School

*Please remain connected as it is vital to comprehend 'the message.' It is so complicated that The Voice of Truth has been guiding me for many years, and I simply failed to recognize it then.*

W hen I was in high school, I helped my mother—so that she could help us—by working in her clothing and jewelry stores on the beach in Bal Harbor, FL. She had two stores, and a warehouse with sewing machines there. My brothers and I would alternate at times, and most times, we would help together. My mother later involved herself in the investing of properties—as most Floridians did from 2000-2007, and prior. I remember once walking into a real estate office in Kendall, Florida and being told by my mother:

"You're going to sign these papers; no questions or answers, just sign, and this will be quick."

"Ok," I said and proceeded as a soldier following an order. And I signed all the documents without reading them to discover four years later that I was a previous homeowner. And that I had a foreclosure on my credit report as I attempted to finance a car. Not surprised, I walked away from the car dealership.

I remember helping my mother with her dry-cleaning business (*Better Life Dry Cleaners*), while my other brothers would help her with her tailor shop (*Ania Sastreria*), which was just a block away on Flagler St. and 59th Ave. I learned practically everything about the dry-cleaning business. I was already 19 years-of-age, and for some reason, my mother couldn't pay me for my work. I desired to make personal funds as must teenagers, but I could not.

## Stealing From My Mother

One day my high school girlfriend, Ada Sarmiento, wanted a *COACH* purse desperately. But I was only being paid with food and shelter, and, therefore, I remained unable to purchase it. This purse was probably $200 to $300, and I just couldn't afford it. She drove me insane with this fantasy, and for some reason, as I was filled with ignorance, I couldn't just tell her, "Do you love me or a purse?" Instead, I decided to break the seventh and the rest of God's Commandments. "For whoever shall keep the whole law, and yet stumble in one point, he is guilty of all" (James 2:10). "You shall not steal," says the God of Abraham, Isaac, and Jacob in The Old Testament (Exodus 20:15). And, "You shall not steal," says the God of Abraham, Isaac, and Jacob in The New Testament (Romans 13:9).

I paid myself and honored my girlfriend, according to the ways of this world system. And in return, I dishonored my mother, and sadly, The One whom I'm not worthy of wearing His sandals—I truly stole from The One, who feeds me daily. I was ashamed when I truly discovered the Voice of Truth years later. Today, I understand that The Voice of Truth remained silent. Or to better explain, that due to my separation from The Voice of Truth and my relationship with The Voice of Lies, I fell for the deception and dishonored the ones that truly love me.

## Brandsmart USA

Here I was, at *Brandsmart USA*, in line, standing behind a man that just paid for a $20 DVD player. And he placed the DVD player on the floor and forgot to take it with him. The Voice of Lies said, "You can take it...it's paid."

"That's right! That's right!" I responded ignorantly and filled with deception. And as I was making payment for my chosen goods The Father of Lies screamed, "Take it! You know you want it. It has been paid for already," and he continued, "why would you pay for it again, or leave it there for the store's profit? This is a multi-million dollar company, and you deserve to own the DVD player—not them.

Deceived by the Voice of Lies I grabbed the bag and walked toward the exit.

"May I have your receipt, please?" said the security guard that stands at the exit.

"Sure. Here it is."

"I don't see a DVD Player in this receipt, sir."

"Uh, oh..., ah, let me see," and I walked away heading toward the return item's window (I don't even remember what lie I said to him prior to walking away).

"May I return this?" with my suspicious face.

"May I have your receipt, please?"

Here we go again with the receipt, I thought, "Uh, oh..."

Suddenly, The Voice of Truth said, "Just return it." But I could barely hear because our relationship remained weak—I needed another bar to connect truly to the Wi-Fi signal.

"I'm just trying to give this to the gentleman that bought this," I said to the loss and prevention man, "he is out there in the parking lot."

"Sir, may you follow me," a new voice behind me. And I turned and saw a 70% tattooed, white and bald headed policeman with hand-cuffs. He said "Sir you are under arrest!" and placed those ugly, metallic rings on my wrist, "please come with me," he said as he led me...

I thought, "He did not voice my rights." At least I remembered that from some ill-advised hip-hop song. Soon after, they locked me in a room with four to five men, and countless questions commenced from each of these individuals. I finally confessed my deception, my sins, my ignorance, my dishonor...and they placed me in the police car. And while on my way to who knows where, the nice black lady said, "Son, do you have someone to call?

"Yes, I do," I whispered feeling hurt because of the disgrace I had just recently experienced.

"Call them now, and tell them you are at..."

"Ok, thank you."

"Mom, I'm here in this situation and..."

My mother arrived at the scene, and I was forgiven by the officer, and by my mother. Thankfully, she took it in a way that I never expected. But most importantly, although I had only a few bars, The Voice of Truth saved me from losing the signal completely.

## Stealing More

Very briefly:

I switched the prices from *Ross*, *Marshalls*, and *Burlington Coat Factory* to give myself discounts and even walked away with new shoes and clothes a few times.

A few times, I purchased some stolen and legal merchandise from Downtown Miami to resell them to my mother in the Dominican Republic. She would then sell them from one of her stores.

## The Voice Whispers

"I'm too tired of putting my information out there. Don't you think this is enough?

"Son, you must go deeper," said the Voice of Truth. "Otherwise, most people will not comprehend MY MESSAGE, MY TRUTH, MY LOVE FOR HUMANITY...and most of My little children will remain deceived, and they will suffer like never before."

"I already told them about my penis problem: Is not this enough?"

"Son, trust in Me—will you?"

"But why do I have to share my personal story when this is not about me—this is painful?"

"My son, you must share your story because it will help many comprehend the big picture and believe in the second half is the book."

"Is this You?"

"I am The Voice of Truth, and all necessary will be given to you."

"All necessary?"

"Yes, I will reveal to you—through the Spirit of Truth—the things to come, and then, I will reveal it to you in My Word—My Word is Truth."

"But how can this be?"

"My son, you will not study this wisdom, nor will you buy it, nor will you steal it."

"Then how will it come?"

"Follow me and you'll see."

"Where to?"

"Keep listening."

"Yes, my Lord. Just lead me, please."

"I've always have, and I'll always will."

## Intercontinental & Dry Clean USA

I worked for *The Intercontinental Hotel* in Downtown Miami as I mentioned earlier. First, I would run about one and a half mile to catch the first bus; then, I would catch the metro rail, and following, the metro mover—which dropped me in front of the hotel. I was late on my first day by 10-15 minutes. And Mrs. Shandani—I think that was her name—almost fired me the same day, but she did not. I was never late again. There, I ironed clothes and did every minor and major work involved in the laundry and dry-cleaning industries. I ate lunch for a dollar with the *City of Miami Police Department* as they had this benefit with the hotel. I had an extra benefit: I could eat all I desired all day for free. Then I found another job with *Dry-Clean USA*, and I kept both jobs for about a year. I remember stealing—from *Dry Clean USA*—some top designer clothes that were hanging on the conveyor rack for over a year already. I figured that the owner would never come back—I never wore the clothes for some reason. I did not even like them, and to this day—besides, now knowing I was deceived—I still don't know the full reason for stealing the garments, when I was supposed to care for them, instead.

Overall, I did perform excellently in all my jobs—except for that one situation with *Dry Clean USA*. Not one employer can state that I underperformed; in fact, this is something I did great in all areas of life—to work.

# Chapter 6
## *Another Stage*

"**D**on't you still want to play football?" The Voice of Truth said.

"Of course! I love football!"

"Call David and he'll tell you what to do."

So I decided to call David Silveira, the husband of my teammate's sister(Marcial and Billy). And David immediately informed me about a soon-to-come college football combine to be held in Long Beach, California. I was thrilled about this life changing opportunity; thus not hesitating, I quickly bought my flight ticket—as well as Clavens Charles, the other Marcial, and Chris. Later, our other friend, Edward, from our high school football team, showed, and then, Newberry, from another school in New York. We attended the college football combine, we all performed greatly, and soon after, we were offered an opportunity to play college football once again for *El Camino College*, in Gardena, California. I ran a 4.60 in the 40-yard dash, bench pressed 225 lbs. about 24 times, and I was clean from steroids for more than three years at that moment. Prior to this, I had taken the *ANABOLEX* during my junior year in high school, and then my brother introduced me to his friend, Camille, who helped me inject *EQUIPOISE*—another steroid.

We all, except Newberry, returned to Miami to prepare ourselves for the season, and within a month or so, we returned to summer camp. We trained hard during two-a-days, and we were all doing great for some reason. But I began to feel a loss of muscle mass and weakness in my joints. I decided to take some leftover *ANABOLEX* pills from high school, and everything seemed to be fine all over again. I'm getting much faster, much stronger, and I'm eating 12 boiled eggs for breakfast. At first, we all stayed for a week in David's friend house, Mark, in Long Beach. And then, we found a 2/1 apartment in Gardena.

Our funds decreased by the time we moved to Gardena, and we were hungry. And we had a grill in the balcony, but it remained empty. I guess I had to steal again. Thus, I told my teammates, "This is what we are going to do: first, I'm going to grab a shopping cart, and then, we will grab all the meat we can and we will fill the shopping cart—I'll take care of the rest."

If I recall correctly, we all went to the supermarket from across the street and began to fill the cart. Then, once I was ready, I asked them to leave through the exit as I walked out through some closed cashier's lanes with a cart filled with meat and food. We rushed to our apartment across the street. And we sustained ourselves with this food for about two weeks.

I also worked part time at a dry-cleaner during summer camp. I was also doing great on the football field. And at some point, I did not have any more money, and I did not want to steal again. I guess I wasn't ready for this life challenge yet. Summer camp was almost over, my mother was horribly struggling back in Florida as she was losing everything rapidly, and I could not help her with my limited income. And, therefore, I made the choice of returning to Florida. I told Mark, David's friend, and he responded, "You are the last one who I thought would leave."

"Sorry, Mark; I have to go," I said with much pain in my heart.

I also explained to Coach Featherstone, our head coach, and he said, "You have to do what you have to do young man!"—the very same man that told me once, "I can't wait to see you in pads!"

### Arriving in Florida

My mother had just lost all her houses, and she was on the verge of losing the businesses. She was no longer living in one-plus-million dollar mansion; instead, she was residing with my brothers, Marcos and Alfred, the younger ones, in a trailer park in Homestead, FL— while Miguel and Angel were practically forced to move to a one-bedroom efficiency apartment in Little Havana. The image shocked me. The next day, I searched for a job and found it at *Big Daddy's Cleaners*—and I worked non-stop there.

I was starting to get closer to The Voice of Truth, but our relationship needed much improvement. I kept hearing these voices saying, "You are a fighter, you are a fighter...you were born to fight." Thus every day my brother Miguel and I attended to the boxing gym at *Tropical Park* and trained endlessly—Coach Rick and Coach Julito trained us.

I left from *Big Daddy's Cleaners* because my mother desperately needed help at her cleaners, and because my brother Angel couldn't do it by himself with the few workers. Therefore, I felt responsible for stepping in to help out once again.

## Working at My Mother's Dry Cleaners

After practically handling everything each day with the help of my brother Angel, periodically, I realized that I was doing the job of three persons. I had been working four months, and the landlord kept telling me that my mother owed her money. She warned me every day about the possibility of my mother losing her business, and I kept reminding her just to be patient with us. I could foresee the loss of the business, and perhaps, the tailor shop as well.

### *All in Spanish*

The landlord returned and said,

"Listen we are going to have to make a deal between you and me. You are the one doing everything here, and I believe, that we must put everything under your name so that you can bring up this business. Don't you worry about a thing! You don't have to pay me anything now since I know that you are tight—we'll help each other. Oh! By the way! If we do not come to an agreement soon, I will then take this business away from your mother—trust me, I will soon."

"I comprehend ma'am; I will think about it."

I was in a rough position, then. "What do I do? If I tell my mother, she won't listen to me as always. And if I don't, then my only option is

45

to sign these papers, and at least, it will remain in our family. And I'll just bring up the business myself and help my mother." I thought about this for many days.

"I know I do not know You well," I asked The Voice of Truth, "but where are You when I need you? Tell me, what to do please?" And I did not hear a thing. I guess The Teacher doesn't speak when the test commences.

I agreed with the landlord lady behind my mother's back because I was afraid of my mother's reaction and the possibilities of losing the business. And I signed the lease on my 21st birthdate, hoping I could truly enhance the operations and growth of the business.

"Mom, I had to do this to save the business."

"Are you insane? I can't believe you!" she continued, "leave! Leave now! Now!" loudly she shouted. I had nowhere to go; I tried to help the family, but I had done wrong in the eyes of my mother. I attempted to save the business, but instead, I just made it worst.

### *In English Again*

"Where do I go Voice of Truth? Where?"

"You'll see when you arrive at the dry-cleaners," The Voice of Truth responded.

"I'm here already. Where do I sleep?"

"Because of what you've done, you will sleep on the bathroom floor—and you will take showers using this bucket every-single-day."

"But the boiler is right next to it; it is extremely hot back here."

"You will also labor day and night until I decide when to cease all things—your sleep shall escape from you."

Then, I was hurting, lost, wondering why I never received or noticed the warnings before all this mess—it seemed unfair to me. Maybe I was floating around in another world? Or maybe it was supposed to be this way? I had to leave the boxing gym because I had no time to train. I labored day and night, sometimes for 30 hours straight, and for some reason, I could not succeed financially. One day, I decided to humble myself before the Creator hoping He will send me The Voice of Truth or something helpful. Knelt down on my knees, as my head remained almost lower than the floor tiles, I said out of the deepness of my heart, "Please rescue me from this mess. I'm lost, I'm begging you. Please help me!" and shouting desperately I continued, "just come now, please."

"Sir, are you ok?"

"Oh, Lord, Is this you? Oh, God. I can finally hear You."

"Sir, are you ok?"

"Yes, yes...as long as you keep talking to me I will be fine," still kneeling and keeping my face bowed I continued, "Oh, Lord just help me, please."

"I'm not your Lord; now it will be nice if you would just stand up to help me find this address I'm looking for." I heard this, and I quickly got up to find myself staring at a man from Pakistan. I thought, "What a disappointment." But The Voice of Truth responded, "No this is your answer." Rapidly, I got myself together, and focusing I said, "How may I assist you, sir? Please forgive me for the inconvenience. I was just having a little moment. How may I truly help you?"

"I'm looking for this dry-cleaner in Hialeah, do you know where it is?" as he handed me the paper, he said.

"Sir, to be sincere, I'm not so familiar with Hialeah."

"OK, ok, don't worry...I see you have a full dry-cleaning plant here. You see, I have a drop-store in Homestead, and I need a full plant to process all my clothes—a plant I can rely on. Are you interested?"

"It depends."

"How is this?"

"How will we work the numbers?"

"Well, I'll pay you 40% of all the orders."

"How about 50% as everyone else does, remember I will have to drive two hours a day, six times a week just to deliver your garments."

"Listen to me, the Hialeah cleaners is willing to do it for 50 percent. Why should I do it with you?"

"The quality of my service will speak for itself."

"Let me see," he said.

"Look at my work, I put my heart and soul into it."

"I like it, but I think I will go with the Hialeah guy to save a little bit more."

"You rather save and give away quality, or do you prefer to pay what everyone else is paying already and receive top quality?"

"Ok, what's your best deal," he said.

"I just told you, sir."

"It's just not going to work out," as he walked away he said.

"Mr. Lakhani," as I extended my right hand I said, "How about you get 55%?"

"OK, I think that's fair," and we shook on it in agreement.

Lakhani's store was generating $10,000-$12,000 in sales, but when it was all set and done I was profiting about 20% of that only. Thankfully, it was just enough to keep me going. I was not expecting a surprise as such to come from The Living God in this way. But it helped a whole lot as I kept this agreement with Lakhani for over a year. The Voice of Truth answered when I humbled myself.

Day and night I labored consistently just to try to cover part of the overhead of the business. The landlord brought me lemonades to keep me refreshed; people called her *La Guajira(The Peasant)*; she was always very nice for some reason. She would always tell me not to worry about the rent money, and I did not comprehend. Months went by, and she would not charge me—I guess she saw my struggles. I wanted to pay her, but I had no way of doing this as I could not even afford to rent a place to live. After about a year plus, I noticed that business started to increase, and suddenly, a Colombian man, walked into the store one day, unexpectedly. And he said, "I'm looking for a partner that can help me pick up lots of clothes all throughout Miami. Would you be interested?"

"I'm listening, sir; feel free to continue."

"Yes, I don't know anything about this business, but I have some money I'd like to invest," and he continued with his speech, "I have $70,000, and we can put them to work here."

"OK, I comprehend, let me think about it, and we'll stay in touch."

Within two weeks, he handed me a check for $70,000 to buy new equipment and to become my business partner. He said, "I hope this works out since I have invested four times and have lost everything."

"Let us try our best," I replied. And within three months we had to close down the store. He wanted to go left, and I wanted to go right. This happened after spending over $50,000 on machinery to maximize our production. I left it alone; he took all the equipment, including, about $100,000 in equipment the store initially had. I guess this was the end of an era and the beginning of another for me. By now, Ada was no longer my girlfriend, but my ex-girlfriend because I was unfaithful to her. And because I was not spending enough time with her. I did not plan to betray her, but one day while shopping at the pharmacy of 57th Avenue and 7th St., I was drawn by a Puerto Rican. I followed her with my *330ci BMW*, which I obtained from a business partner that owed me money, and snatched her phone number.

## More Women & The Dealership

Within a year, I slept around with various women. But thank God it did not exceed the amount of fingers on both of my hands. By then I was living in Doral, Florida, driving the latest model BMW, visiting the night clubs where my brother worked as head of security, and it felt like paradise.

"You need to stop," said The Voice of Truth, but I didn't care since I didn't have a relationship with Him. It felt good, and I could barely hear The Voice. Slowly, I began to feel different in my heart—I truly wanted to stop. And one day, my brother called me to tell me about some fine ladies that were going to be at some night club. I insisted that I preferred to pass the opportunity, but he persisted instead of resisting himself, and convinced, I finally said, "Ok, I'll go."

After a year of sexual intimacy with the young Colombian lady I had met at the nightclub—she was pregnant. By then, I was working as a sales consultant for *Maroone Dodge of Miami*—I learned how to sell from selling merchandise of the back of my van, for my mother, from 15-19 years-of-age. I was making, $8,000-$12,000 every month as I treated people as I'd like to be treated. I took what other salesmen called flakes and made a living assisting these people. These were the people that drove-in in old cars, the people that had very rough credit, and the people that were rejected by most sales people just because of their appearance. Instead of following the trend, I decided to embrace them and helped them sincerely—I guess I was becoming a better person. When asked by clients if I believed in God, I would rapidly answer with a "yes!"—Not thoroughly knowing what the word 'believe' meant. I desperately wanted to know the real God, but I didn't like to sing in church and act crazy. I was ignorant, filled with deception to some extent, and wanted to live my life. I remember thinking about football and boxing all the time; these sports would never leave my presence. I wanted to help many people, but did not know how to. I thought that the more money I made, the better for me and others.

Carolina was pregnant with a child—my son—and I was turning insane because I was still trying to figure life out. I was lost and worried because it was my first time, and I believed, I had not signed up. I was running away; I didn't want to be with her anymore as she remained pregnant. I can't believe I was acting like this over an unborn harmless creature that only wants to be loved, but I was. I considered myself a "good person" because I was not out there robbing banks and murdering people. I would see her periodically just to see how she was doing, but I truly wanted her to have an abortion. In fact, I told her to have one. I was not ready for a child in my life. I was so wrong as I can clearly see today, but I was so right "in my own eyes" then...

For some reason, I remember how I usually spoke with some retired *NFL* players, *NBA* players, as well as college football players throughout the course of my sales consultant career. I sold to them the *Dodge Chargers*, the *Magnums*, the *Challengers* and referred them to a friend to make extra money as he sold wheels to them. They always advised me to return to college, and it was what my heart desired, precisely. I also sensed, periodically, The Voice of Truth directing me along the college path as well. But I felt responsible for my soon to be born son.

One day, Carolina called me and said, "I'm having an abortion." And I panicked and said, "Please don't, I just lost my mind; I'm trying to get myself together here...please don't."

"I am...I am," crying she continued.

"Please don't, do it for him and not for me, please. It is not his fault, please don't," extremely concerned I replied.

"She will give birth to your son," said The Spirit of Truth suddenly.

## Another Woman

In the midst of the turmoil, one day, I was hungry while at work. And I was on my way to the vending machine. But my party friend and co-worker, Robert, said, "Why don't we go to *Pollo Tropical* instead?"

"Nah, I think I'll be fine, brother."

"Come on, let's go; let's eat real food."

"Ok, fine."

It was *Father's Day*. And we were at the fast food restaurant about to place our order, and suddenly, I saw what appeared to be a family entering the restaurant. And within that family I saw a gorgeous young lady. I'm pulled by the strong energy moving within me. We ordered; they ordered, and Robert and I sat a couple of tables across from them. I did not know if one of the men, sitting at the table with them, had anything to do with her. My soon to be born son, the dilemma with his soon to be mother, and everything else on my mind seemed to disappear. We were having eye-to-eye contact as we ate, the fire appeared to progress within us, and finally, I heard a voice saying, "If she gets up, go after her." And not knowing if it was The Voice of Truth or The Voice of Lies I followed her as my carnal desires agreed.

She got up right after "the voice" commanded and walked outside pretending she was on a phone call. I followed her—hypnotized by her perfection—and waited for her supposed phone call to end. I was hiding behind a post as I was not sure about the relationship between her and the man sitting inside. And suddenly, I said, "May you please come over, I'd like to speak with you?"

"You come over; you're the man," she replied.

"I do not know if the man sitting inside is related to you somehow."

"No, that man and the rest of that family are just friends—you may come, we just came from church." And I introduced myself by my name and not by my history. We conversed for a moment, and she said, "I'm looking for a car." And immediately, I wanted to help her with her shopping experience, not just because I liked her, but also, because I desired it in my heart. We quickly exchanged phone numbers and we left it at that. There is a scripture in The Holy Bible located in Proverbs 16:4, and it declares:

"The LORD hath made all things for Himself: yea even the wicked for the day of evil" (KJV).

I truly did not know if I was on the wicked side or on the side of the righteous, or maybe, somewhere in between. I realize today that during these times in my life, I did not care because of lack of wisdom. I was just immersed in the river called "flow," and the water was too sweet to refuse to swim—I just did not know Him.

The sun was setting, and I had Bianka on my mind. The image of her remained embedded in my memory—just as when we chatted at the restaurant. I decided to phone her by 7pm, and asked, "Would you like to go to the movies, and have dinner with me?"

"No, not really. I appreciate this, but maybe another day."

"Are you sure? Listen, I comprehend we just met today, but would you please allow me to."

"Thank you for the offer, but not now."

"OK, no problem, maybe another time," I said and we disconnected.

In Proverbs 16:2, one can find a scripture mentioning, "All the ways of man are clean in his own eyes; but the LORD weigheth the spirits" (KJV).

I followed my clean ways in my own eyes and disregarded The Lord, who weigheth my spirit—The Lord that judges righteously. I just did not comprehend then what I fully comprehend today. Thus, I was determined to call her again a few hours later since she had said, "Maybe another time." And I called her and said, "You said another time, and I believe this is another time..." She smiled and said, "Fine, this is my address..."

"I'm on my way!"

When I arrived at her house, she was dressed beautifully according to the ways of my "clean eyes." I was seating in my *Chevy Corvette*, she got in, and soon after, we were on the way to the movies. We talked, and talked, and talked some more and then got lost—we could not find the movie theater. When we finally found it, it was closed. Plan B: "How about we dine somewhere," I proposed.

"Fine."

So I drove to Ocean Drive in South Beach. Thus, we both enjoyed dinner, then she grabbed my hands as we walked down the beach shores—hearing the amazing sounds of the ocean—and we sat on the sand. And after conversing for a while, I stole a line from my friend Robert, and said:

"I bet you 20 dollars that I can kiss you without touching your lips if you just close your eyes!"

"Yeah right, that's impossible!"

"Do we have a deal then?"

"Yes, but you're losing your money."

"Let's see," as she closed her eyes I said. And I kissed her for about a minute, and soon after, she stopped me and said, "You did touch my lips! So how is that...?"

"I guess I lost my bet," smiling I replied. We kissed, and kissed till the point where her purse was stolen as we were so distracted, and the sounds of the ocean waves did not help. Then, we walked by the beach shore again, and it was getting late, so I asked, "Would you want me to take you to your house this evening? It's kind of late?"

"I don't know, I wouldn't want to wake up my family."

"Ok, I comprehend, then how about we find a nearby hotel and we stay there for the night, and then I take you home tomorrow morning?"

"Ok, but don't you get any ideas."

"No problem," I said, and we headed to *Intercontinental Hotel* for *Father's Day*.

## At The Intercontinental Hotel

"I'd like to reserve a room for a night, sir."

"We have a room available; it's just three hundred and..."

"Ok, no problem."

## In The Room

"Wait here I'm going to shower," Bianka said.

"No, problem."

I waited and waited, and waited to the point where I decided to ask, "Are you ok?" as I neared the restroom door.

"I'm coming!" she shouted. And soon after, she came out with a bathrobe, and I was hypnotized once again by the curves of her body, her gorgeous face, her curly hair—I was in another world.

"Why didn't you come in?" she asked.

"I respected your decree."

And one thing led to another, and we mixed our flesh and souls—all this in one day, one night. We continued with the mixture for about a week, and one day, as we laid in my bed at home I said, "There is something I must tell you." She panicked, and as she stared into my eyes, "What is it?" she asked.

"I will soon have a son, my ex-girlfriend is pregnant."

Stunned, speechless she remained for about 30 seconds and then she said, "I take you as you are." And now I was stunned, speechless, but I reacted much quicker, and said, "No please, you do not know what you're saying..."

"I insist, I take you as you are."

## Something Crazy

I told her not to purchase a car because I knew the risks involved. She ignored me and purchased a used Corolla, at *Lehman Toyota*—for the price of a new one, and an interest rate of 28% (from a special finance bank called *S.A.F.C.O*). And instead of just returning the car—as I could had easily done because the deal was not funded—I decided to place myself in the other salesman's shoes. And I promised the sales manager to sell him three cars—just to have him receive her car, and cancel the deal. He agreed and one day, strangely, the power went out at *Maroone Dodge of Miami*. And I decided to take all my clients to *Lehman Toyota*. I sold three cars that day, and we returned her car. And they wanted to hire me on the spot, but I refused. Therefore, afterward, I sold to her a *Honda Civic* for a third of the price and half of the interest rate.

## Leaving From Maroone Dodge of Miami
## And Starting at Kendall Toyota

Thankfully, I met a sales manager there called Luis who later referred me to Angel Rodriguez—a sales manager for *Kendall Toyota*, and now friend. Thus, I decided to leave from *Maroone Dodge* as they had deported my friend, Ray Ulloa, the general manager, and overall, the sales were dropping—they closed down the store soon after.

# Chapter 7

# *The Battle Begins*

*You may be wondering, "What does this true story has to do
with me and my future and the future of this world?"
The answer is: it does not, directly. But only and as long as I
leave my personal story by itself. But when I unite it with the
soon-to-be shared message—coming from The Voice of
Truth—you will see the Big Picture; the Message from the
Voice of Truth; the mystery behind most events soon to unfold,
and most importantly, you will know the Truth.*

**M**y heart is changing for some reason. I could hear the Voice of Truth saying, "Come to Me, and I will give you true life." And, of course, I kept going the other way thinking I was going insane—thinking that "this voice" wasn't real. I was selling lots of cars and making a six-figure income. And mostly everything seemed "clean in my own eyes," but The Lord held the balance of the spirits within me (Proverbs 16:2).

## A Star is Born

October 24th, 2006, a child is born. His name: Brandon A. Ferreira. I was there, crying like a baby while Carolina was bringing him into this soon to pass away world system. Bianka was parked downstairs waiting for me to share with her the news. And as I was carrying him in my arms and gazing into his God-given eyes, The Voice of Truth surprisingly declared, "This is My son, I demand that you love him with all your heart. But you will not love him as you remain without Love— for I am Love; not the ladies."

I was trembling because I was confused about this dilemma. And I replied, on my mind, to the Voice of Truth, "I want to care for him, but

I'm in love with Bianka; I want to provide for him, but I can't do it separated from him. Please just take away this fight within me." I walked downstairs, filled with this moment in my heart, and I said, "Bianka, I'm going to have to move in with the baby's mother." And now she was crying; she was terrified. I was devastated; I was terrified, but I felt that I could not exist without my son. Bianka said, "It's ok, I'll be here waiting for you always; do what you have to do."

## Pain

I want to stay with her,
but my son pulls me away.
I've heard many stories
about children living without their parents
from my clients,
and I did not want to be a part of it.
I'm in love with Bianka,
but I want to do the right thing.
My heart wants to divide into multiple pieces,
but it can only remain in one place.
I wish all of us could remain united;
this wouldn't work today.
I long for peace,
but peace seems to remain far away.
I remain far away from The Truth,
as The Voice of Truth departed away:

"O son, why don't you seek Me as I have been here today," said The Voice of Truth suddenly. And I trembled in fear and left with an undecided heart. The wind was taking me all over as The Voice of Truth sought for me day and night. Worried, lost, and going crazy—I moved in, with Carolina and my son, Brandon. I was happy because I had my son with me always, but I was miserable because the love of my life remained far away. Two to three months passed, and I could not eliminate my feelings for Bianka. I still had not graduated from

"The Love College," but I, at least, comprehended my love for her somewhat. At this point, I also wanted to remain united with the baby's mother for the sake of my son, but for some reason, Bianka had captivated my heart. I thank my son's mother for bringing Brandon to this world. And also, because I once loved her "in my own eyes." I wanted to care and provide for her, but "something" kept telling me to walk away. Could it be The Voice of Truth or The Voice of Lies? I didn't know, but "something" just kept telling me to walk away.

## Walk Away or Stay

"O Voice of Truth, where are you?
No answers seem to remain,
I'm seeking,
but I can't find you today.
I'm asking for signs,
but they remain out of line.
I'm searching for true guidance,
and she remains too far away to find.
Away, away, away...
I see a light at the end of the day—
it just seems to be delayed;
delaying the process I am,
by not choosing today.
What do I do O Voice of Truth?
Where do I go O Voice of Love?
Do I leave or do I stay, today?
Or tomorrow You'll explain?

I decided to move in with Bianka—back into my mother's house. And we resided in Homestead, FL—as we are all "doing ok."

# The OK

The OK.
The "OK" did not remain
for as long as the baby's mother battled for her place.
She showed up to the house...multiple times,
threatening to burn down the whole place:
O Lord, do I stay?
Or do you want me to leave today?
I miss my son;
I'm missing my son!
She's not letting me see him today.
I'm trying to explain my position,
but my words seem to fall out of position
'in the cleanness of her own eyes.'
My heart is failing due to the distance from
my new star,
my new star doesn't have a clue
of what's really going on,
on and on time passes,
as I remain undelivered from this pain,
O pain, O pain,
will you just go away?
O Love, O Love,
will you just come back today?
O peace, O peace,
will you just visit me...just for today?
O today, O today,
why don't you escape from my way?
Again and again,
and not receiving your 'Answer.'
I concluded to move in
with my son's mother again.
Again and again,
Mr. Suffering came to my place

while Mrs. Answer delayed,
But O how I loved holding my son,
over and over again.
And each day I carried him in my arms
not wanting to let go again.
Again and again,
I suffered because of my current state.
O pain, O pain, why won't you just walk away?

## The Feast and The Song

Months pass by, and the spirits within me
are having a feast,
as my heart runs away.
He hears, he feels,
but no feast for him today;
Today, today, I said!
Why can't it just go away?
Bring me a feast,
bring me a song,
just something to take this away.
O Voice of Truth,
where may I find Truth?
O Truth,
where are You?
O Voice,
why won't you speak to me today?
"As much as I love you, my son,
I may have to step away, again."

I decided to move out again from the house of my mother's son. Her step-father and her mother said to me, "We gave you a second chance, but after this, we will not accept you in the place." And I walked away again in pain. Again, I moved in with Bianka into my mother's investment apartment in Cutler Bay, FL. I still had not committed my life to the Voice of Truth. However, He said, "I'll be waiting for you, today."

## I Want Peace

I'm working hard each day,
but my peace seems to dissipate.
There's joy here and joy there,
but the moments seem to escape.
O good moment! O scarce joy!
Why won't you come my way and stay?
Why don't you bring me love, peace, joy,
and patience to endure this, today?
Today!
Today, not tomorrow:
Today! Seems to be the best day.
The day escapes and escapes,
as my terror never agrees to disintegrate.

# Chapter 8

## New Business, Boxing, And Football Again

While I sold cars, and sent clothes, shoes, jewelry...to my mother, in The Dominican Republic, I started to hear The Voice of Truth again. He followed me, but I did not fully comprehend. Then I was making $12,000 to $17,000 each month. I had football and boxing on my mind. I thought, "If I go far in sports maybe I can help countless families around the world. I was talented, I knew I could make it in both sports; I was fast and skilled..."

Though I did not perform well enough on the football field—according to my potential—at the beginning of my high school season, by the end of the season, Coach Rodriguez had prepared me for college football. He only said this once with excitement, "That's how you tackle! That's what I want you to do every single time!" as we practiced our tackling drills.

Unfortunately, my senior year season was over soon after, but, fortunately, my life wasn't. I thought about these moments—the moments when I trained at night at the high school every day when no one was there. When I consistently dragged the sled, sprinted across the field, did push-ups and pull-ups, backpedaled, and jumped over things—when I lived a block away from the school with my brother, Miguel. Often, I thought about the three years I consistently trained to be told, "You cannot join the football team," by my mother. Periodically, I thought of my days at *El Camino College*. How, perhaps, I had an amazing opportunity to transfer to a *Division I* university by just remaining there. I would see myself boxing in a big championship—becoming the new light-heavy or heavy-weight-champion of the world. And I would also receive signs periodically from The Voice of Truth—signs that began to make more sense as time progressed.

When I worked for *Maroone Dodge of Miami*, I went to our local *Chevy* store to take a client there, and I bumped into Milton (Shannon Briggs boxing trainer). They were all there—including Shannon Briggs with his entourage. Milton and I conversed briefly; I expressed to him my desires to train to fight, and he provided me with his phone number and offered to train me. We spoke three to four times, but I never allocated the time to commit truly to him as there was always something in the way. Another opportunity came by one day, as I was driving down Old Cutler Road when I noticed that Glen Johnson—the boxer that knocked out Roy Jones Jr. in, 2004—was running down the road. I immediately made a U-turn, stopped and parked at a street corner and asked my girlfriend to wait for me there as I ran after him.

I jogged next to him, I introduced myself, and he did the same politely as we continued to jog. And soon after, he replied, "You can come to *Thump Gym*, where I train, and I'll help you."

"Thanks a lot, I'll be there tomorrow," I said.

I trained every-single-day with him and DaThomas—a four-year amateur champion just turning pro. Coach Hamlet Mckency and Coach Orlando trained us every day. I trained with Glen 'the champ' every day also, and then I would run with him down Old Cutler Road since we were neighbors. I never missed, and every day I learned something. Thus, I was training twice-a-day, working at the dealership, going through my personal dilemma, and planning for a new dry-cleaning business.

## The New Business

One day, as I was working at the dealership, I noticed that all the sales staff dressed in long sleeved shirts, ties, and slacks—and some, in two-piece suits. The voice of Truth came and said:

"Customize a logo for your new company; just hang a hanger on top of the world—this is your logo. Also, order yellow custom-made bags from *Cleaner's Supply* so that each sales person has their own—with their name, phone number, and instructions to process each garment. You will then make a price list—convenient and fair to all—as I will give you most of the dealership's business. This business will be unique, above all dry-cleaning businesses because you will make an agreement with each store owner or general manager, and establish a custom-made system within the premises of each edifice. This way, all sales staff will save fuel as they will no longer have to drive back and forth to the cleaners to pick up their garments. They will spend this extra time with their families, and you will make enough money as you pick up multiple filled bags from each store. Create a form to keep all the information needed for your new clients, and give it to each person after you process their first free $20 order. When you have all the supplies ready, find a dry-cleaner like the one you and your mother had before, and pay them a fair amount—thus in return, your amount will remain fair. When you have all this ready, I will speak through you at the Friday meeting—as you stand in front of all sales staff—to help you introduce this convenient new service. Most will trust in you, and will give to you all you need to succeed, freely. Most importantly, trust in Me as I will deliver the message."

"Yes, Lord; I will follow You."

Friday's meeting came, and prior to the meeting, I began to hand over the free and folded yellow bags—with the $20 gift order within—to most sales consultants I knew personally. The buzz was spreading quickly as the rest desired to have a yellow bag. The meeting time arrived. And in a 3-minute speech 80% of the staff signed up for The Voice of Truth's services. Every week, I received calls from other car dealerships wanting to have The Voice of Truth's services. And within three months, we purchased our first dry-cleaning store to process all garments. With the help of Dodanin, Bianka, and the true guidance of The Voice of Truth, the work was timely-honored.

Then, I was picking up all garments in the morning; working at the dealership from 2pm to 9pm, and boxing during morning time also and running at night—I remained extremely busy constantly. And, for this reason, I told Coach McKency, and Glen Johnson 'the champ,' "I will bring up the business and then come back. This way, I'll have more time to train."

Coach McKency looked at me with pain in his demeanor and said, "You're a good man, God is with you." And The Voice of Truth replied in my heart, "Something new is coming into your life, be ready."

By then, I was no longer working as an internet sales manager because upper management changed the internet manager's pay-plan— after I habitually hit the $5,000.00 monthly bonus (plus $10,000.00-$12,000.00 in commissions) while I sold over 45 cars monthly. I noticed that some of my superiors were complaining because my pay was higher than theirs. The Voice of Truth said, "Go back to the sales floor, and you'll have more time for the dry-cleaners and your family," and I did just that. And about three months passed, and the Voice of Truth said, "You have to be late for work every day, you'll comprehend later."

"Late?"

"Yes."

Soon after, I was managing the dry-cleaning business; exporting goods to my mother; showing up late for work—as the sales staff did not have to clock in or out, and as The Voice of Truth commanded— and I was preparing myself to buy Lackani's drop-store along with two other stores, and a $1 million facility, in Opalocka, FL, for cents on the dollar.

Since I had purchased an investment property in Orlando, FL, minutes away from *Disney World*; and since, I had given a down payment for a $678,000 two-story penthouse with a rooftop jacuzzi, and since I have paid off a few cars and carried multiple credit cards— my personal credit skyrocketed to an 849 score. To me, then, and to a deceived world, now, this sounds like I was on my way to glory—like I was living the "American Dream." A kid that pedaled his way throughout the streets of *La Romana* to make 2.5 U.S dollars weekly was about to explode quickly.

## A Choice

Financial freedom is at hand,
and the worries of life will dissipate.

The car collection will increase,
as the increase of previous headaches decrease.
My previous life will fade away:
Go away! Go away! Fade away!
The Father of Lies shouts in vain,
and I can say to my past today.
Today! And not tomorrow, but today!
I can live the life I desired yesterday,
O yesterday, O yesterday,
thank you for leaving today.
Today, really today:
Is this what I truly want? And through this way?
I don't know, but it sure feels true,
Oh, yeah, it feels so good;
Although the Truth, and yes,
nothing but the whole  truth,
remains at a distant place.
But is it distant or is this Truth truly close?
I don't know, but perhaps is a choice.
Oh, choice who are you?
What are you?
Are you a man or a boy?
Are you a woman or a girl?
Are you a house or a home?
Are you a thing or a...?
I don't know.
But do I choose, or do You choose,
or do we both sign on the dotted line?
Talk to me! Talk to me!
Whoever or whatever You are.
But please do it now!
As I intend to choose the true path,
right here and right now.

# Chapter 9
## *A New Opportunity*

I almost fell for it. But The Voice of Truth interfered.

### At Kendall Toyota

I was standing in front of the dealership calling clients, and seeking for business opportunities, when suddenly, The Voice of Truth interfered, and declared, "Call David Silveira, your friend who helped you to get into college, and open up your heart to him."

"Yes, Lord, but what do I tell him?"

"Your heart contains all you need. Trust in me." And I walked away a little bit lost, but also somewhat comprehended that that moment and decision could become a life-changing journey. A few minutes passed, and I made the choice.

"Hey, brother; how are you? I asked David.

"I'm doing great, thank God."

"Listen, I know that this may be ridiculous but I have to tell you."

"Talk to me, brother."

"I know that I made the choice of leaving from *EL Camino College* about five years ago, but I long to play college football again."

"How will you do it? You have your son now; you're working, and if I find for you an opportunity, it will probably be out-of-state. You're going to have to leave a lot behind. Why don't you go back to boxing, I thought you were doing great there?"

"I truly comprehend, brother, but I can always do boxing later. But for football, I have to act now."

"Listen carefully, there is a football camp every Wednesday in Homestead—it starts at 3:30pm. If you want, I'll talk to Coach Noah, he's a straight up man, and I'll tell him about you."

"Oh, man...this could be great! If you could just help me again. Oh, but there is a problem?"

67

"What is it?"

"I'm not in such of good shape."

"Don't worry brother; you know you'll get in shape in no time— just go."

"Thanks a lot, brother."

"I'm here for you brother," David said and we disconnected.

Now I was filled with something I truly did not recognize—I was thrilled by the opportunity. And, "I can't wait to go!" I shouted in my heart. And right after this, reality struck through The Voice of Truth:

"You have to quit your job; you're going to have to leave your son, and your girlfriend, Bianka, behind. You'll have to leave everything for this—it's the only way. But don't you worry; I will reunite you with your family again."

I was silenced for a moment, nervous, but also, I knew that this was the right thing. The Voice of Truth returned with news:

### Eternal

"This cannot be it.
You may work and work, and never truly work.
You may live and live, and never truly live.
You may fight and fight, and never truly fight.
You may win and win, and never win a thing.
You may lose it all, and have it all again.
Again and again, a decision must be made today.
Today! Yes, today!
I will bless you with My love and grace.
Follow Me, and you'll see
the amazing thing I bring.
Bring me joy, bring me peace,
and I will sing on to you a melody.
Fight for me and not for flesh,
and I will give unto thee My Key.
Obey My message; obey Me,
and I will take you to a new place prepared

for thee with Me.
Follow Me, O son, follow Me,
and you will find yourself through Me indeed.
Through me, O yes, only through Me,
the gift of life can be found eternally and free.
Fear not! Fear not! My little flock
as you keep your eyes on Me—O My sheep.
Don't you worry, O don't you worry,
just cast all your burdens unto Me.
Through Me, through Me, and only through Me,
you can find your true gift surely:
A gift, given by Me
is what I have waiting for thee.
Just choose life,
and only through Me,
and I will provide for all your needs, truly.
Don't be afraid.
Don't run away.
Away! Away! Away!
You may only find evil and pain.
Come close, very, very close
as I long to keep you with Me.
With Me, and just with Me,
you can find everlasting peace.
Yes, peace!
I give to thee!
As you hold on to My family.
No family will ever die,
as long as they keep Me as the center of their lives.
Within, O yes within,
and only with Me,
there's a place I want you to see.
See it all, see it now,
and you'll live eternally with Me."

I'm trying to comprehend...everything,
but it sounds like a Chinese melody.
Although Chinese melodies
seem far from me,
somehow, I comprehended clearly.
Clearly, is the Voice,
That Voice that says,
"My sheep hear Me."

## The First University of Miami Promise

It was incredibly hot and dry that day, and I sensed The Voice of Truth whispering:

"Go to The University of Miami, now!"

"Yes, Lord."

"I'm on my way now; what do I do?"

"Just walk in."

"Where to?"

"Just follow My lead.

"Stop," said The Voice and continued, "approach that lady, and ask her about enrolling here."

"Are You sure? Did You forget about my high school GPA?"

"No son, just trust in Me."

"OK."

"Ma'am what must I do to enroll in this Institution?"

"What's your GPA?"

"I think I had about a 2.7...plus."

"Oh, you won't qualify, you need at least a 3.5 to be considered, or maybe through a sports' scholarship is another way."

"Don't you have any special programs that perhaps may help me in this time of need?"

"I don't work for the admissions office; it's over there," she said as she pointed her finger to it. "But based on what you're telling me, I think you're wasting your time."

"OK, thank you for your help," discouraged I replied.

"What is this supposed to mean?" I asked The Voice of Truth.

"I will give you a scholarship, and you will come to this place. In this territory, I will show you many things. I will use this place; will you just trust in Me?"

"Yes, Lord. But what do I do now?"

"You've done your job; you may leave now."

## Chapter 10
# *A Real Chance*

I showed up to Noah's Football Camp (from *Fellowship of Christian Athletes*), and I saw Coach Noah Wilbanks gathering all the football players. But it appeared to me that most young men were much younger than me—they all appeared to be 17 to 21 years young. I must had been in the wrong place.

"Are you Marcial?" said Coach Noah.

"Yes, coach; I am. But I think I'm in the wrong place?"

"No, no you're not, please join us," he said as we all sat on the track bleachers.

"Today, we're going to do our 15 minute Bible study as we always do", said Coach Noah in his speech and continued, "When we give God the best?" he shouted.

"He'll bless us with the rest," the crowd responded.

"I must be in the wrong place," I thought, "is this a set-up from David?"

"You remain there; this is the beginning," said The Voice of Truth.

### My Heart's Desires

Coach Noah continued speaking as we all sat quietly:

"Psalm 37:4 says, 'Delight thyself also in the LORD; and HE shall give thee the desires of thine heart.' You see, when you delight yourself in God, He truly gives you the desires of your heart. He changes your life; delivers you from potential catastrophes; changes your direction; blesses you in all His ways; comforts you in the midst of pain; protects you in times of trouble, and most importantly, you join His everlasting family. But you must delight yourself in Him—that's the key!

"Clear so far?" with boldness and love he asked.

"Yes, coach!" everyone shouted as soldiers respond to their leaders.

"Now, we may find the key in the word 'delight;' let's see what this word means. Any suggestions?"

"To believe!" shouted a young man.

"To care," said another young man.

"To love!" whispered a kid with long hair.

"To trust!" said a big black kid challenging Mike Tyson's voice.

"To depend on Him in everything you do," a short skinny white kid with his pants sagging.

"To never give up," said a brown skin kid with authority.

"To seek Him!" shouted an abnormally tall kid.

"To follow Him," said the crew's grandpa, but he did not know where he was truly going.

"OK, I guess I should be sitting there, and you guys should be up here," said Coach Noah with a smile on his face. "What if I tell you that all those words you just shared with me will help you understand better your new journey with God—your new relationship. Is that fair?"

"Yes, coach," we all shouted.

"Alright! Alright! Alright! Let's huddle up and get readdyyyy!" coach shouted and continued, "we ready!?"

"Yes, coach!" all of us shouted again.

"Are you sure?" loudly, Coach Noah said, "Repeat after me!"

"No, weapon!"

"No, weapon!"

"Formed against me!"

"Formed against me!"

"Shall prosper!"

"Shall prosper!"

"I'm the head!"

"I'm the head!"

"And not the tail!"

"And not the tail!"

"I'm bless going and I'm bless going out!"

"I'm bless going and I'm bless going out!"

"Alright! Alright! Alright! Everyone—to your coaches," with a high level of caffeine he continued. And some kids were coming in late, and Coach Noah shouted, "Oh, no, you all missed the Bible study; you all going to be hungry later!" He continued shouting, "what's my first rule team?"

"No profanity!" they all shouted.

"And my second?"

"To make it on time."

"You all heard that?" he shouted to the young men as they were walking in late.

"Yes, coach," they all responded.

"I'll forgive you all today, but don't 'do me like that' tomorrow," he continued, "Is that fair?"

"Yes, coach!"

"Hurry! Hurry! You all late."

## A New Man is Born Again

I walked out of that field a different man that day. Most things began to make sense suddenly—most things were becoming clearer. What I desired prior to this moment wasn't exactly the way to go. The Voice of Truth was leading me all along. I can detect it much better now—a vital component was needed for true and everlasting life. I discovered, on that day, the truth behind many deceptions.

## The True Light

"O Voice of Truth,
thank You for being You.
For You, and only You
it's all I want from You.
You remain in my heart,
and I hope I remain in You.
O Truth, O Truth,
just keep telling me the whole Truth.
O Voice, O Voice,

never leave me without Your choice.
I hold on to You today
hoping You'll never fade away.
The journey seems so far away,
but I know I'll get there someday—
even without a train.
I may see it now or later on,
but what matters is that You're with me on and on.
Thank You, Voice for guiding me;
without You, I would have never arrived.
I know I'm far from Your delight,
but I'll delight myself in The Light.
O forgive me for being blind while having eyes;
for Your Forgiveness, is truly One of a Kind
now in my sight."

# Chapter 11

# I Lost It All to
# Gain One

### They Let Me Go

I was at work, and my friend and sales manager, Angel Rodriguez, called me and whispered, "Brother, I'm going to have to let you go."

I knew he did this out of respect and kindness because he knew about this internal decision already. I understood that he just wanted to be the one to inform me—to keep our friendship perhaps. I believe he did the right thing with honor, and The Voice of Truth will reward him. I understood that this had to be part of the plan, the reason for being asked to show up late for work, and because of The Voice of Truth' petition. Somehow, I knew that transformation was coming in my direction.

### Mom Won't Pay Back

I was working hard at the dry-cleaners; picking up clothes throughout most car dealerships; then things began to improve slowly, and we bought a *Hyundai Bering Box Truck*. Business was increasing, and clients kept coming. I was buying more merchandise, and sending it to my mother in The Dominican Republic.

This time, I decided to send to her a large amount. I figured, "Once she pays me back, I'll be able to buy the warehouse and the other stores, and then, perhaps, even help some people in need."

One week passes by, and I couldn't reach my mother via telephone. Two weeks; three weeks, and she answered and hanged up continuously. Four weeks; no connection whatsoever...

"She will no longer answer; for you must go to her," said The Voice of Truth.

"But this can't be happening, I've given almost everything to buy all this merchandise?"

"You must go quickly."

"Yes, Lord; please help me now?"

"I've always have; I will always."

"I can't believe this is happening to me; my only mother is running away from me: This must be a dream?"

"No, is not, My son; you will learn from this."

I arrived to Santo Domingo, in The Dominican Republic at one of my mother's stores, and there she was, selling all the merchandise I recently sent to her faster than I can eat. She finally recognized that I was there waiting for her, and she stepped out and said, speaking in Spanish, "Oh, my son; I've been so busy. Listen: go to the apartment, and we'll talk later. As you can see, I have to get back to work," and she kissed me and walked away.

"I'm here, she just sent me to her apartment: what do I do?"

"Just honor your mother."

"Honor her!?"

"Yes."

I walked away not comprehending this option. I didn't comprehend this whole thing, and suddenly, my mother arrived at her apartment and said, "Oh son, I'm so glad to see you! I've been in all sorts of problems. I tell you what: how about you come with me to the store tomorrow, and we'll chat? I need to get some rest; as you can see, I'm exhausted," and walking away she kissed me and said, "God bless you, son!"

"Blessings, mother."

Her store was a beauty salon/spa/clothing-store/jewelry-store. And when we arrived there, I noticed that the workers were complaining about their pay—while they were fixing hair. One lady shouted in Spanish, "I work hard for my money! I need it now!" with a strange facial expression.

And another lady elaborated, "Bills don't wait for me! You know!"

"It's been four weeks, and I have not gotten a cent," said the other lady behind me.

"We want our money now! No excuses!" they all shouted together in much distress.

"O Voice of Truth what am I doing here? O Voice of truth is this your reason for sending me here?"

"I need you to get up from that chair and speak to them. I will speak through you; don't be afraid."

"Now?"

"Yes. Right now!"

And speaking through The Voice of Truth I said:

"Ladies, ladies, I am the owner's son. I truly cannot comprehend your frustration because I'm not you, but please know that I'm trying. In the midst of this turmoil, would you be kind enough to follow me upstairs, please?"

And they all gazed at each other quickly, and in agreement some of them replied:

"Sure."

"Of course."

"Why not?"

"He's kind of cute!"

They followed me upstairs to the spa area. And inspired by the Voice of Truth I said, "My name is Marcial, and I can already see that money is owed to you..."

And they quickly interrupted me and shouted:

"Yes! A whole lot of cash!"

"Lots of money!"

"This isn't fair," said one of the ladies screaming as she stood in the back.

"Please, allow me to help you," I said.

"How?"

"Yeah, how?"

"May you all just let me try, please?"

"Go ahead," a leader said, and silence hovered the spa area.

"I know that you are all in desperate need of your well-deserved money. You worked hard for it, and you all have earned it. I do not promise you anything but this..."

"What is it?" one of the ladies interrupted.

"False promises again," another shouted as she stood by the bathroom door.

"Let him talk," said the leader standing in the back row.

"...Love never fails."

And they soon calmed, or at least it appeared to be the case.

"Thank you for your words," one lady said.

"I feel much better," another nice lady replied.

"Thank God you came," shouted one in the back.

"Let's get to work; we're losing money!" shouted the beauty salon's leader and the rest followed along.

I did not offer money, but the Word of Truth came through with healing. Here I was attempting to collect my "misplaced" money, but instead, I was asked to calm the debt storm. I was dealing with my personal storm, but I guess The Voice of Truth knows best. I was losing everything back in Miami, but I assumed The Lord had another plan. I had been there a week, and my mother kept avoiding me. And thus, I said to her, "Please, just tell me what's happening?" And her response, "I'll tell you in another moment."

And then I initiated a conversation with The Voice of Truth, "I'm lost; don't know what to do. Should I get another job, and recover from all this mess? Should I sell everything I have remaining? What do I do?"

"Just go back home," said The Voice of Truth.

I was broken because my mother avoided me, and not mainly because of the money. I could not comprehend how this was possible. I wondered when it all went wrong. I thought, "How could a mother, not even explain to her son, the reason for such calamity?"

We did not speak for months after this—just because she could not say, "Son this is what truthfully happened." Maybe I deserved this for trying to help the family when I put the dry-cleaner under my name to save it—for the best of us all. All I desired was for her to say, "I'm sorry, son; please forgive me," but this did not happen. Day and night I prayed about restoring my relationship with my mother, but time passed, and we did not communicate. I couldn't punch her because she brought me into this world. I couldn't fight her because she is a woman. But I chose to forgive her because The Voice of Truth told me multiple times:

"For if you forgive others for their transgressions, your heavenly Father will also forgive you. But if you do not forgive others, then your Father will not forgive your transgressions," (Matthew 6:14-15, NASB).

# Chapter 12
## *The Training Begins*

Soon after, I lost the dry-cleaning plant—I was practically forced to sell my contracts for cents on the dollar. Also, I gave my car to someone I met once—to take over an $876 monthly payment. And my box truck's engine blew up, I slept in it till sunrise, and then sold it for nickels soon after. I lost my apartment in Orlando, FL as well. Everything vanished in an instant. All I had left was part of my family and The Voice of Truth.

"You have all you need," The Voice of Truth said.

"I can get back on my feet, many people lose and win," I replied in hope.

"No. For now you have to remain there with a humble spirit because soon I will take you somewhere."

"With a humble spirit?"

"It will help you attain true wisdom."

"True wisdom?"

"The kind I give freely."

"And where am I going to?"

"Somewhere new; somewhere different—somewhere to prepare you for your next battle. You'll know when the time comes."

I didn't know where I was going, but I knew that, perhaps, it was connected to football. I also knew He was right, but it was hard to swallow. Within a few months, the mayhem between my mother and I was out of my system.

### At Noah's Football Camp

"Marcial," said Coach Noah, "let me introduce you to Coach Orlando from *ASA College* in Brooklyn, New York."

"It's a good thing to meet you, coach."

"Likewise, young man!"

"Marcial is one of a kind," said Coach Noah, "he's special; trains after all of us leave, a father, a leader..."

"A father?" said Coach Orlando.

"Yeah you know coach," said Coach Noah, "responsible also!"

"How old are you, young man? Coach Orlando asked.

"I'm 26, coach."

"Coach, he's like wine you know; a good kid!"

After practice, I was offered an opportunity to become a student-athlete for this college. And I said to the visiting coach, "I'll be glad to join your team; I'm thankful for this chance, coach." But there was only one problem: I had injured my right shoulder's ligament by trying to exceed over twenty repetitions with 225 lbs. prior to proper warm up. At first, I thought this was minor, but then, I couldn't do a single push up. And the time arrived for the new football season, and for me to leave to New York, but my shoulder remained injured. I was forced to turn down the opportunity. And soon after, I returned to the car business while my right shoulder recovered.

## South Motors BMW

By then, I was working for *South Motors BMW,* and I was doing fine. Every day, I was visiting *LA Fitness* next door to improve my strength and cardiovascular conditions. I was paying the bills, and I was making maybe: $5000 to $6000 each month. And I was desperate to play college football already because the Voice of Truth kept revealing it to me. I had to lose one season due to the injury, and about seven seasons due to my departure from *El Camino College.* I was already 27 years young, and I was fully aware of this. But The Voice of Truth kept telling me, "You'll see, son; you'll see" and again He spoke, "I know you want to leave for College already, but *South Motors BMW* must let you go first."

"Again?"

"For My thoughts are not your thoughts,

Nor are your ways My ways," says the Lord" (Isaiah 55:8).

Soon after this, one day, one of the sales managers disrespected me, and I lost it with words. The rest of the sales staff believed that I was right, but I knew, I had failed by not retaining my peace—even though he had disrespected me. Everything after that changed, within a few weeks after this they let me go. The Voice of Truth did tell me that they were going to let me go, but I still did not completely understand.

## Slip & Fall Deception

"Watch, I'm going to sue somebody," said my father-in-law, David, speaking in Dominican Spanish, as we sat in his backyard lounge area, "and take some of these rich people's money—it won't hurt them, they got too much."

These words found their residence in me, and it began to develop within me. I figured, "This makes sense! Insurance companies 'legally steal' from hard laboring and honest citizens; a builder may spend $70,000 to build a house and then sells it for $350,000; pharmaceutical companies bribe government agencies to keep better-healing drugs off the market—just to steal more money from you and me; the U.S Government spends more money than it brings in, and they also keep borrowing and not paying back; we're told that we have to file a personal income tax when this is against the U.S Constitution, and, therefore, against the law." So then, I believed that, "slipping and falling was not going to hurt anybody." The Voice of Lies captivated me with much truth—it just wasn't the whole truth.

While living in Homestead, FL, I shopped at *Publix Supermarkets* often. And one day, as I was shopping, I noticed a wet spot on the floor. I walked by it, analyzed it, walked around a couple of times, and finally I slipped and fell, intentionally. And the first thing I heard, was a man shouting, "Call 1-800-something; [you gettin'] some money!" I acted as if I was hurt, and the store manager approached me right away and said,

"Are you ok?"

"Yes, I'm ok; it's just that my knee is hurting me," I said as I acted better than Denzel Washington.

"Here, put this ice on it, would you want me to call the rescue?"

"No, no, that's ok; I'll get home somehow."

My girlfriend was waiting for me outside, and then we returned home. And within a few days, I received a call from *Publix Supermarkets*:

"Hello, may I speak with Mr. Marcial Ferreira, please?"

"This is he."

"We noticed that you slipped and fell in one of our stores, and I'd like to offer you a $50 gift card to help you in this time of need. What do you think?"

"No, no, it's ok?"

"Are you sure?"

"Yes, thanks for the generosity."

"Well...you have a good day!"

"You as well," and we disconnected.

The Voice of Lies said, "Now you'll be able to help others; you'll have all you need. Just tell them that your right shoulder injured also, and you'll have a surgery free of cost. Plus, you'll receive money to help many people."

So far, I was filled with the deception, and I made the decision to call *The Robert Rubenstein's Law Firm*. They sent to me one of their representatives, and quickly, I signed an agreement to hire them as my representatives. By then, I was receiving therapy each day for my knee, and I remembered what The Voice of Lies said about the free surgery— so I asked them to inspect my shoulder. And next thing you know, the physician said, "You have a torn ligament in your shoulder, and you need surgery."

So we scheduled the surgery for Friday the 13th. I did not like the date at all, but I was fearless—I was just getting to know The Only One I must fear. My shoulder was feeling way better, almost, as if I felt no need for a surgery. But I was blinded by The Voice of Lies and proceeded with the pre-surgery procedures.

"Go on, you'll be alright," said The Father of Lies. Thus, I believed and followed through with the surgery. And for a whole month a sling sustained my healing arm. I desired to heal quickly for the upcoming season as I had been offered to play football for *Dakota College at Bottineau*...

## Steroids Again

One day, while training at *LA Fitness*, in Doral, FL, the front counter fellow said, "How's your shoulder doing?" And I responded, "I'm ok, but it is not healing as fast as I desire."

"Just tell your doctor to give you testosterone."

"No, no...I don't think that's a good idea."

"Listen, I've had three surgeries on my knees, and steroids have worked miracles. You see my knee?"

"Yeah, I can see you just had surgery as well." And with a smile on his face he said, "And what do you think I'm taking to recover?"

"I'll think about it, brother," and I walked away.

## Training with Illness

By then, I was training very hard every day, and I noticed that my joints were very weak. I felt that I had much more strength, but due to the weakness of my joints, I remained constricted. I was drinking all kinds of over-the-counter products, and nothing seemed to help. I was ordering all kinds of teas from countless websites, but a cure remained far away. I kept on asking The Voice of Truth for direction, but my connection had reduced true connection. I was also attended different football fields, and performed drills, jumped on tables, ran up and down the bleachers with my 40 lbs. weighted vest, flipped and slammed my tractor tire, pushed my truck in the parking lot...

I was training twice a day, and swimming once, and nothing seemed to help. I pleaded persistently to The Voice of Truth, "O Lord, please heal me!" every-single-day, but everything remained the same...

I dealt with this excruciating pain—arthritis is what they call it nowadays—and I just didn't know when I'll be ok. I was becoming an expert in the medical field by all the studying I was doing consistently. I tried all the teas and remedies, but nothing seemed to heal me....

"O Spirit of Truth and Love, please heal me," is all I kept saying every day, but the pain remained.

"Testosterone is your best choice," whispered The Father of Lies.

"Is this you, Voice of Truth? I repeated, "Is it you?"

"Take it, you'll recover what you've lost," whispered The Voice of Lies again.

I was in a test and didn't even realize it. There was a battle within me, and I was failing to comprehend fully. I just longed to be ready for this upcoming season, but my healing ran away from me that season. I was praying, reading The Bible, believing that one day I'll be touched, but nothing had happened yet:

"Steroids," The Voice of Lies whispered again.

Not yet graduated from "The Listening University of Heaven," I sought after a tutor.

## At the Physician

"Doctor, do you think that testosterone will really help me recover, and perhaps, make my shoulder strong again?"

"I think that you'll be fine by doing your therapy, but if you want, I'll give you testosterone to help you recover faster" the physician replied.

"Testosterone is all you need," whispered again The Voice of Lies.

"OK, I just hope this helps," I said to the physician facing me.

"Sure, you'll be fine, here's your prescription" he replied.

"Thank you," and I walked away confused, but with hope in my heart.

I decided to take testosterone, and regained my strength. I joined cross-fit with Coach Guido Trinidad at *Peak Performance 360*. And even *Channel 7 News* came once to interview us, but my joint pain remained. I was 218 pounds and to everyone around me, I appeared to be strong due to my performance. But I knew that I was weak because of my shoulder weakness and my joints.

## Thundering At Tropical Park

I remember being at *Tropical Park* with my good friend Melvin Brownlee running up a hill with my 40 lbs. weighted vest, and pulling my sled attached with 45 lbs., and carrying the sled on my way down. And The Voice of Truth showed up unexpectedly, and said:

## Lost and Found

"You were lost
and you found Me.
I see you're trying,
just keep trying with Me.
My words are medicines
for the one who seeks.
You've been forgiven,
since you're trying to follow Me.
In Me, and only in Me you'll find the healing you need."

## Noah's Football Camp Again

"Marcial," said Coach Pete Monzon, "There is a college in North Dakota, in a very small town—it's in a place called Bottineau. What do you think?"

"It's a small town you said?"

"Yeah, not much around. And 99% white people, but if you want to be focused, I think this is a good place for you."

"You've said all I need to know. Thanks a lot, coach, this means much to me. When can I sign up?"

"Just go to my job tomorrow: it's the school for special needs kids—on Miller and just past 107$^{th}$ Ave.—and I'll help you with the paperwork.

"Thanks, coach; I'll be there."

I had to make a tough decision. My son was only two years young, about to turn three, and I was accustomed to spending time with him frequently. I had been living together with Bianka for about three years now since I met her when my son's mother was pregnant. Also, we were not legally married, but we were doing what most do when living together. I loved her dearly 'in my own eyes,' and we have bonded since day one in the midst of the turmoil. Every single day, I read my *Fellowship of Christian Athletes Bible*, and a Spanish Bible my father-in-law and I found next door—in an empty apartment. I was also receiving tutoring, as much as possible, through 'The Listening University of The Heavens' and I was trying my best to pass all tests. But The Voice of Truth's tests were getting harder and harder.

Suddenly, while I was reading the Holy Bible, a verse in Matthew 6:21, hit me with a left hook by stating:

"For where your treasure is, there will your heart be also."

The Voice of Truth visited me a second later and shouted, "Your treasure is in Bottineau, North Dakota, and you will find your new heart as you seek for it."

I was blown away by this response, I thought, "Why will I need a new heart?" and The True Voice responded, "To finish the fight of your life." And He continued, "Now tell your girlfriend these words: 'I must leave to follow the will of God; this will destroy us, but it will restore us.'

"And tell your son's mother these words: 'I must leave now, but I'll never leave nor forsake my son.'"

"But this is very hard for me, Lord. I love them with all my heart; how can we separate like this? You're telling me to tell them that I'll never leave them nor forsake them but isn't this exactly what I'm doing by leaving for college now?"

"I chose to separate myself from My Father—for over three decades—to provide salvation for you and the whole world..."

"You did?"

"...And I died for you, and the whole world—to provide eternal life through My blood and sacrifice..."

"Blood and sacrifice?"

"...Now, I'm here—alive and filled with glory—with My Father."

"Our Father?"

"Yes.

"And I'm also within you through The Spirit of Truth. Will you continue to follow The Voice of Truth?"

"What does football and college have to do with this?"

"Will you trust Me to discover then My everlasting glory?"

"How I'm I going to support my son and help my girlfriend from over there? You know I'm not going to have time for work since I will participate in school and play ball?

"Remember when I asked you to be late to *Kendal Toyota* and *South BMW*?"

"Yes, Lord."

"And then they let you go?"

"Yes, Lord."

"You will call the unemployment agency tomorrow morning. And through those funds and My infinite power, I will provide for all your needs."

"I have a request."

"I'm listening."

"I promise you that I will always remain faithful to my girlfriend, but if she sleeps with another man, I will leave her."

A moment of silence elapses and no answer.

"I can't hear you? I asked and no response.

"I can't hear you?" Again and again I said, but no response.

"Unconditional Love," I heard after a while.

"What do you mean by 'Unconditional Love'—do we have a deal, or do we not have a deal?"

"Love her," He said.

"I will, I believe I always have."

"This is my commandment, that you love one another as I have loved you." (John 15:12)

"I still don't understand, do we have a deal or do we not?"

"This is my commandment: Love her." I gave up and left Him alone.

## Speaking to Bianka

I told her everything that The Voice of Truth asked me, and I added, "Listen, I'm going to do this for God, for us, my family, and for those who will, one day, need my help."

"What is it?"

"This is extremely painful for me, but I know it's the best thing to do. Please, I'm only going to ask you for one thing."

"And what's that?"

"I'll never be able to forgive unfaithfulness, so please, if you love me, remain faithful to me as I will do the same. Are we in agreement?"

"I'll never do that to you, I love you with all my heart," she said.

"OK, I trust in you."

And I thought, "Why am I worrying so much, she's always remained faithful to me? Maybe I'm just overwhelmed..."

89

## Chapter 13

# Marcial J. Ferreira
# vs.
# Publix Supermarkets

Before I left for Bottineau, North Dakota, I had to meet various times with Mr. Soto, the attorney from *Rubenstein Law*. I went to depositions, dealt with mediators, visited their offices various times, and even told them the truth when asked all kinds of questions. They just never asked me if I had truly slipped and fallen; I guess lawyers believe this question isn't important. And I guess I related the truth without the whole truth. As I visited these offices more and more I began to sense a strong force pulling me away, asking me to drop the case—to leave it alone. Another force was pulling from the opposite direction, it was telling me:

"You'll get the money and help many people; you can establish a church one day and help the poor; you're only getting this from the rich: do you think that the insurance company will even feel this? You'll get at least a couple of hundred thousand—don't you think you can use these funds for a good cause?"

"Yes. Sure."

"So what's the fear?"

By now I was still an undergrad student at "The Listening University of Heaven" so discerning between the Voice of Truth and The Voice of Lies remained as a work in progress. I had taken classes, quizzes; I had gone to lab, a test here and there, but still had not been fortunate enough to take a final, "So what's the fear?" made sense to me, and I continued with the process...

# Chapter 14
## *Dakota College*
## *At Bottineau*

After two days of traveling through cars, airplanes, and trains, my teammates and I, arrived at the Rugby, ND *Amtrak* train station. Coach Tim Pfeifer, our soon-to-be head football coach, was there waiting for us, gladly. With a smile on his face, he received us and provided transportation for us. And he drove away to a place where I was soon going to experience a radical modification in my life. It was cold, and all I could see was a long road and endless grain fields:

"They [ain't got] no buildings around here?" said Melvin Brownlee, "and how about some girls?"

Coach Pfeifer smiled. And The Voice of Truth whispered, "This is it! No turning back. Give all you got. I'll never leave you nor forsake you."

"Coach Mooney!" said Coach Pfeifer.

"Yes, coach."

"This is Johan Betancourt, Melvin Brownlee, Marcial Ferreira, Keith Osgood, Paul Holliday..."

"It's a great thing to have you all," said Coach Mooney, "the rest of the coaches and I will be shooting hoops at around three o'clock today. You all coming?" as he walked away he asked.

"Yes, coach" we all replied. And that afternoon we bonded, and I noticed that the coaches were studying some of our athletic abilities. One of the coaches pointed his finger at me as he spoke to Coach Mooney. And soon after, Mr. Mooney invited us to his house for supper, introduced us to his wife, Mrs. Tania Mooney, and his children also. And thanks for their generous support, we were fed. All along I thought, "I can really adapt to this!"

Soon after, I was with my roommate and good friend, Melvin, just organizing our stuff, and preparing for two-a-days. And suddenly, The

Voice of Truth whispered, "You give it your all, and I will reward you."
And I thought, "OK, I really have to do this."

Thus, I immediately began to train on my own, eating raw eggs, running around town, and I was also running away from the volleyball team girls. I tried seeking for The Voice of Truth and living through His requests—and rapidly, two-a-days commenced.

## Two-a-Days For The Lumberjacks

We were all out in the practice field—behind the baseball field—and suddenly, I heard Coach Pfeifer screaming louder than a rock star. He shouted,

"Alright, alright this is what we're going to do," he continued, "linemen, you all go to that corner of the field.

"Wide receivers, and cornerbacks, and skilled positions—that corner over there.

"Linebackers and Quarterbacks—to that one.

"Safeties, running backs—that one.

"And kickers! Where are my kickers?"

"Probably kicking something," Coach Mooney said and they laughed.

"I'm here, coach," responded the kicker.

"Just go where you think you belong!" said Coach Pfeifer, "Hurry! Hurry!" and he continued addressing the team with his rock star voice, "You will run around the field as fast as you can.

"We're going to warm up well today!

"Ready! Go!"

First lap: we took a break, and many seemed out of shape.

"This is college football; high school is over," he shouted, "let's try this again. Ready! Go!"

Third lap: now over half of the team was panting; most appeared overwhelmed. Fourth Lap: I was running with all my heart, and I heard Coach Ken Keysor say, "That's a future captain," as I turned the final corner.

We practiced and practiced, and practiced some more, and came back a few hours later to do it again.

## Penny "The Superstar" And the Crew

Now we're in the cafeteria, and The Voice of Truth said, "You won't have to steal food again, just eat all you can."

I laughed in my heart and thought, "They're in big trouble leaving all that turkey out there in the salad bar."

"All you can eat, son," said The Voice of Truth.

"I'm Penny," said a nice lady, about my mother's age, as she served us.

"I'm Marcial, thank you for the food, Penny."

I figured she owned the cafeteria by the smile on her face and her expressions of appreciativeness. Soon after, a group of us sat together, we were eating, and suddenly, I noticed something: Most out-of-state and Miami players were on one side, and most, white, North Dakota players were opposite to us. Rapidly, The Voice of Truth said,

"I will unite, and not separate."

"How," I asked.

"Just follow Me."

My legs were sore—from getting up so many times for turkey—so I decided to walk to my dorm and rested.

## Daily Routine

The Voice of Truth said:

- "You will pray and worship The Lord in the morning
- Eat breakfast
- Attend to class
- Have lunch
- Stretch in the sauna room
- Exercise prior to practice
- Practice with your team
- Have supper

- Visit the library from 6pm to 10pm, and study.
- And lastly, study your Bible, drink enough water, pray, and rest."

The True Voice continued, "All this, you must do in this order. Do not forget to come to me every night. I will give you rest, and most importantly, wisdom."

I was doing great in class, and on the field; I liked the staff and my coaches, and the green and white scrimmage arrived.

I was still feeling moveable bone spurs on my right shoulder, but I had labeled it "classified." I was able to do everything just by dealing with the pain. The doctor said, "9 to 12 months to recover," and over nine months had passed. And I thought, "I should be fine."

The scrimmage commenced; I tackled many times, and I figured, "I'm doing just fine." The second scrimmage came, and everything repeated. The first official game arrived, also. And during that game, I had over 14 tackles, 2.5 sacks, two pass deflections, and I was enjoying the game. Suddenly, this happened: I was hit on the back of my unrecovered shoulder, as I was chasing down the ball carrier—who was escaping multiple tackles from the opposite side of the field...

## With All

"...but I continued in the Battle Field
with all my strength,
and soon, all warriors called it a day.
Some tired, some defeated, some heartbroken,
and some wounded today
I guess tomorrow will bring a better thing,
the thing I need to remove this pain away.
A pain not seen, for is not of blood and meat;
a pain not heard, for words cannot explain.
O pain, O pain,
I've come from so far away.
Take my shoulders, take my bones,

but why my life away?
You see my life from up in the sky
so what do I do now to try?
Do I try some more?
Or do I head back home?
Or do You have a better thing for me to find?
I know that You and only You
can take this pain from life in these times.
O Voice of Truth, I'm waiting for You:
Will you just share with me The Whole Truth?
Don't give it to me all, if that's what you want;
just take this pain and I'll be just fine."

## At the Coaches' Office

"Maybe you can help us coach the defense," said Coach Pfeifer as he sat next to Coach Mooney and Coach Sathre in the coaches' office. I looked at them, and said, "I comprehend I'm 27 already, almost 28, but not yet, this is not the time."

"I mean you know your stuff in and out, you're football smart, we can use you here, you can count on us," said Coach Sathre, our defensive coordinator.

"Hey, coach," said Coach Pfeifer to Coach Mooney and continued, "Aren't we in need of a team equipment manager?"

"That's right!" said Coach Mooney and rapidly stared at me.

I said disappointed and broken, "I mean...," and The Voice of Truth came rapidly, "...I mean: yes. Sure, I'll be the one.

"Thank you, coaches," as I got up and shook their hands.

"We'll show you what to do later on," Coach Pfeifer said as I walked away.

"Thanks again," walking away, I said.

I was still conditioning, and doing most drills, and helping after practice with the training equipment. Suddenly, Coach Sathre shouted, "All defensive players follow me," as he walked to the baseball field.

"I hear all kinds of numbers in the air," he said and continued, "today we'll see who's the fastest." And we all lined up ready to race, and the braggers remained whispering their brag.

"Usain Bolt got [nothin'] on me," said one.

"My grandma can beat you back pedaling," said another player. And I thought, "I can't even move my arms." But The Voice of Truth said, "Just run, and don't move your right shoulder much."

"Ready!" shouted Coach Sathre, "Go!" And the race commenced. I gave my all, and the race ended.

"An injured Grandpa is beating you all; I can't believe it!" He continued shouting, "Now the top three, line it up again." And we lined up quickly, and coach shouted:

"Go!

"Unbelievable! Graaandpa took it again."

"What in the world did you do to get this fast?" said Bubba, my friend from Florida.

"Just trained brother," I responded.

"You see, you didn't even use your arms," The Voice of Truth whispered.

## The Classroom

Every day, I was doing everything I could to follow the daily schedule The Voice of Truth custom-ordered for me. I attended the lectures; trained twice a day; visited the cafeteria punctually as well as the library from 6 to close, and most importantly, I continuously attended my one on one meetings with The Voice of Truth.

## True Guidance

"He's guiding me in all my ways
in the midst of this pain.
I'm seeing another chance
completely fading away.
Girls are chasing me down,

but I'm chasing Him up instead.
He and only He
seems to carry this pain for me.
O load, how heavy;
who can carry you alone?
O Lord, how tough;
is this real stuff?
All I wanted was some football,
but you wanted more than fool's balls.
Should I leave now, or should I stay here
in the midst of THE ALMIGHTY?
O Voice of Truth, what should I do,
for a moment; for now, or when to?
I don't know how, but I know it's true
that You are the Only Whole Truth
I searched The Bible when I found You,
and You gave me The Spirit of Truth.
O Truth O Truth, O Truth O Truth,
keep telling me, where to find Thee anew."

## Away Games with 116 Clique

I was seating in the bus, bumping to Lecrae, Da' Truth, J.R, Tedashii, and so many other Christian Hip-Hop artists from the *116 Clique* that Coach Mooney introduced me to.

## The Game Away

It's our first away game, and I long to play,
but playing seems to fade away.
I'm trying to help with everything I can from the sidelines,
but simultaneously,
I'm seeing The Promise fade away.
I'm out with an injured shoulder;
my friend Melvin; O broken ankle—
I guess the two roommates will cry together today.

Through a song The Voice of Truth sings:
"O son, you'll be just fine."
I see the grain fields as I travel across the states,
The animals eating and living freely,
The birds flying and not afraid of the cold and free weather,
The trees without fruit, and The True Voice says:
"Follow these, and you'll be fine."
"How can I without the wings, without the coat,
 and without the grass?"
"Follow Me to the heavens and see."
"But how?"
"Eternity through Me is all you'll ever need."

## Attending Church

Coach Mooney said, "I'm going to be preaching next Sunday at the little church just across the railroad tracks; you're all welcome. Just bring whomever you like and tell the rest of your teammates."

"Yes, coach," some teammates replied.

"We'll be there, coach" I replied.

"We'll have some food!" Coach Mooney said.

"Now you really know we're going to be there," all of us agreeing responded.

Sunday came, and a group of about 12 of us headed to the little church right across the railroad tracks. Pastor/Coach/Professor Mooney preached intensely with truth, and then we assisted in the congregation with our appetite. Every Sunday after that, I followed the routine. Sometimes The Voice of Truth delivered the message through Pastor Bob and sometimes through Pastor Mooney. At the church, I met so many lovely people like Georgia; Duane and Marilyn Moen, and their children; Tim and Patricia Bryantt, and their children; Rob and Charlotte Bedlion, and their kids; (Tall) Mike and his family, who always invited us for barbeques; Maynard Mosher; Beth Rose; Jack & Sonja Kana; Judy Wall, and many more lovely people that I wish to recall their names. And they became my family, and not just part of it, but my family. I felt the genuine love every single time I visited.

# Chapter 15
## *A Surprise*

It had been over two months since I had been in the lovely small town of Bottineau. By then, I almost knew every resident, pet, and personal habits of most in town. People left their cars unlocked; everyone greeted their closest and farthest neighbors—a true humanitarian atmosphere could be a way to put it. An overwhelming presence of The Spirit of Truth encountered me and said,

"More pain is coming your way."

"More pain?" already in guard, I responded.

"Yes, son; more pain. But I will use it for My glory."

"What!?"

"Yes. Your heart will be broken, but I will give you a new one, no longer made of stone, but instead, made of flesh."

"Stone? Flesh?"

"Flesh. And I will fill it with My Spirit of Truth, and you will be guided through all things and find The Whole Truth (John 14: 17, 26).

"The Whole Truth?"

"Pain and discipline are coming your way, but I will reward you with wisdom through My Spirit of Truth."

"Wisdom?"

"Yes. My true love gift for you."

"How about the pain?"

"Pain is the beginning; you see it as pain, I see as discipline."

"How about You give me the discipline with the wisdom, and take away the pain?"

"Believe in Me, and THE TRUTH SHALL SET YOU FREE."

"Yes, Lord; I will follow You."

I was alarmed, restless, and attempted to make sense of what appeared to make no sense. And suddenly:

## Preparing The Bride

"Hey," said my girlfriend, Bianka, on a phone call, "Is it ok with you if I leave to The Dominican Republic—to see my mother and family?"

"Sure, why not? But do you think this is necessary now?"

"Well...I would like to see my brother, and my mother—I haven't seen them for a while."

"OK, but be very careful. Remember, we are on a budget, and also, what I asked you to honor."

"What's that? she said.

"The only thing I asked you to do before I departed from Florida."

"Oh, of course, babe; I'll never betray you."

"Ok, I love you; please remember always."

"I love you too."

She left the following week to Santo Domingo. And we communicated two to three times per day. I prayed day and night for her and asked God to guide her in all her ways.

I was still in Bottineau, with almost two months remaining in the semester. And all of the sudden, The Voice of Truth said, "Call her and tell her to be careful with the baseball player from *The New York Mets*."

"Listen," I told Bianka, on a long distance call, "please be very careful with your neighbor friend from your youth—please be careful with him."

"I can't believe you're jealous?"

"No, I'm not," I continued speaking, "I just know what I know. And I know what the love of money and the desires of the flesh can do. Also, our separation of over two months doesn't help us much."

"You're worrying too much."

"I can't forgive adultery, and I'm only warning you before a disaster strikes."

"I can't believe you do not trust me," she said.

"I do. But I also comprehend that I'm following another path now."

"I love you," she said.

"I love you, Bianka," I responded and we disconnected.

"You did your job," said The True Voice.

"Ok," I said and proceeded in my daily walk.

The next day, I called Bianka, and she answered not. I called her at her uncle's house, and all I got from her mother, brother, and cousins was this: "She's not here now." I called various places, and had no success. Finally, I got a hold of her the following day, and she admitted she was at a nightclub with her friends. Immediately, I knew she was an inch away from a disastrous fall. She said, "There is nothing wrong with dancing."

I knew that she was lost and ready for a deception, but I couldn't do anything else—I had already done my job. I left her alone, and my journey continued at the college.

A few days later The Voice of Truth reappeared and said:

"Go to *Facebook*."

"Ok, I'm logged in now."

"Now, find Bianka."

"Ok, there she is."

And she was with her friends in the picture, coming out of a nightclub and holding a drink. I began to feel a sense of betrayal, and it was eating me alive. There were no men in the pictures, except in the background, but I knew something was wrong. I was hurting, confused, disappointed, and rapidly, I was touched by the warmness of the breath behind me that said:

"She dishonored you."

I unplugged my ears and said, "May you repeat?"

"She dishonored you," said The Voice of Truth.

Engulfed by still-to-discover emotions, I ran out my dorm room and headed to the emergency exiting stairs. I sat, attempted to relax, but my attempts decided to relax instead. One minute, two minutes, seven minutes went to the past, and suddenly:

"Why?" destroyed, I shouted in my heart to not wake my teammates, and I continued, "Why?" I murmured wanting to shout desperately. "Oh, why? Oh, Lord, I can't continue?" I said, and no response. And I sat there for about an hour and decided to return to my dorm room as

I wiped away my tears. I entered, closed the door silently, and many thoughts circulated through my mind.

"That's it; this is over. I asked her for one thing, and that one thing, the one and only thing, is the very thing she does. I made a commitment to You, Voice of Truth, and You allowed this to happen? Enough is enough! I've been faithful since I met You, I just don't comprehend anymore."

"Phone her and ask her if she dishonored you," said The True Voice.

"Call her?" I asked, "I'm leaving her, I told You that this was the only thing I'll never accept."

"Just call her and I will speak through you."

"Please leave me alone; go away."

"My son, just follow Me. Would you?"

Broken into a million pieces, I decided to call her and said:

"Where you unfaithful to me?"

"What?" she responded surprised.

"Please just be honest with me; I will repeat what I just said, "Were you unfaithful to me?"

"No, why would you ask me such a thing," she said.

"Why am I wasting my time?" I asked The Voice of Truth.

"Just follow Me," The True Voice said.

"Now, what if I tell you that I just know?" I said to Bianka.

"Stop it already! I'll never do such a thing," she said.

"Ok, you cheated on me with that baseball player from *The New York Mets*."

"Are you kidding me?" she said. And I got furious and wanted to tackle the phone; then hit it with my jab, but I couldn't, it was too tiny. Furiously and in pain, I said:

"I'm going to hang up, and you'll never get to see me ever again."

"Wait! Wait! Wait! I just popped kissed him."

"You, just what?" I responded and said, "you lost a whole lot, but one day you'll realize it. Don't call me ever again."

"I'm sorry, I'm sorry!" she shouted, "we did it all; I was so stupid. Please forgive me?"

"Forgive! I asked you for one thing; one thing, Bianka; and you just couldn't..."

"Please forgive me. It's just that I had some wine, and one thing led to another, and..."

"You're such a prostitute. I can't believe you," and I hung up. And from that moment on, she drove me insane with all her phone calls. And I just avoided them all. One, two, three days go by, and a week arrived. And out of nowhere, I saw a ghost, identical to her, standing in front of me in Bottineau, North Dakota. I couldn't believe my 20/20 vision, I must replace my urologist; I mean my ophthalmologist.

"Is it her?" I asked The True Voice, "Is it her?"

"You must forgive. And yes, it is her."

"How did you get here? Did you spend the only money I...?"

"I'll pay you back; I promise you," in much desperation she responded.

"I don't know what you're doing here, but you're in the wrong place." And in the midst of my message The Voice of Truth interfered and said, "You must provide a shelter for her."

"A shelter? She can go back to Miami."

"Please forgive me, I didn't know what I was doing. Let's start all over, I promise..."

"Stop wasting your time," I said as I walked away.

"She must sleep in your dorm room," said The Voice of Truth as I was about 10 yards away from her.

"STOP!" The True Voice said louder than ever before. And in fear, I froze—outside as we both stood in the snow.

"Now turn around," The Voice said and I turned immediately. And there she was standing, staring at me with hope, and with the desire to be rescued.

"You will take her into your dorm room and provide a shelter for her."

"Now?"

"Now!" The Voice responded.

And desiring to walk away from all things, and standing between True Love and his daughter, I chose to follow Him. I wanted to sleep on the floor, but to hide the situation from my roommate, Melvin, we slept in my dorm room bed together. For almost two weeks, The Voice of Truth demanded to offer hospitality services to the woman that had just recently broken my heart and dishonored me and God. She showered late at night, in the men's showers, while I watched the door and avoided other men from coming in. We ate from the same plate in the cafeteria. She spent some of her time wandering around the college, and in the admissions office while I studied. And I was going insane with the situation. The time came for her to leave when The Voice of Truth said,

"You have done your job; she leaves tomorrow."

"Hallelujah," I shouted silently.

"You will see her again," said The Voice of Truth as I attempted to rejoice—I was disappointed; I took back the Hallelujah.

Three. Two. And only one week remained for the college semester to end. Soon after, the time to return to Florida became a reality, and therefore, I returned for a break.

# Chapter 16

# Back to Florida

A s I was riding in the *Amtrak* train on my way to the Minneapolis Airport, sitting right next to me, The Voice of Truth said, "A test is coming your way."

"A test?"

"Yes, a test."

"Another test?" I asked, but He departed without responding.

Soon after, I entered into the airport. And I was excited about spending time with my son, Brandon, and my brothers—it was all I had on my mind. But suddenly, an interruption occurred by a light brown skin, God-made sweet apple pie for my appetite. She froze, when I encountered her presence, as I waited and stood behind her in line at the security checkpoint. She broke her neck once, twice, and a third time to eat me alive with the power of her eyes. Her appetite was far greater than mine as her eyes described the hunger. All this within a three-second round—I looked away. The Voice of Lies whispered, "You deserve her; you are free now."

"Are you sure?"

"Sure, just like the Chinese buffet you love: all you can eat!"

Quickly after, I was seating in the waiting area, just patiently waiting for my flight to depart to Florida. And suddenly, as I was fighting back my carnal desires and The Father of Lies, The Voice of Truth visited me and said:

"You have failed My test."

"What test?"

"You broke my one-second rule."

"What second?"

"Yes, you have allowed darkness to enter into your temple."

"What temple?"

"Son, you must look away—in less than a second—when your desires overcome you with evil."

"What evil?"

"The intentions of your heart and mind."

"But she was checking me out first?"

"You are My servant and friend, and you must remain prepared at all times—be perfect as I am perfect."

"This is impossible."

"All things are possible according to My will, and only through Me."

"It was stronger than me."

"But I AM is the strongest, My son."

"Who is I AM?"

"I AM, WHO I AM."

"So what am I supposed to do?"

"Next time, look away within a second or less from the moment your eyes attempt to deceive you."

"In less than a second, but that's...?"

"It is my 'one-second rule,' son."

"But I'm free. I'm hurting. She cheated...?"

"You are free through Me, and you're saved through Me."

"And how about the temple?"

"Your body is your temple, where I also reside and speak to you."

"I thought you were in heaven?"

"At the Right hand of our Father, and My Perfect Spirit is within you" (1 Corinthians 3:16).

"So how do I overcome this?"

"Son, the day a child learns to control what I gave him to procreate, on that day, and on that day alone, he will initiate his journey to manhood."

"But I'm 28; I'm a man."

"I repeat: the day a child learns to control what I gave him to procreate, on that day, and on that day alone, he will initiate his journey to manhood."

He left me thinking for a while trying to make sense of this. And suddenly, I was flying by Him in a manmade flying metal, but couldn't truly see Him.

## My First Son: Brandon

So far, I had only spoken to my son, Brandon, via a cellular phone, and through *Skype*. We conversed daily, yet I couldn't demonstrate affection to him—through these technologies—the way I desired. I supported him financially and sent him a toy every month, but that never made up for hugs and kisses. I kept him in my heart throughout the marathon, but now I desire, even more, to show him my love. I only had three and a half weeks to nurture him, and then, I must leave from his presence again.

The time came and I loved him, and enjoyed the limited time given by The One Who controls the real clock. We were playing at the park, and suddenly, he looked at me while he ran sprints and shouted, "Never give up!" And The Spirit of Truth interfered and said, "Remember this essential moment and his words." And over and over again he shouted, "Never give up!" as he ran in all directions throughout the field. And I became curious and said,

"Why do you say this, son?"

"I don't know, but all I know is that: 'you should never give up!'"

That day, I was moved by him, and the simultaneous message delivered from The True Voice—I understood that this was important.

Quickly after, we all sat in the car again, and rapidly, my fleshly desires told me, "Why not work, or establish another business, or just stay in the sunshine state, and remain with your family?" And answering The Voice of Truth replied, "I am your Vine, and you are my branch, abide in me and you will bear much fruit" (John 15: 5).

## The Voice of Truth Says: Forgive

As I held on to those words, I continued on my three weeks' journey. But guess what? I had to see Bianka again since we lived in the same place in Florida—we lived together for about four years before I departed to Bottineau. I wanted to run away, but The Voice of Truth kept pulling me back, and kept saying,

"Forgiveness is your duty."

'Forgiveness' became The Voice of Truth' top choice. Over and over, again, 'forgiveness' was the word He replied. I had been in Florida for over three weeks already, and one day, I said to The True Voice,

"OK, I'll forgive her. But may I please move on with my life now?"

"You may, but you truly need to forgive her first."

"I did," I replied.

"Just hold on to The True Vine, and you will bear much fruit."

"What does fruit has to do with forgiveness?"

"True forgiveness fertilizes your fruit."

"Fertilizes my fruit? My fruit? And fertilizes?"

"You are my friend, if you do whatsoever I command you." (John 15:14)

"I'm trying my best to understand: what do you mean?"

"This is my commandment, that you love one another as I have loved you." (John 15:12)

"Of course, I love all people you send my way."

"Love your neighbor."

"I do it all the time, don't I?"

"Isn't she your closest neighbor?"

"But how can I love a...?"

"Forgiveness without love amounts to hatred, and love without forgiveness remains conditional."

"We've been living together for all these years, but we're not even married. Why can't You just find me a clean woman—a woman I can trust?"

"I'm cleaning her for you as I am cleaning you for her. True Love makes you clean and sets you free."

"Please let me move on with my life."

"You can move all you want, but true everlasting life, only resides in Me."

# Chapter 17

# Back to Bottineau

I arrived again at the small town called Bottineau. My shoulder remained injured, my heart remained shattered, The Voice of Truth kept disciplining me, and rapidly, He said,

"You made the Dean's list with a 4.0 GPA."

"Me?"

"Yes, you."

"I graduated with a 2.7 from high school; how is this possible?"

"Remember, just keep following Me, and I'll show you the way."

"What way?"

"I am the way, the truth, and the life. No one comes to the Father except through Me" (John 14:6).

"Why me, what do I have?"

"You have what you have willingly accepted from Me."

"And what's that?"

"My Spirit."

"OK?"

"And you're following Me everywhere."

"Why do you keep showing to me boxing and football?"

"You are a fighter; I made you a fighter."

"But I have arthritis, my shoulder remains unhealed, and I'm almost 28 years-of-age?"

"Son, pain doesn't exist unless you allow it to come in."

"But I am the definition of pain?"

"Discipline and pain aren't the same things."

"But I'm in pain."

"Only until you fully comprehend the difference between pain and discipline."

"I'm listening."

"Keep listening and I'll take you to a place called wisdom."

I walked away somewhat confused as usual, and with a renewed mindset (Romans 12:2) I became triumphant in the classroom: received awards habitually, and maintaining a 4.0 became a habit. The Spirit of Truth Hand-picked my classes, directed me through my studies, counseled me through my pain, guided me in the community, provided for all my needs, and I just kept on going, somehow. Once, He said, "Just think of the 'Big Picture,' and you'll stay in the fight," and I attempted just that, multiple times a day.

He guided me through the journey. In dreams, He shared what was coming worldwide; through signs, I followed along with His freely-given codes; His voice, kept me alert as I retained vision through it; and most importantly, his unconditional love, I attempted to imitate daily—attempting to comprehend fully, the mystery.

### Elevate 1 *(E1)*

Once a week a group of us gathered to talk about life. We often used the Holy Bible to answer many questions and to find healing for our concerns. The Voice of Truth led Coach Mooney through a journey which later became *Elevate 1. Embracing, Encouraging, and Equipping* others remains as the focus of it to this day, as Pastor Hershey leads now. Some of the college staff, student-athletes, and Bottineau residents regularly attended. Coach Mooney, as the leader, had arranged a meeting with the leading students, and soon after, they had elected me as president. It quickly became a habit for Coach Mooney and I to sharpen each other. Three to four times a week we met in his office, home, or at the little church building in the morning—to embrace, encourage, and equip each other. So much was happening so rapidly, but I knew I had to remain in the race to win it—no matter my personal circumstances. I understood that I had many personal issues, but that The Voice of Truth had a global concern. And Mankind, for the most part, remained in silence. The True Voice always showed me boxing and football, and, on the other hand, He showed me love and peace. I just followed along in my attempt to fully discover.

# Chapter 18
## *The University of Miami*

One day He said, "Apply to the University of Miami."
"Is this you?"
"Yes, and don't be afraid."
I did just that, and an acceptance letter came in quickly. But there was only one problem. What was it? They only had offered $21,000 of the $42,000 in tuition cost. I asked the Voice of Truth,
"What's this all about?"
"It is just the beginning."
"The beginning of what?"
"THE REVELATION."
"What's a revelation?"
"I will speak to the Nations through you."
"But I'm not a pastor, or a prophet, or a...?"
"You are My servant, and my servants serve Me."
"But I don't know the whole Bible yet, what's this all about?"
"Follow Me, and you'll see."
"But, how about boxing and football, and these *University of Miami* visions you keep revealing to me?"
"Step by step, follow Me."
"How about Bianka? What do I do with her?"
"Go to church tomorrow, and you will know," He said and departed.

### The Little Church: The Next Day

It was Sunday morning, and I was walking to the little church building behind the railroad tracks, and suddenly, The Voice of Truth approached me and said, "Focus as Pastor Bob speaks."
"Focus?"
"It's all you have to do—focus," He said, and sat next to me in the church.

"Today, I'd like to talk to you," said Pastor Bob, "about one of the most vital subjects lacking in the Body of Christ, today. What is it? The answer is in 'forgiveness.'" And he shouted:

## Forgiveness

"Forgiveness! Forgiveness! Forgiveness!
'Forgiveness' remains as one of the most difficult decisions to make, yet, an   essential component—for those that desire never-ending growth as servants of The Lord.
Forgiveness! Requires for you to choose to love that person in the midst of your betrayal and pain.
O Forgiveness! She seeks for the author of dishonor,
and cures it with The Author of Love.
O forgiveness! How painful she is,
but O how vital is she.
Some of you have faced forgiveness
and departed away from her,
some of you have faced her and looked another way,
some of you still have some youth and have jumped over her fence;
I challenge you today to face her with Love.
With Love and only with Love you may forgive and find your heart again, with Love and only with Love, you may find yourself again, only through The One that is LOVE may you face her face to face.
You may not completely forget,
but I know you won't remember over and over again.
Again! Again! And again! Is what we are trying to eliminate.
Though a scar may remain,
the main thing—is that you found your way again."

He took a ten-second water break, paused for a moment, opened up the Bible and said:
"The Living Word of God declares the following in Mark 11:25-26:
"And whenever you stand praying, if you have anything against anyone, forgive him, that your Father in heaven may also forgive you

**113**

your trespasses. But if you do not forgive, neither will your Father in heaven forgive your trespasses."

By then those words had confronted me. I was starting to get the point, but my feelings had not arrived yet. I noticed that this was about a decision, and not some special-made miraculous feeling coming from an unexpected place. My desires wanted me to get up and leave immediately, but The Voice of Truth longed for me to stay, permanently. Holding my hands He said, interfering Pastor Bob's speech:

"Forgive, and you'll see."

"What will I see?"

"You'll see what you can't see."

"I can see, clearly."

"But not through My reality."

"Reality?"

"Not through my realm—just follow Me and you'll see." And I attempted to rise and leave, and suddenly He said, "Following Me is the key." And not fully comprehending I decided to sit once again as Pastor Bob continued with his message, saying:

"Who has not received forgiveness here?" and he paused. And continued,

"Once, twice, or hundreds of times we've all been forgiven. Will you choose to forgive that person one time—who has caused pain in your life—in exchange for the immeasurable times you've been forgiven? Will you choose to focus on the various wonderful moments you've had with them, instead, of focusing on the few undesirable moments you've experienced with them? Maybe they've done one horrible thing to you. And through your personal laws and regulations it remains impossible to overcome and forgive. I tell you the whole truth today and challenge you to choose 'forgiveness' over any other alternative established in your heart's agenda; to then receive the complete forgiveness of your Father in Heaven—The One, who sent Everlasting Forgiveness for Mankind."

"Forgive, and I shall press delete to all your old files," said The Voice of Truth as He sat next to me.

"Forgive?"

"Yes, just choose through My infinite strength, and not through your own."

"This is impossi..."

"Son, I make all things new."

"Keep me old then."

"Wine may taste better when old, but you'll feel better when renewed.

"Just take this pain away please, and I'll keep following You."

"Attend to the little church every Sunday," he said, and the conversation was over.

It was Pot Luck Sunday, and all of us—some football players with Coach Mooney, and Coach Hershey—were enjoying the God-given meals.   We're gathered in the little church's basement where the cafeteria is located.  And out of nowhere, The Voice of Truth invited Himself and said to me, "I'm preparing your bride, be ready!"

"What?" almost panicking I responded, "What was that?" and no response.  I guess He wasn't hungry and walked away.  And for over two months after that Sunday, something related to 'forgiveness' was mentioned at the little church—over and over and over, again.

## Bianka Calls

Bianka called and said, "Listen, I've been genuinely thinking about going back to school again."

"Great," I said, "that's a very good thing."

"I'm talking about going to *Dakota College at Bottineau*."

"Oh, no! This is not the place where you want to be, please just stay away from me."

"Well, I think I deserve to go to college just as you decided for yourself as well."

"Sure, sure, but not here, please."

"OK, no problem," she said and we disconnected.

"Please, keep her away from me," I mentioned to The True Voice.

"I'm preparing your bride," He responded.

"I don't understand?"

"He who finds a wife finds a good thing,

  And obtains favor from the Lord"

(Proverbs 18:22).

"A good thing? Favor from the Lord?"

"You need a helper."

"A helper? But aren't You helping me?"

"You need another kind of helper."

"Another kind? But I'm fine with You alone?"

"My son, just taste and see my goodness—follow Me."

Another week passed by and, unexpectedly, I saw a shadow, but it wasn't mine. Then, I heard a voice that declared, "Hey, how are you?"

Quickly, I turned around and saw what I did not want to see. It was her, Bianka, standing in front of me carrying luggage. Again, she said, "How are you?"

"What are you doing here, you're supposed to be in Miami?"

"I know, but I'm here?"

"We're not sleeping in my dorm room bed again."

"Please forgive me?"

"Please leave already."

She remained standing there, and rapidly, The Voice of Truth said, "Asked her to go to the little church with you on Sunday."

"But I don't want to go with her," I replied.

"Just ask her. Will you follow Me, My son?"

"Will you go to church with me on Sunday?"

"Yes! Yes! I'll go wherever, please just forgive me, please?"

"Ok! Ok! Please calm yourself, I'll see you on Sunday."

"You forgive me?"

"No. We're going to church on Sunday."

"You must provide a shelter for her as you previously did."

"Again!?"

"Yes, son, as I always provide for you."

"Bianka, follow me and we'll go to church this Sunday."

## The Little Church
## Across the Rail Road Tracks

Sunday came, and there we were: walking across the football field on the way to church. We walked in, sat next to The Voice of Truth, and Pastor Bob initiated his speech.

"Today, I'd like to talk to you about repentance."

"Pay close attention," said the Voice of Truth.

"O salvation, O salvation. None of us chose to be born, and none can choose to escape from Judgment Day." And he continued, "The Lord says in His Living Word, 'Behold, I stand at the door and knock. If anyone hears My voice and opens the door, I will come in to him and dine with him, and he with Me' (Revelation 3:20).

He continued with his sermon, and said:

## Knock and Knock

"I knock and knock at the door of your heart, saith The Lord.
Whoever longs to invite True Everlasting Life into their hearts just open the door,
no money can buy this gift,
no gift can amount to it,
no mountain is greater than it;
only this, and only this gift,
it's what is promised within.
Within these words, you have found Him.
In Him, and only through Him,
you may receive it."

Pastor Bob continued, and said,

"Will you choose today, to open the door of your heart by coming up to this altar and kneeling before The One Who knocks? Will you choose Eternal Life in this very moment—to enjoy paradise with The King of kings? If you believe you carry the keys of your own heart feel

**117**

free to open it, and welcome Your Master as He comes in. Just come...
And follow Him, Who gives freely."

The Voice of Truth said, "Ask her now."

"Why don't you tell her Yourself," I responded.

"Be perfect, as I am perfect."

"Bianka."

"Would you like to go to the altar?"

"I'm scared?" she whispered as we stood in the midst of the little
church.

"Of what?"

"I don't know, but can you please go with me?"

"Me?"

"Hold her hands?"

"Her hands?"

"Now!" said The Saving Voice. And we walked to the altar, knelt
down before the presence of The One Who knocks, and another new
child was born again, on that day.

"The bride is almost ready!" He whispered into my fighting ears as
we departed.

# Chapter 19
# *Please Give Me*
# *A Sign*

I was training very hard attempting to recover from my shoulder injury and joint pain, but I had not achieved optimum results. And I remembered that I had some leftover testosterone from my first surgery. I figured that by taking some of it I will speed up the healing process and get back on the field quicker. So, right before I went to the weight room to train, I got on my knees in desperate need and said, "Lord, please, do not allow me to take this stuff if this is not part of Your will for my life. If I do not hear from You by the end of the day, then I will inject myself with this stuff. I honestly do not want to do it, so please, speak to me now," and I walked toward the weight room.

Soon after, I was in the weight room looking for some 40-50 lbs. dumbbells to step up and down from a wooden box, but I couldn't find them. And instead of waiting for one of my teammates to finish, I had decided, to grab some heavier ones. I was on my third set, and as I attempt to step up one more time, "Ah!" I shouted loudly. I felt like someone stabbed me in my inner thigh. My friend and teammate, Johan, helped me to stand. I was in pain, couldn't move my leg, the football season was 3-4 months away, and all I kept thinking was, "What am I going to do now?"

Johan helped me get to my dorm room as I couldn't walk on my own. And he attempted to alleviate the pain by bringing me a sports medicine cream he had. We talked and talked, and he compassionately supported me—he left soon after. I was alone in my dorm room, and all kinds of thoughts were entering into my mind. Unexpectedly, silence hovered over the surface, and then:

"I allowed it," said The Voice of Truth.

"You allowed this?"

"Yes, this was the answer to your prayer."

"What do you mean?"

"Now you won't inject yourself with testosterone as you planned since you're hurt."

"I asked You to give me a sign—not an injury?"

"It was the only way you'll listen, My son."

"What am I supposed to do now with an unrecovered shoulder and a messed up leg?"

"Son, I make all things new?"

"Can you make my whole body new?"

"In due season, you'll get a new one, My son" (1 John 3:20).

"How about for this upcoming football season?"

"My son, you will be ready when the time comes?"

"For this season?"

"For your fight?"

"How can I fight limping and with a messed up shoulder?"

"Follow Me, and you'll see."

"And what will You injure next?"

"Don't be afraid, My son; for Love overcomes all things," and He left me alone in the dorm room.

# Chapter 20
## *The Encounter*

I was still training hard twice-a-day, attempting to recover from my right shoulder injury.  And I was doing all types of exercises to strengthen my weak joints, and torn groin muscle.  I ordered all kinds of teas and natural supplements attempting to recover.  And I tried praying and walking according to the Living Word of God daily.  But I still felt loose bone spurs on my right shoulder and joint weakness throughout my whole body.  Thus, I decided to call Mr. Soto, the attorney that handled my case in Florida, to explain to him my shoulder discomfort.  He soon arranged a second surgery, but this time with a sports medicine doctor.  He said, "You will have to take two to three weeks off from school right after the surgery for proper healing."

"Fine, I'll be there," I said, "I need to get ready for this upcoming season."

Soon after this, I was in the airplane—on my way to Florida—speaking to a new friend I just met.  We talked about The Voice of Truth throughout the whole flight, and we discussed many current events around the world.  I shared with her many of the revelations given by The Voice of Truth.  And suddenly, we landed at the Fort Lauderdale Airport and separated.  The Voice of Truth whispered as I descended from the escalators, "Two physically beautiful women will soon come your way: be ready."  And I continued walking toward the airport's exit to meet with my brother, Miguel, who was picking me up.  But suddenly, The True Voice whispered again saying, "Those two young ladies will come after you."  And soon after, I glanced and noticed that one of them looked like Beyoncé in her prime, and the other one was not that physically attractive.  I quickly went to the men's restrooms, and suddenly, I noticed that they were behind me.  I exited from the restroom, and soon noticed that they were behind me once again.  And while standing outside by the airport's sidewalk The Voice of Truth said,

"They will come, and ask you a question—be ready." And in the midst of His instruction they silently came from behind me, bumped into me, and one of them said, "I'm so sorry," and smiled.

"It's Ok; no problem," and I kept on bumping to Lecrae. But they interrupted me again, and one of her said, "Listen, we're from Charlotte, I'm Naphtali, and this is my friend. Do you know of any place where we can have some fun—a place to party?"

My wild side kicked in as Naphtali had just made the cut to my personalized menu. But The Voice of Truth's power pulled me away with unparalleled strength and voiced quickly, "Tell her that you party with me at the little church."

"Seriously?" I asked The Truth.

"My Word remains forever."

"It depends on where you like to party; I like to go to the little church in a place called Bottineau to party with The Truth: what do you think?"

"Oh! I see! We were thinking like South Beach; the night clubs—something like that. You must be a Christian then?"

"I follow The Truth and apply His messages to my life. Here, listen to this song by Da' Truth, I said and handed her my headphones.

"Oh, cool; so you do music?"

"Not really. But I follow the words of this song you just listened to."

"Oh, that's pretty cool."

"Consider following The Truth, and you will be set free," I said and my brother arrived to pick me up.

## The Day of the Second Surgery

I was on my way to the surgical center in Weston, FL. And suddenly, I saw a man running that was almost identical to my friend, Glen Johnson. I remained focused, and I couldn't take my eyes off him as he reminded me of Glen—the champ. The Voice of Truth soon spoke to me and said, "You will fight for the world title, you will be a champion." Quickly, I turned my head the other way and noticed a sign on a public bus that stated, "You're the champion." Right away, I felt that The Voice of Truth had initiated a process within me. Right after this, I arrived at the surgical center, and the nurse assisting me said,

"Wow, you have the blood of an Olympic caliber athlete—seriously." And right after, The Voice of Truth said, "I will come to you today, and you will feel My presence."

"Are you ready?" said the Anesthesiologist.

"Let's do this," I said and the anesthesia kicked in. And I woke up a few hours later, and the nurse said:

"These are narcotics, you must take them today, and every day for three weeks—thirty minutes prior to bedtime. Do not take them if you do not plan to rest because these will knock you out."

"Fine, I'll follow your instructions."

It was around 11 o'clock, and I decided to take the pills to rest soon. I laid in the bed, turned on the TV, and decided to watch *The Trinity Broadcasting Network*. Joel Osteen was speaking, and he said something that touched me. Then, I flipped the channel to *The Church Channel*, and T.D. Jakes said something else and impacted me. Again, I flipped to another channel, and Dr. Charles Stanley delivered a message and touched me deeper. All the messages were correlated to "fighting." I took the medicine at 11 o'clock, and it was already 3am, and I couldn't fall asleep. I was trembling and shaking because of joy, and crying and smiling simultaneously, and couldn't seem to comprehend the reason for this. The nurse had said clearly that the medicines will knock me out, but something was dancing inside of me. The Voice of Truth showed up unexpectedly and said, "Son, you will fight for Me."

Now the trembling and crying was shifting into another gear. I was trembling and a pill was not causing it. I was crying, and I just couldn't figure out what may had been producing these tears. The encounter intensified, and the revelation revealed a bigger picture. Hollywood can't contain it. The government can't control it. The prince of the power of the air can't stop it. And rapidly, came The True Voice and said, "You must wake up Yosi and Isabel (Bianka's cousin and aunt), and allow Me to speak through you."

"But it is almost five in the morning; this will be impolite?"

"Trust in Me," He said as I trembled continuously. And I tiptoed my way to Isabel's room and whispered in her ears, "You need to follow me to the room."

"What happened?" she replied in Spanish nervously.

"Nothing, just wake up your daughter and ask her to come to the room, also."

"Ok," she said filled by fear.

All three of us were gathered in the room, the TV was no longer on, and the only light coming in was the light penetrating through the window from our neighbor's backyard light bold. The Voice of Truth grabbed the microphone and used me as speakers—as I declared His message to both of His daughters. And when The Voice of Truth finished, I said to Yosi and Isabel, "Forgive me for waking you up at this time to talk about these things."

"I needed to hear this," they both said simultaneously, thanked me, and returned to their beds.

"You must obey at all times," said The Voice of Truth, "they desperately needed to hear this—I planted a seed in their hearts."

I looked at the clock, and it was 6:57 am; I laid in bed once again, and The Voice of Truth whispered, "By 7am, you will fall asleep because this day was perfect. And in a few hours you will receive one more sign—a fighting sign..."

## Few Hours Later

The phone rang:

"Hey how are you?" said Bianka calling from Bottineau.

"Great, thank God."

"Listen, I have Damian here next to me, and he wants to tell you something important."

"Ok, good; put him on, please."

"Marcial!" Damian shouted.

"Hey, where's my child support money?"

"Ha, ha, ha!"

"What's going on brother?"

"Listen, I don't know, but I've been feeling something strange all day, and it's telling to tell you that you should go back to boxing."

"Really?"

"Yeah, brother."

"Ok, I'll think about that, thank you brother," and we disconnected.

I sat there on the living room couch, stared at my sling and shoulder, and The Voice of Truth said, "Count the signs."

"How?"

"Begin from your trip to the surgical center."

"Ok, the man running that looked like Glen, the champ, that's the first sign; the sign on the bus stating, 'You're the champion,' that's the second sign; the nurse that said, 'You have the blood of an Olympic caliber athlete,' the third sign...and our encounter last night, the sixth sign."

"You're missing one."

"Which one?"

"You just received it."

"The call? The phone call?"

"The seventh sign."

"The seventh sign?"

Although I was supposed to rest for three weeks, I realized that I was going to get behind in the classwork. Therefore, three days after the surgery, I booked a flight and departed for Bottineau—to finish the spring semester.

## Chapter 21
# *The New Shelter*

I had just arrived. And the summer break was almost at hand. The Voice of Truth said, "You will seek for a new shelter to live in."
"Yes, Lord."
"You will move in with Bianka."
"With Bianka!?"
"Yes, with her."
"But we are not married yet, I thought the Bible was completely against this?"
"You lived with her for over four years in Miami, and I allowed it—though it was not My perfect will. You fornicated with her, and I allowed it—though it was not My perfect will. You committed adultery with her, and I allowed it, yet this was not My perfect will. None of it was part of My perfect will for you both, but I allowed it."
"Why did You?"
"Because, 'The Lord has made all for Himself,
Yes, even the wicked for the day of doom'" (Proverbs 16:4).
"So I'm wicked?"
"You were for a season, and your fleshly desires still cry out for wickedness, but your spirit is winning the fight..."
"Why?"
"The Voice within you."
"I can't see it."
"...You lived wickedly, and you were lost until I chose you—you finally listened."
"I thought I chose You?"
"It is too deep to explain now. But go to your friend from the little church, Tim, and ask him to rent to you the house he's remodeling."
"How will I pay for it?"
"I always provide."

"Yes, Lord."

Sunday service was over, and I asked Tim, "Hey brother, I noticed that you were remodeling a house by the college—will you be renting it?"

"Yes, I will."

"Oh, ok, because I will need a new place to stay with Bianka when I return for the fall semester."

"With Bianka?"

"Yeah, she's thinking about enrolling."

"Oh! Ok. Listen, how about you stop by the house tomorrow, and we'll talk for a little bit."

"I'll be there, God willing; thank you, brother."

"You're always welcome, brother." And Bianka and I departed from the little church after our conversation ended.

## The Following Day

"Hey brother, how are you?" I said to Tim as I entered into his for-rent house.

"Everything is great, thank God."

"I'm glad."

"Listen, Marcial, I'm surely going to think about this as this is something I must go to the Lord to confirm."

"I comprehend brother, in fact, I still don't understand what's going on, personally."

"Hey, I have all these collectibles from the guy that lived here before I purchased this house: Do you want any of these?"

"Sure brother. Thanks a whole lot; I haven't seen one of these Michael Jordan jerseys since I was 12."

"You can have it. And take this one from Shaquille O'Neal as well— plus these signed magazines."

"Thanks, brother; I'll see you this Sunday—God willing."

## Sunday at The Little Church

"Hey, brother how are you?" I asked Tim.

"I'm doing great, thank God."

"Did you have time to think about it?"

"Marcial, I'm not going to be able to rent you the house."

"I understand brother," I said, and we shook our hands.

I knew that something was happening beyond the comprehension of my intellect. Somehow, I comprehended that The Voice of Truth was preparing the territory for a new shelter. I just did not fully comprehend how all this was about to unfold. But the following Sunday, Tim referred me to Georgia, our other sister from the little church. And Georgia said, "I have a property I'd like to show you."

"Oh, great!"

"Yes, please stop by tomorrow if you can, I'll be home after five o'clock."

"Great, we'll be there, Georgia," and I returned to the college with Bianka.

## Speaking to Bianka

"Bianka, I certainly don't know what this is all about, but I just want you to know that God is the Protagonist of this whole dream."

"I believe so," she said and we arrived at the college.

## Walking to Georgia's Apartment

As Bianka and I were walking to Georgia's apartment, I said to her:

"Bianka."

"Yes," in humility she replied.

"I truly don't know what this whole thing is all about, but I know that The Voice of Truth is directing me."

"The Voice of Truth?"

"Yes, The Voice of Truth."

"What do you mean?"

"Yes, The Voice that leads me to The Whole Truth."

"Why do you need to know the whole truth?"

"If a truth is not whole it can convert into a lie."

"I don't get it?"

"Truth sprinkled with 'minor lies' gives birth to deception."

"That makes sense. But what about The Voice of Truth?"

"The Voice of Truth will speak through Georgia as she helps us now."

"Really?"

"Let's see," I said and knocked on Georgia's door.

## Georgia Greets Us

"Hey, you guys come on in."

"Thanks, Georgia."

"Excuse my dog, he's always biting everything, but he's friendly."

"No problem at all."

"So tell me, what are your plans?"

"Well, as you already know, we are attempting to move out of the dorms. Bianka, is considering to enroll at the college, and we are not so sure of how this will all unfold."

"Oh, you are not married yet, right?"

"Sincerely speaking we're not, and I'm truly trying to comprehend all this still. We lived together for over four years in Florida, but legally we're not."

"Oh, ok. I'm not going to stand in the way of whatever God is doing in your lives, so with that being said, I have this apartment over here."

"Great, I think this will be great," I said.

"Are you sure that this is...?"

"It's perfect," I insisted without consulting it with The Voice of Truth first.

"Ok, if you insist, then all I need is a $350 check and that'll get you covered for the first month."

"OK, much better than the $600 for Tim's house," I said and began to fill out the check. And as I was signing the check, she said, "Wait. Wait."

"Sure," I replied puzzled by her reaction.

"I think it will be unfair if I allow you to sign that check before I show you another property that will become available in a month or so."

"Where is it, Georgia?"

"Oh, is the little house down the street."

"I think you're very fair; I guess I'll hold on to this half-way-signed check. Is that ok?"

"Perfect, let's go see the little house."

## At The Little House

"Is this the one?"

"This is it," she said with a smile.

"Do you like it?" I asked Bianka.

"Sure; it's perfect."

"Ok, Georgia, we're going to hold on, and we'll wait till we return from the summer break. Is that fair?"

"I think is a wise decision."

"Thank you much, Georgia."

"You're always welcome," she said, and we went our separate ways. And as I walked away The Voice of Truth said, "Just continue to follow Me, and you'll see Me face to face" (John 16:16).

"I don't know what this is all about," I said to Bianka, "but I do know that The Voice of Truth is behind all of this."

## Another Assignment

The following day, Coach Mooney approached me and said, "Hey Marcial, there's a Presbyterian Church down on Main Street that is in need of a youth pastor...you know, leading the junior high and high school kids. What do you think?"

"I'll think about it during this summer break, coach."

"Great."

"Thanks a lot, coach."

"I'm here for you, brother."

"Coach remember to sign me up to help out with the Armory Sale, this fall."

"I'll put you down."

"Thanks again, coach," I said, and walked out of his office, and visited Coach Pfeifer in his office.

"Coach, is it a good time now?"

"Sure, old man."

"Ok, ok I'll get you one of these days," I said and we both smiled, "coach, if it's ok with you, I'd like to change my number from 52 to 7, for the following season: Is it ok with you, coach?"

"That's for the skinny players, I don't think you'll fit in that one."

"I'll make it fit, coach, it just means something for me."

"OK, you can have it."

"Thanks a lot, coach."

"Get that shoulder healed quickly," he shouted as I walked out of his office.

"Hey, coach!"

"What's that?"

"What happened with the team's prayer that Paul and I built? It's no longer posted out here?"

"Ah, I had to take it down because someone complained, but don't worry, it's right here posted in my office now.

"Oh, I see, coach.    See you after the break, coach—thanks for everything."

"See you old man," he said.  And I headed back to Florida for my first summer break, but this time, accompanied by Bianka.

# Chapter 22

# My First Summer Break: Another Sign

As I was riding in the *Amtrak* train, on my way to the Minneapolis Airport, and I laid down on my back, on the train's floor, in between the train seats, and I closed my eyes, and without voicing a word, I communicated the following to The Almighty God:

"My Father in Heaven, you know all things. You keep showing to me football, boxing, *The University of Miami*, world championships, and professional sports. I know You gave me much talent, but I just don't fully comprehend how all this will transpire into my reality. I will follow You forever, but please show me, already, if this is what You truly want from me. You say in Your Word to be specific. So tonight, as I lie on this train floor, I'm asking you to show me tomorrow, at 12 o'clock exactly, what You want from me, completely—Your perfect will."

I laid there for a while waiting for an answer, and unexpectedly, He responded, saying, "Stay in a *Motel 6* tomorrow with Bianka, turn on the TV at 12pm, and you will see My majesty."

"Bianka."

"Yes."

"You will see God's majesty tomorrow."

"Really?"

"You'll see."

We arrived at the *Motel 6* at around 10 in the morning. I was eager to turn on the TV, but the hour had not yet come. It was 11:25am already, and suddenly, The Voice of Truth showed up and said, "I won't just show you what I desire for you at noon, but I will show you a sign at 11:30am, at 12pm as I promised, and another one at 12:30pm. It is 11:29am now, find the *ESPN Channel*." And I quickly found the *ESPN*

*Channel*, and suddenly I saw a *30 for 30* documentary on Mike Tyson. Then 12 o'clock arrived, and a documentary on the 1980's *University of Miami Football Team* was airing. 12:30pm came, and another *30 for 30* documentary about Nelson Mandela was airing. And in the end, the narrator said something like, "Through Sports we can change the world."

By then I was speechless, didn't know how to react, and I was just waiting for The True Voice to explain the whole illustration. He sat next to us in bed and said:

"The Mike Tyson documentary is to remind you of the fight, and for you to go back to the boxing gym. The UM football documentary is for you to re-apply to this institution once again. And the Nelson Mandela documentary: just keep it in mind, and you will comprehend in a near era."

"Can you believe this?" I asked Bianka.

"It must be a 'coincidence.'"

"The timing of our trip; the timing of the train; the timing of the cab; the timing of all three shows; the timing of my prayer, and asking for a specific time when I prayed; the timing of The Voice of Truth... it's a coincidence?"

"I guess."

"Think again. I'm not a mathematician to figure out other probabilities..."

"Did you really pray last night, and ask God to show you at noon today?"

"I'm 100% sure. He said He will show me, and here we are now living this moment."

"This is just a beginning son; follow Me, and you will see."

Chapter 23

# Just Let Me
# Feed Him

## Thundering at the Park

I had just arrived at the Sunshine State, and I comprehended that finding healing for my leg and shoulder was essential. Besides this, I decided to enroll in online classes to speed up the graduation process. During these times, I was living in Homestead, FL, with my mother, some of my brothers, and Bianka—by a place called The Redlands. Every day I trained twice, ate nutritious food, and rested my body sufficiently. The main goal was to recover rapidly.

One day, I was at *Tropical Park*, and it began to rain while I was running up and down the little hill there—then, it began to thunder. Soon after, I noticed that no one, but me, was still in the park—not even the dogs. For some reason, I wasn't thinking about the possibilities of being energized by a lightning bolt as I ran up and down the hill. And as the deadly flashes intensified, and the park increasingly flooded all-around, I unpredictably heard The Voice of Truth say,

"Remember what your son, Brandon, said."

"What's that, my Lord?"

"Never give up!"

The thundering increased as I ran up and down faster and faster, and then I stood there wondering, "How is all of this going to unfold?" and The Voice of Truth kept silence.

## Meeting with Mr. Soto

I continued to have various meetings with Mr. Soto, the attorney, and I began to feel that no matter the amount of money received by this legal case, for some reason, I had to drop it. I didn't know what to do since I had already started the process; the easiest thing to do was to

134

continue, simply, to receive the large amount of funds. During the process, I clearly remembered how my friend, Fred, told me not to have this surgery prior to everything. Sometimes, I wanted to go back in time to just have my God-given shoulder again. But, on the flipside, I thought about the many wonderful things I could have done with the funds received. I thought about immediately helping the poor since my heart had changed. The process continued, and I followed along with it...

## Spending Time with My Son, Brandon

Three summers ago, before I moved to Bottineau, ND, Brandon was on a vacation trip with his family, in Colombia. His mother said to me, "I will return in two weeks" before she departed with my son to her country of origin.

"Fine," I said, "God is with you."

I called her every day to speak with Brandon, and we stayed in touch. And quickly, the two weeks expired, and I decided to phone her. She said, "I will take another week since things have changed."

"OK, no problem," I said as I desperately desired to see my son. And another week passed, another month, and finally after two months she said, "I will be there tomorrow."

"Fine, if it is ok with you, I'd like to pick you up at the airport so that I can see my son immediately?"

"Fine, I'll arrive by noon; see you at the airport, thanks a lot."

"Thank you. I'll be there."

Here I was, searching all over the airport and couldn't find them. I had walked for over an hour, asked about the flight, and she was nowhere around. She finally answered her phone and said, "Oh, I decided to come with my mother, we are at the house already."

"No problem, I'll be there shortly."

I drove for 35 minutes, arrived at her residence, and knocked on her door. Her mother opened the door and said, "Come on in."

"Thank you."

I noticed that my son's mother was attempting to feed him, but he rejected the food over and over, and I said to her, "May I...May I try?"

"For what?" with hatred in her speech she replied.

"Maybe he'll eat it with me."

"Here," she said and handed over my son and the food. And within seconds he stopped crying and soon after he began to eat. After not seeing him for over two months, I was having a special moment with him. I wanted to cry, but I was holding it in. Suddenly, she said, "How long will you keep him for?" with an attitude.

"I don't know, but may we talk about this later—when I finish feeding him?"

"How long?" again she repeated aggressively.

"I don't know; just for enough time I guess." I responded attempting to hold my peace.

"How long, I said?" she said.

"I don't know, maybe a week, or two, or three...you just spent two months with him, I think, I, at least deserve to be with him now."

But as I was feeding him, and as he smiled, she came and interrupted me with a slap on the face, and snatched him away from me.      I didn't want him to experience this craziness, so I snatched him away as gently as I could from her, and placed him by the door. Then, I carefully placed her on the floor(no I did not body slam a woman, I was really careful not to hurt any of them) and ran toward the door to take him with me. Unexpectedly, her mother took my son away, and as I attempted to hold him again, without hurting anyone, Carolina, came from behind me and pierced her nails through my back—tearing my t-shirt. Bianka was waiting outside sitting in our SUV, and I ran out carrying my son, Brandon, to the SUV—in the attempt to leave with him. I shouted to Bianka while attempting to escape from Carolina's presence, "Sit on the driver's side and drive away!" But she froze as she watched the scene. I then handed over my son to her, shut the passenger door, and as I attempted to come around to drive away, Carolina, was already inside of the SUV—driving away with both of them. She almost ran me over.

By then, I was furious, I wanted to hit something, and the nearest thing I saw was the mailbox—I treated it like a punching bag. I thought:

"All I wanted was to spend time with him as I deserve, and this is what happens?

"Where is he now? When may I see him again? What am I going to do?" And I was phoning her, and she didn't answer. Then I called Bianka, and she said, "A cop is pulling us over right now; I'll call you later."

Soon after that, the police arrived at her house, where I was waiting, and the policeman said, "We're here because we just received a call on a domestic violence issue. We were told that you hit a woman."

"If I hit a woman, then why isn't the woman here to explain the assault?"

"We're going by the allegations."

"May you take a look at my back, sir?"

"She did that?"

"I guarantee you it wasn't me." And the policeman wrote a report, handed it to me, and said, "We know you're a good man," and drove away. And soon after, Bianka returned by herself, and we drove away. The next day, I tried to spend quality time with my son once again, but Carolina didn't allow me. Instead of attempting to run away with my son again, I said to Carolina's mother, who received me at the door, "It's ok. This world isn't fair, but The Living God is," and walked away with a broken heart once again.

Within a week, I received a restraining order. Then, I received a letter from the court that demonstrated a hearing. And Bianka worried more and more as the date approached. I did not have such a close relationship, yet, with The Voice of Truth, but He said, "Do not fear; I will go with you to the court of law."

# The Court Hearing

The hearing arrived. And the judge allowed her hiring attorney to speak first, and the attorney focused on the falsified story of a domestic violence issue—by asserting that I hit a woman. The judge then said, shortly after:

"Enough! Enough!" And He stared at me and said, "Now Mr. Ferreira, will you like to explain?" And I got up, and The Voice of Truth took over for over ten minutes. And the Judge said, "Enough. Enough. Just follow that gentleman standing next to you," and the hearing was over. I followed, the young man standing next to me, and he said, "One of one thousand men that come through this court come out again, the rest go straight to jail."

"My friend, I'm learning that when you live by the Truth it truly sets you free."

"Really?"

"These words come from my heart."

"Ok, ok. Listen. How much can you give her monthly?"

"I don't know; I've been giving to her more than enough every month—since my son was born."

"Is this amount ok for you?"

"Sure, I think that's fair."

"Ok. Good."

"When will you like to see your son?"

"Every day if possible."

"I can't do that, but you may pick a weekday, and you may see him every other weekend."

"OK. No, problem."

I was asked to give just under half of the amount I was willingly giving her—for the provision of my son. And I was now allowed to see my son—all accomplished through The Whole Truth, and without a dime.

# Chapter 24
## *Returning To Bottineau*

It was the seventh day of two-a-days. And I was running up and down the field with a hurting groin muscle, and I noticed that I couldn't continue. The Voice of Truth came quickly and said, "Tomorrow you will speak; first to your teammates, and then to your coaches. And you will no longer play football for *Dakota College at Bottineau* after that moment."

This situation was not syncing in because I just could not comprehend how I kept receiving all these revelations about football and boxing, and then, I had to stand in front of my teammates and not play football again. The signs, given at *Motel 6* after I prayed, would not amount to this outcome. All the signs given through dreams and directly by The Voice of Truth will no longer make sense. All the training, all the effort, all the listening, all the praying, and all the following of The Voice just wouldn't add up to this decision. I, to some extent, comprehended that He knew what He was doing. The next day, I gathered my teammates, we prayed together, and then, I shared the news. I said something like, "This is it," as my eyes could not retain my tears, "this is it," I repeated and said, "The Lord has another plan for me. I just received this academic scholarship from *The University of Miami*, so maybe, God allows me to go there one day."

I noticed that some of them felt my pain by their facial expressions, and I said, "I love you all," and we hugged as brothers. Soon after, I walked into the coaches' office and repeated my words as the True Voice instructed. Within a few weeks, I developed a program, to physically train my teammates, from 5am to 6:30am—with the help of Coach Eugene. And prior to this, I received some good news.

## Finding a Shelter

Before leaving to Florida for the summer break, I had applied for some apartments that were right in front of the college. The lady called me and said, "You're approved! When can we meet at the apartments?"

"Whenever you're available works for me."

"It's 1 o'clock ok?"

"Sure. I'll be there."

## At The Apartment

"Nice to see you again."

"Likewise."

"Ok, this is a lease for a whole year. Are you ok with that?"

"No, problem."

"Good."

"Where do I pay for the water and sewer and the electricity?"

"That's included in your rent payment."

"Oh, how much is the rent?"

"Let me see, let me see, oh, here it is: It's $22 a month."

"May you repeat that again, please?"

"Sure. $22 per month."

"There's probably a mistake..."

"Not really. It's just that we are calculating this rent by your personal circumstance."

"Really?"

"Yes."

"And...how about the deposit to move in?"

"Well, if you do not give us a deposit then you just won't receive anything when you leave."

"Amazing!"

"Please sign here, and these are the keys."

"Thank you so much," I said as she walked away. And I sat there thinking about this gift. My rent was half of my cell phone bill. I regularly paid $1200-$1400 a month in Florida, but this time I had to pay $22 only.

"I always provide for my little children," said The True Voice, "Tomorrow, go to The Armory Sale and help them with all your heart." And I did just that, and when I finished they said, "Do you need anything?"

"No, no; that's ok." But they insisted and furnished the entire apartment, freely—they even delivered the furniture.

## The Next Day: The Bride is Given

"Can you pick me up from the train stop, please?" said Bianka.

"Are you here?" surprised I asked.

"Can you please pick me up?"

I asked my friend and teammate, Derrick Woods, for the favor, and we were on our way. We arrived at the college, and The Voice of Truth said, "I prepared the apartment for her yesterday."

"You can stay in this apartment if you like," I told Bianka.

"Really?" surprised she responded.

"Yes. I have been given orders."

"How did you get this, I thought you we're going to deal with Georgia?"

"God gave me this, and I took it with joy."

"And how about Georgia?"

"We spoke. And she completely comprehends."

"How did you get all this furniture?"

"God provided, and I took it with joy."

"And where will you sleep?"

"At the dorms; you may stay here if you'd like."

"Thank you, sincerely; thank you." And The Voice of Truth sat next to me and said, "When she was on her way, you were preparing this apartment—I did it simultaneously," and He departed. And I slept in my dorm room for about a week, and then, The Voice of Truth said, "Move in with her."

"Are you sure?"

"Move in with her."

I did just that. By then, we were both attending the same college, studying together, and The Voice of Truth began to open up my heart: to marriage. In this point in my life, 'marriage' was the last word I had on my mind. We soon began to mix our souls and flesh again, over and over, and one day she said, "I don't feel so good."

I quickly bought a pregnancy test, and the results came back positive. Here I was confused and still hurt by her betrayal, but the Voice of Truth preferred forgiveness. And one night, after a marriage Bible study the Lord began to move in my heart intensely. He showed me the importance of marriage, and forgiveness. But I truly didn't feel like accepting this message. Soon after, Bianka and I returned to the apartment. And one thing led to another, but right before we mixed our souls again The Voice of Truth said, "If you look at the clock and it is 3:07am then I recommend that you get on your knees and ask Bianka to marry you." And I was nervous; I didn't even want to look at the clock, but His power was much greater. "Do not touch my daughter unless you look at the clock," He said, as we kissed intensely, and our bodies navigated through the bed. Our souls weren't mixed yet.

Filled with fear, I turned my head, and I saw a three and a zero and a...and a seven: It was 3:07am on the dot. I couldn't hear a thing, but I felt that something lifted me up from the bed, and placed me in front of Bianka—in the custom-made rugs of our $22 a month one bedroom apartment. And The Voice of Truth returned and said, "You may get on your knees now and ask her to marry you."

"Are You serious?"

"Or you can walk away from her life now."

"Ok good."

"This is not what you truly want, My son."

"I'm sure it is."

"My will is perfect."

"What do You want from me?"

"Everlasting life."

"Everlasting life?"

"My son, will you follow Me?"

"But I don't even have a ring?"

"Excuses are the excuses of a man with many talents."

"Excuses are the excuses..."

"I will provide."

My knees were trembling, and weak, but it was not my arthritis. And I fell, suddenly, on my knees.

"Say it without fear!"

"Will you marry me?" erupted out of my lips, and I just don't know how.

She was shaking and filled with joy or fear, I don't know, but she was smiling and couldn't contain herself. A tear escaped from her left eye. And I just remembered, "Where's the ring?" I asked The Voice of Truth.

"Take off the $5 stainless steel ring you purchased from your friend when you worked for BMW, and give it to your bride."

"What!?"

"Follow Me."

"That's a men's ring."

"Will you follow Me?"

While my arm was already extended, on hold, waiting for the message from The True Voice:

"Yes!" she said with a facial expression I truly didn't recognize. And I loosened my ring and placed it on her finger, but it was not her size. She held on to it regardless. And we hugged, cried, and laughed; I couldn't believe the phenomenon.

"Congratulations," you may kiss and mix your soul with your bride.

"Are you sure?"

"I declare you husband and wife."

Soon after, He spoke once again and said, "Go to the Bottineau courthouse and make it legal according to men."

"And how about at the church?"

"One day you'll comprehend."

Not only did He ask me to forgive her, but He also asked me to marry her; not only did He bring her from over two thousand miles away, but He also provided a shelter for her; not only did He allow her to fall, but

He also extended an opportunity for her to repent of her wicked ways; not only did she find a new beginning, but she also started all over in college. But most importantly, I was given an opportunity to forgive, and the rest was born from it.

## The Youth Ministry and the Training

I decided to take the position as the youth leader at the local Presbyterian Church, *United Parish*. By then, I was attending to class, attending to the *Elevate 1* Bible studies, leading my wife, and leading the youth group at the church. I was also training every day as The Voice of Truth kept showing to me boxing. I remember coming out of the church's youth group, and walking down Main Street, and seeing a store called *Ali's Coffee Shop*. The Voice of Truth used it to remind me of boxing and 'the fight' I was in. I started training at the local gym to isolate myself, late at night, or also, early in the mornings. And I was also running around town, and developing my stamina as The Voice of Truth commanded. Thank God, many awards, and multiple college scholarships kept coming. Wholeheartedly, Bianka and I were studying every day and making an effort in search of a complete life restoration.

The final semester ended, and I graduated with a 4.0 GPA; I made the *All-North Dakota Academic Team*, and they hung my picture on the college's main hall—it was time to go home.

Practically, the whole town wrote letters to us, and some gave us money as well. I was forced to buy a car to drive back to Florida since Bianka was pregnant—we found a *Ford F-150* with the help of our Math Professor, Scott Johnson. And we bought it with our school loan and financial aid returned money. I was offered about three jobs at the college, and I had an opportunity to continue in nearby universities as they all offered me full scholarships. I knew that my time was up at *Dakota College at Bottineau*, and that I had to reunite and father my son, Brandon, once again...

Chapter 25

## *An Interruption*
## *Occurs*

I am no longer at the $18-a-day hotel room, instead, I've been in my mother's apartment home, in The Dominican Republic, since The Feast of Tabernacles (The Festival of Sukkot)—a Biblical Holy Day described in Leviticus 23:33-44—and, since the recent Blood Moon, which reflected gloriously, on the same biblical appointed day. I finally saw my brother, Angel, who I had not seen since he departed Miami to come live in this island—over seven years ago. My mother, Angel and his significant other, and my brother Marcos and I—enjoyed a God-given meal together at a local restaurant. We all gathered in the living room afterward, and my mother initiated a conversation that contradicted my personal faith. I was hurt inside and attempted to explain my relationship with The Voice of Truth, but she wouldn't pass the mic. But at least, something worthy came out of this situation. She said, "You weren't supposed to be here today!"

"How's that?"

"Allow me to explain," she answered and continued, "I kept pushing and pushing, and the doctor said to your grandmother:

'Ma'am, you have to make a tough decision, it's either the child or your daughter—you make the call. And your grandmother immediately got on her knees and said, with her arms pointed to the heavens: Oh, Father, O Holy Spirit of Truth, You are The Most High; bless this child and my daughter, and breathe on to them Your breath of life—in this very moment.'"

"And what happened?"

"'Hurry! Hurry!' said the doctors to the assisting nurses, 'call all the local radio stations and ask them to send all people willing to donate blood—explain the emergency!' The physicians shouted. And I was dripping more blood than this water here."

She stopped and opened the kitchen faucet to display an example, and said, "Do you see all that water?"

"I can see," I responded.

"Just picture that," she said and continued with the story, "Your grandmother was praying; she and your father wouldn't sign the document to let you go, and suddenly, I passed out."

"What do you mean?" I asked her.

"I was out! Out of this world," she said with larger eyes this time. "Suddenly, I saw a white light, and a bright sun."

"A bright sun? I asked.

"Yes."

"And then out of nowhere, I woke up, and I noticed that they were giving me blood."

"Please tell me. What do you remember from the scene?"

"Then I looked to the right, and there was your 300 pounds-plus grandmother next to me. And slowly, I then glanced to my left, and there were over 40 individuals standing in line. I found out later that these people were all willing to donate blood.

"After all of this, then your head got stuck—that's why you have that bump on the back of your head—and then you finally came out; you were born. But the story didn't end there. Those doctors from those days injected me with some stuff, attempting to alleviate my pain, but they made it worse. And your father had to call his Chinese colleague physician who later injected me with a special shot right in my lower back—I couldn't walk for eight months. And because of all that, you are here today."

I knew I had caused trouble when I was born, but not that kind of trouble. I was so overwhelmed that I could not write one word the following day. I thought about not continuing with this book; I thought about maybe deleting everything written so far, and starting all over. I earnestly thought about taking another approach, but The Voice of Truth used a phone app from where I receive scripture daily, and it read:

"And David said to Solomon his son, Be strong and of good courage, and do it: fear not, nor be dismayed: for the Lord God, even my God, will be with thee; he will not fail thee, nor forsake thee, until thou hast finished all the work for the service of the house of the Lord" (1 Chronicles 28:20, KJV).

Then I remembered another scripture that beautifully declares:

"Shall I bring to the time of birth, and not cause delivery?" says the Lord. "Shall I who cause delivery shut up the womb?" says your God (Isaiah 66:9).

Soon after, in the midst of my turning point, my younger brother, Marcos, said:

"Hey! Have you seen *God's Not Dead*, with the college kid and the professor?"

"I haven't," I said, "but I'll love to watch it."

"Good, because they have it on *Netflix*," he answered joyfully. And we watched it. It was the push I needed it to continue with this book.

*Please hold on for the ride because, soon, we will uncover the message The Voice of Truth has for Mankind. But first, let's take a road trip from Bottineau, North Dakota, to the City of West Park, Florida.*

Chapter 26

# Our Trip Home

I t was our last day in the small Town of Bottineau. And The Voice of Truth said, "Give away the furniture and take with you some clothes, and some of the books Coach Mooney gave to you."

"But won't we need most of it later?"

"I will provide."

Thus my wife and I did just that and drove away toward the Minneapolis Airport with my friend and teammate, Sid, so that he could catch his flight. Once we dropped him off at the airport, we continued in our journey. I noticed that my expecting wife was already uncomfortable, and, therefore, we decided to stop at a hotel in Minneapolis. And I asked,

"How much is it for the night?"

"Let me see...it is...$89 for the night, sir."

"Ok, here it is," I said as I pulled out from the donations I had just received from friends in Bottineau.

"Oh, we cannot accept cash to reserve," she said, "only credit cards or debit cards, please."

"Well, you can try this card."

"Ok."

"It declined it, sir."

"Are you sure?"

"Let me try again."

"Yes, sir. I apologize for the inconvenience."

As she was saying all these things, I was simultaneously praying. And The Voice of Truth appeared quickly and said, "Ask her for a discount, and then go to the truck and pray more with your spouse." And I followed His orders, and once I returned to the counter, I encountered her manager, and she said, "I can make an exception for today, and lower the price to $79; will that work for you?"

"All I can do is try."

"Ok. Let's see...oh, it went through."

"Thank God. Thank you for your help."

It was *Mother's Day* that day. And we were in the room, and I grabbed some loosed diamonds I had purchased through *EBay* with some Financial Aid cash back, and I said to my ring-less wife as I knelt down, "I know I have not been able to purchase you a ring yet, but please have these diamonds as this is all I can give you at this moment."

"You didn't have to do this, honey."

"Please hold on to them, and God willing, one day we'll build your ring."

She held on to them, and she said, "You hold on to them; I might lose them."

"Please just hold them as this is all I can give in these moments."

The following day, we filled ourselves with the free included breakfast and headed to another hotel that took the cash we received from all the wonderful people in Bottineau.

By then, we were tight on funds, so we decided to sleep in the highway's truck stations a couple of times. I was driving to Florida, but we did not have a place to live in yet. After four days, we finally arrived at Emenelia's house—the house where Bianka's brother, Dodanin, resided with his girlfriend, Nisy—the same house I ran from in the second true story in the first chapter. Dodanin said, "You know, the people that were living back there just left a few days ago, and we just cleaned it today. How about you guys stay here until you find a better place?" And The Voice of Truth said, "This is the better place."

Dodanin brought us a TV, and silverware he had received from tenants from his job. He also referred us to his co-worker, who gave us a practically new bed, and within a week all we needed was given.

I was in Florida and ready to attend to *The University of Miami* as they were covering about 75% of the tuition with grants and scholarships. And the government was temporarily covering the rest with student loans. Thus, I soon sold a 99' convertible *XK8 Jaguar* to *CarMax*; which I had purchased at wholesale price over a winter break—to pay the rent on time, and to continue to provide for the family's need. But before we enter into this territory of revelations at *The University of Miami*, I must first prepare you. So that you may fully grasp the message of The Voice of Truth—allow me to show you where the original sign birthed.

# Chapter 27
## *The Sign: 16*

It was summer time around 10 o'clock at night, and Bianka sat on the passenger side, as I was driving toward my mother's house, in The Redlands, in my old Lexus. And as I was nearing the street corner where I regularly turned left, The Voice of Truth whispered, "Do not turn, instead, continue until the road ends."

"Is this You?"

"It is the Spirit of Truth, My son?"

"Ok, so when do I stop?"

"Continue until the road ends."

I was driving and driving for over 10 minutes already, but the road appeared to be limitless. Suddenly, from about a football field away, I saw darkness approaching, and The Voice of Truth returned and whispered again, voicing, "Continue, till the road ends."

"What are we doing?" said Bianka.

"I don't know; I'm just following."

"But what are we doing here?"

"I honestly don't know. Hold on! Hold on! He's talking again," as we arrived at the end of the road I said.

"Do you clearly see the two gates in front of you?"

"I do, my Lord."

"These are two paths."

"Ok."

"I brought you here to show you what appears to be almost identical paths, but completely different ones."

"Almost identical, but completely different?

"Yes."

"Why?"

"Because even those who claim to know Me are following a path of worldly success, and the false church accepts it as Godly success."

"What should I do now?"

"Are you ok?" said Bianka as she appeared lost.

"As you can see, both gates have a lock, and you will not trespass."

"So what's the point of driving blindly, all the way to these gates?"

"Keep this picture and vital moment in your mind, and now return to your mother's house."

"Yes, Lord."

"Why did we just waste our fuel; it's expensive you know?" said Bianka.

"He's talking, and I'm following."

"To the middle of nowhere."

"Trust me, we're going somewhere."

"I know we just got home."

"Wait, wait...," I said as He approached me once again.

"Go to your room, and search through your old wallet."

I was searching desperately for something that I couldn't describe, and He sat next to me and said, "That one."

"This one? This business card?"

"Yes, the one from *Robert Rubenstein Law Firm*."

"This is the law firm handling my case."

"Yes, it is."

"What's this all about?"

"Count the letters."

"What letters?"

"Robert Rubenstein."

"16 letters."

"Count them again."

"16."

"Keep this vital number in your mind."

"Why You made me drive to the end of the road and showed me two gates—then asked me to remember the number *sixteen* from a business card?"

"Just remember it as this is the key to unlocking the other sign."

"Are you ok?" said Bianka.

"I need to make sure that I'm counting these letters correctly...wait...wait."

"What letters?"

"It's too complicated, but I'm following regardless."

I sat there for hours until I couldn't, anymore, attempt to comprehend this adventure. Over and over I thought about it, asked Him, and nothing seemed to return. After four years of connecting the dots by the guidance of The True Voice, I began to realize that this moment remained connected to the year of 2016. I believed that something was about to occur even with my joint pain, and that, at the given time, The Voice of Truth was going to make me whole again. My shoulder was doing much better after the second surgery; I was already days away from attending to a Division 1 University, and all I had to do was to continue listening.

Many questions constantly repeated through my mind, questions like:

"Will I represent the US in Boxing in these upcoming Olympics by 2016?"

"Will I make it to the *NFL* by 2016?

"Will I turn pro in boxing by 2016?

"Will this be the year where I finally get a break?

"Will God bless me and my family in 2016?

"Will I finally do what I love to do in 2016?

**"Will something BIG happen in 2016?"**

Questions after questions flooded my mind daily about this year. And The Voice of Truth kept leading me, and I'm still following. The number 16 was all He continuously showed me, and it's the same number He continually shows me to this very moment. Sixteen, sixteen, a mystery, but a key to unfolding the Big Picture...

### John 3:16 Revelation

I was at the license plate agency now attempting to register my *Ford F-150*, in Florida. And, of course, a license plate is required to drive it. I had 'BOXIN' on an Olympic license plate—on my repossessed *X5*

*BMW*—since I believed that by 2016, I was going to represent U.S.A in the sport. And I was trying to acquire it again. But the nice lady said, "Someone else already owns it now."

"Are you sure, I have to have that tag?"

"Positive."

"You have your Bible with you," said The True Voice. And I looked, and I was carrying it, and He immediately said, "Find a scripture and apply it to your license plate."

"Do you have 'Psalm 37:4' available?" I asked the counter clerk lady.

"Sorry; too long."

"How about this one...?"

"Taken already."

"I have selected the perfect one for you, My son," The Voice of Truth whispered.

"Which one is it?"

"John 3:16."

"My Lord! I'm in the State of Florida?"

"I chose it for you."

"There's almost 20 million residents living here. Don't you think someone else has the most famous scripture in the entire Holy Bible?"

"Are you ready; there are people behind waiting?" said the nice lady.

"Oh! Yes! Well...I think."

"Which one now?"

"I know that this must be a stupid question, but do you have JOHN 3:16 available?"

"Let me see...oh, that's weird, I do?"

"Are you sure? Let me spell this correctly again."

"I have it! Unbelievable! No one else has this tag in the entire State of Florida?"

"I have chosen this license plate as another sign, for you to continue to follow Me."

"Out of almost 20 million people living in Florida, you're giving it to me?"

"To you."

"And why me?"

"You are following me blindly, yet seeing, and because of this, I've chosen to reward you with a glimpse of My vision and wisdom."

"But I'm sure many more are doing the same."

"Many more, but I've chosen you."

"What am I supposed to do with this tag now?"

"The license plate will do something for you instead."

"And what's that?"

"It will remind you that out of entire State of Florida, I have chosen you."

"And how is that important?"

"What does My Word state in John 3:16?" He asked me.

"For God so loved the world that He gave His only begotten Son, that whoever believes in Him should not perish but have everlasting life."

"Now, think about these words stated in this verse; think about the license plate; think about the odds; think about boxing; think about the decisions you've made by listening to Me; think about it all, all things, and you will find the next key."

"What key?"

"You'll see."

# Chapter 28
## *Temptations or Options?*

I was still in Florida, and I had to make another decision before I finally attended to *The University of Miami*. I was meeting periodically with Mr. Soto, the attorney; I was no longer receiving the unemployment benefits; I was still supporting my son, Brandon, and spending more time with him. Also, I was sustaining my family from the $5000 I had received from the sale of the *Jaguar*, and there were many strong temptations on the table.

First Temptation: I may choose to attend *Florida International University*, instead of *The University of Miami*, and receive about $10,500 in returned funds every semester, due to the amount of scholarship I had received.

Second Temptation: I can return to the Car Business and immediately make a six-figure income while working around my class schedule.

Third Temptation: Not going to school at all, and just providing for my family.

Fourth Temptation: I was sent by Mr. Soto's paralegal, Nancy, to visit a physician on 88th Street S.W. and the Florida Turnpike—to check up on my shoulder. And while in the waiting room, suddenly, I saw Mr. Mario Cristobal (head football coach for *The Florida International University*) walking in. They soon called me; I met with the physician, and on my way out, I spoke with Mario quickly about the possibilities of walking on to his football team. He asked me a few questions, and we soon went our separate ways.

"I know that you can use the money, but remember, that I will provide," said The True Voice.

"Isn't FIU a great institution?"

"You will miss the next sign."

"But doesn't your own Word says that, 'if anyone does not provide for his own, and especially for those of his household, he has denied the faith and is worse than an unbeliever?'" (1 Timothy 5:8).

"Yes, it does, My son."

"I'd like to provide for my family if this is ok with You?"

"Haven't I provided since the beginning of times?"

"Yes, Lord."

"Do you prefer to provide for yourself, or do you prefer to receive My provision?"

"Your provision."

"Do not fear, and follow Me."

"So don't attend FIU, even if they're giving me $10,500 every semester?"

"Does the key have a price? Does your life have a price? Would you like to receive My freely given wisdom? Are you ready for the next sign?"

"Yes! Yes!"

"Then you must remain connected to the True Vine" (John 15:1-27).

# Chapter 29

# Arriving and Leaving:
# UM and Football

Collage classes had commenced. My wife and I decided to take our newborn son, Jonah, for a 35-minute ride to *The University of Miami*—to prepare myself properly. As I was approaching the prestigious institution multiple flashbacks hit me, suddenly. The first was when my third generation, 89 *Ford Aerostar*, died on me right in front of this institution, and the security guard helped me by allowing me to borrow his fuel container. The second was when The Voice of Truth directed me, and the lady said, "It is impossible for you to attend to this institution." And the third was when I came to the coaches' office during a summer break, and attempted to speak to the defensive coordinator. But instead, I bumped into the linemen's coach outside, and he said, "Oh, we're too busy right now—the best of the best in the nation are visiting. Sorry, we're too busy."

I parked and said to Bianka, "Please wait here, and call me if anything happens." Then, I resolved all the necessary procedures to fully enroll, and we returned to our efficiency apartment.

## The First Official Day
## At The University of Miami

It was Wednesday, August the 22nd, 2012. I had just arrived at the *TGI Fridays* Restaurant across the street, because the parking was over $300 for the fall and spring semester—this wasn't covered. I was walking around, and I began to think about everything that I had to go through just to make it to this place. The sight was amazing, everything appeared perfect, and it felt as if I was living a dream. I began to sense The Spirit of Truth guiding me as I walked on campus. He would say,

"Go here; go there," and I followed along. And then He said, "Your time here is short."

I was beginning to worry, even though I was not supposed to, and the message was not making any sense to me. I made it to a Sociology class, and the professor began to speak about evolution, and immediately, the spirit in me wanted to initiate a debate regarding this matter. The professor said:

"The only difference between us and other animals is that we have learned to make tools," and he continued, "this makes us different, and of course, we can stand on our legs as apes do."

I was boiling inside, I was about to stand and let him have it, but The Voice of Truth said, "Not yet; not yet, son." And I looked around and noticed that 9 of 10 students owned a very expensive device—an *Apple, MacBook Pro*—just to come to class. I wondered, "With the cost of one single laptop, a whole school may be established in another country."

## The Second Official Day
## At The University of Miami

The Voice of Truth said, "Soon, you'll have to make a difficult choice," and He departed. Soon after, I was at the coaches' office speaking to Ryan McNamee and he weighed me, measured me, and asked me all kinds of questions. Finally, he handed me over some paperwork and said, "The tryouts will be in a few weeks; try to get all things ready." I walked out thinking, "I'm 28, and here I am about to play football at a *Division I* level Institution in the *ACC*. My shoulder is completely healed, and my joints are a little weak, but I can manage the pain."

I was in class again listening to another professor and The Voice of Truth said:

"Some of these professors have multiple Ph.D.'s and consider themselves bright, but a child that knows Me has already found what most of them will search for throughout all their whole lives."

"Really? Why can't they find You?"

"Because they search in all the wrong places?"

"Why do they?"

"If they will only humble themselves as little children."

"Then what will happen?"

"They will acquire wisdom, given by The Creator of it, and not the limited knowledge of men; they will receive a heart of flesh, and I'll remove their hearts of stone, and they will find true everlasting life, and no longer perish."

"How is this possible?"

"I'll show you later," and He departed.

### The Third Official Day
### At The University of Miami

I was walking around campus, and I noticed that the girls competed in exhibiting their bodies. Every time I failed the "1-second rule" The Voice of Truth said, "Remember: on that day; on the day you control even your sight—you shall become a man."

I remember being at the *Patti and Allan Herbert Wellness Center*, training, and I felt The Voice of Truth approaching me. I couldn't focus for some reason as I attempted to train. And suddenly, I met my first friend there—a nice black guy from the Music School. We talked for a little bit; he was also on a scholarship, and I continued with my workout. Suddenly, The Voice of Truth said, "Go for a jog around campus," and now I was jogging by *The BankUnited Center* (the basketball arena). And out of nowhere, I felt a sharp pain in my right knee, causing me to slow down, and The True Voice came and said, "Go up and down the stairs."

"Yes, Lord."

And about 30 minutes passed, and He continued, "Now jump rope," and I followed the order. Suddenly, He said, "Now shadowbox," and I continued, "Stop!" unexpectedly He said. And I was filled with an unexplainable feeling as I stood by the Arena's main entrance. I saw the train stop at about a football field away, and the people walking around. I saw the trees from a different viewpoint; I felt pretty tall from up there, and silence hovered around me abruptly. Suddenly,

"Look to your left," said The True Voice, "do you see *The University of Miami'* flag?"

"Yes."

"Now look to your right."

"An American Flag?"

I was motionless and attentive to The True Voice because I suspected that something was coming, and unexpectedly, He said, "Who will you like to fight for?" Immediately through the True Spirit, I understood that the UM flag symbolized: Football, a Ph.D. in something, a 'bright future,' etc. On the other hand, I comprehended that the American flag represented not only the U.S, but also the entire world.

"This is the third day," said The True Voice, "I resurrected on the third day."

"And what's that supposed to mean?"

"You may resurrect today, or you may choose to remain in your current state?"

I was still standing there blown away by the phenomenon, and He said, "Would you like to fight for a dying country, or would you like to play at the *Sun Life Stadium*? Will you choose an 'amazing career,' or will you choose a true and everlasting life? Will you hold on to all this, or will you lose it all for Me?

"Are you serious?"

"It's your choice, My son."

"Why all the revelations, the dreams, the signs, the promises, the drastic decisions, the unemployment dilemma, the time in North Dakota, the drama, the suffering...why?"

"My son, no matter where my sheep go; no one can snatch them away from me."

"But why did You allowed me to enroll, to meet the coaches, to walk around campus, to go through the hassle, to taste and live a fantasy moment? Why?"

"It was all part of the plan."

"You even showed me all this after I prayed that night, at the train, on our way to Minneapolis, remember? Through the *30 for 30* TV shows; remember? And even countless revelations, remember? Through countless dreams, remember? Why are You asking me to leave, now?"

"It is your choice, My son; you may pursue your goals and achieve much?"

"But I thought these were Your goals?"

"My will for you resides in the consistency of following Me."

"And staying in this prestigious institution isn't following You?"

"Arriving here is part of My perfect will for you, but staying here is your choice."

"I just don't get it?"

"Remember The Story of Abraham?"

"Which one?"

# Chapter 30
## *The Story of Abraham*

"The one in Genesis in the 22<sup>nd</sup> Chapter."

"Not really."

"Let me refresh your memory:

### Genesis 22:1-18:
### Abraham's Faith Confirmed

Now it came to pass after these things that God tested Abraham, and said to him, "Abraham!"

And he said, "Here I am."

Then He said, "Take now your son, your only *son* Isaac, whom you love, and go to the land of Moriah, and offer him there as a burnt offering on one of the mountains of which I shall tell you."

So Abraham rose early in the morning and saddled his donkey, and took two of his young men with him, and Isaac his son; and he split the wood for the burnt offering, and arose and went to the place of which God had told him. Then on the third day Abraham lifted his eyes and saw the place afar off. And Abraham said to his young men, "Stay here with the donkey; the lad and I will go yonder and worship, and we will come back to you."

So Abraham took the wood of the burnt offering and laid *it* on Isaac his son; and he took the fire in his hand, and a knife, and the two of them went together. But Isaac spoke to Abraham his father and said, "My father!"

And he said, "Here I am, my son."

Then he said, "Look, the fire and the wood, but where *is* the lamb for a burnt offering?"

And Abraham said, "My son, God will provide for Himself the lamb for a burnt offering." So the two of them went together.

Then they came to the place of which God had told him. And Abraham built an altar there and placed the wood in order; and he bound Isaac his son and laid him on the altar, upon the wood. And Abraham stretched out his hand and took the knife to slay his son.

But the Angel of the Lord called to him from heaven and said, "Abraham, Abraham!"

So he said, "Here I am."

And He said, "Do not lay your hand on the lad, or do anything to him; for now I know that you fear God, since you have not withheld your son, your only *son,* from Me."

Then Abraham lifted his eyes and looked, and there behind *him was* a ram caught in a thicket by its horns. So Abraham went and took the ram, and offered it up for a burnt offering instead of his son. And Abraham called the name of the place, The-Lord-Will-Provide; as it is said *to* this day, "In the Mount of the Lord it shall be provided."

Then the Angel of the Lord called to Abraham a second time out of heaven, and said: "By Myself I have sworn, says the Lord, because you have done this thing, and have not withheld your son, your only *son*— blessing I will bless you, and multiplying I will multiply your descendants as the stars of the heaven and as the sand which *is* on the seashore; and your descendants shall possess the gate of their enemies. In your seed all the nations of the earth shall be blessed, because you have obeyed My voice."

"And what does this story have to do with me?"

"I asked Abraham to sacrifice his son to test simply his faith and to test his love for Me."

"But he never killed his son?"

"But through love and faith he was willing to go even that far just because I asked him and because he believed."

"I still don't understand?"

*My son, I brought you this far to show you a country and a world which I will soon judge, righteously.* And to show you an amazing career in sports and academics—what most people consider an amazing dream. Abraham chose to listen to Me, and then, I provided for him. And then, I also blessed all his descendants and the nations through him because he obeyed My Voice."

"But why me?"

"I'm not asking you to sacrifice your son, but I'm showing you that through you, as my servant, I can sound My alarm to America and the whole world. I am giving you an opportunity to deny what seems to be an amazing achievement, and instead, to choose to remain following Me, wholeheartedly. And we may warn the people together—not just in America—but in all the Nations."

"Why such a drastic decision in this specific moment?"

"Remember why I gave to you the *John 3:16* license plate?"

"Somewhat?"

"I chose you because I know you're capable."

"I'm capable?"

"Which one is greater?"

"Which what?"

"Which flag?"

"I know you know all things, but isn't that a dumb question?

"My son, you've given me a wise answer."

"Wait! Wait! I'll take that back, The UM flag could be a great flag."

"Follow Me, and you'll see."

"So do I leave, or do I stay?"

"It is your choice, My son?"

"It appears like You prefer for me to leave?"

"I prefer to see the nations repent from their wicked ways before I judge them righteously."

"Why can't you just speak to all people and let them know directly?"

165

"Because all people aren't listening to Me; their sins have covered their ears."

"But can't You just do something about it?"

"I have, since the beginning of times."

"I mean, can't You just make a perfect world?"

"Soon it will be, but until this hour comes, My Creation has the freedom of choosing."

"Do I really have to leave?"

"If you love Me, keep My commandments" (John 14:15).

Here I was, knowing that I could triumph largely in sports and excel in academics. But somehow, I understood that the encounter was divinely appointed and that I had to make a tough choice—to somehow assist The Voice of Truth on Earth as it is in Heaven. My third day at the university landed on a Friday, and I comprehended that I had to make this decision quickly. Throughout the entire weekend, my mind was consumed by this encounter. I used math, science, history, Bible prophecy, economics, family counseling, and a whole lot of tutoring with The Voice of Truth to conclude my decision. To the world and my carnal ways this was insane, but to The Voice of Truth and The Spirit of Truth in me it was a choice of valor. Classes were suspended that Monday due to the *Storm Isaac*, and it allowed me to think it over, again.

The time came. I arrived, and my wife and Jonah waited for me in the car.

"Are you sure about this?" said Bianka.

"I don't know yet, but I'll know soon," I said as I slowly closed the door.

I went to the financial aid office and canceled; then to student account services and canceled everything, and then as I was on my way to the advisor's building I began to doubt. I quickly sat down nearby the president's office, away from all the advisors, and I looked around to make sure that no one was around. And I prayed, "O Father in Heaven, if this is what you want from me, then please send my personal advisor, to me, now, please, as the final confirmation?"

My head remained bowed, and unpredictably, "Do you need any help," said Bethany Angiolillo, my corresponding Advisor, as she touched my shoulders.

I wanted to run away from the scene, but I knew that something was happening behind the curtain, and I had to decide finally in that very instant.

"I can sure use your help, Mrs. Angiolillo," and I followed her to her office and we sat down.

"How may I help you?"

"This will be quick..."

# Chapter 31

## The Department of Children and Family

I had $50 in my family's name, and we were on the way to *The Department of Children and Family* to inquire about some assistance in that time of need. I genuinely desired just to go back to work, and to produce funds to provide for basic needs, but The Voice of Truth kept directing me in this journey.

"Is this the place where I may find help in a time of need?"

"Yes it is, may I have your address, please?"

"Sure, it is...in West Park, FL"

"Oh, you're in the wrong office, you must go to this one, in Broward."

"Oh, ok, thanks for your help," and I walked out. But as I exited the edifice, a gentleman came out and said, "Did anyone help you?"

"Well, they did, but we're in the wrong office."

"Please come on in, I sense that *something* is telling me to help you. Please come right in!"

"Thanks much, sir."

"It's a good thing to meet you; here's my business card."

"Likewise, sir."

"Listen, I'm one of the county's commissioners, and I do not work directly with *The Department of Children and Family*, but I believe that *something* just asked me to call you."

"Oh, ok."

"Please have a seat."

"Thanks."

"Now, tell me about yourself."

"Well, we've been here in Florida for weeks only, sir."

"Well, I'll put it this way: why are you here?"

"Well, I believe I need help in this time of need."

"Listen, let me introduce you to my friend here."

"It's a great thing to meet you, sir."

"Same here, my friend."

"Bo! You came at the perfect time. Let me introduce you to Marcial and his wonderful family:  This is Bo Leonard, the chief of the police."

"It's a good thing to meet you, sir."

"Likewise, my friend."

"He's a boxer", said the commissioner.

"Oh good, I'm opening up a boxing gym soon; not that far away from here.  Would you like to see it?"

"Sure!"

"Follow me," said Mr. Leonard.

"Is this it?" I asked as we arrived.

"This is it, Marcial."

"This is not the time yet, My son," said The Voice of Truth.

"Why am I here?"

"Just keep all this in your long-term memory, son."

"For what?"

"You will need it soon."

"Hey, are you alright? Bo asked.

"Oh me, yeah, yeah, I'm fine thank God, Bo."

"Oh! You believe?"

"I do everything I can, to walk in The Spirit of Truth, Bo."

"Listen, maaan, when God called me I was 'doing me'...and everything was fine: the women, the money...*and one day...*

"Get my cell number," Bo said.

"Thanks a lot for your time, Bo."

"We didn't receive any financial help, but we received something much greater," I said to my other half.

"Really?"

"God is with us," and we smiled and I drove away.

## Chapter 32

# Marcial J. Ferreira
# vs.
# Publix Supermarket:
# The Case Proceeds

Bianka's cousin, Yosi, was going through a case of her own as she was facing possible jail time from a real estate issue. It was past 3am, and suddenly, a loud knock at her front door:

"Police open up! Now!"

"Oh, God! Mom! It's the police; don't let them take me," as she was hiding in her closet panicking.

"Police open up now!" they shouted again.

"Don't worry daughter," crying in fear her mother said as they hugged each other.

"Don't let them take me, mom, please! No! No!"

"I have to open up now."

"No, no."

"Open up! Police!" as they knocked harder and harder.

"On the floor! Now! Now!"

Yosi went to jail, and The Voice of Truth said, "You're going soon, also."

"Me?"

"Yes son, you must."

"Why?"

"You will cease your case against *Publix Supermarkets*, and you will tell Mr. Soto the whole truth."

"But why now, and why couldn't You tell me this before I purposely slipped and fell?"

"You did not truly know Me, son, and I allowed it to happen."

170

"I can't do this now after I've taken away so much time from Mr. Soto, and they're about to pay me in the next few weeks?"

"This is for My glory, son."

"But can I just wisely use those funds for Your Kingdom's purposes?"

"What's Mine belongs to Me, and what's wicked belongs to the Father of Lies."

"I just can't; I'm sorry."

"Don't be afraid, and return what was never yours."

"But how about all the people involved in this, currently waiting for this lawsuit to settle, to receive their funds?"

"They will be fine."

"This isn't fair."

"Life isn't fair, but I AM HOLY, and as you seek Me, you'll also find holiness."

Bianka and I, Yosi, Yosi's mother, Yosi's attorney, and other friends were at Yosi's court hearing.

"All rise," said the temporary judge, and we were all there, and I was praying for her freedom as I was getting a taste of what was about to unfold in my life.

"You will come to a court like this one," said The Voice of Truth.

"Please help her from this now, and help me also, please."

"You're going to jail."

"I have kids, and now a wife; do something else please, but don't separate me from my kids again, please."

"You will become a better fighter in prison. And then you will fight for Me."

"Can't I just go back to the boxing gym, and simply be with my family?"

"You are My warrior, and My warrior only trains in My training camps."

"Are you serious?" I asked, and He soon departed as Yosi's hearing continued.

"And I sentence you to 28 months...", and most were crying, most were sad, and I was in a multi-emotional state.

"You're going after," whispered the Voice of Truth.

"If this is Your will then let it be done in my life."

"Go to Mr. Soto's office, and tell him the whole truth."

"When?"

"Tomorrow morning."

"Do I call him first?"

"Just show up."

"Yes, Lord."

"Bianka!"

"Yes."

"I must drop the case."

"But we can use those funds for great things—for the Lord."

"It is not my will, but His will."

"I thought His will was for us to help the poor and to feed the hungry, and just love one another?"

"It is, but not with these funds."

"I'm afraid."

"Don't be; He is with us."

"Well, you do what you have to do."

## The Next Day

"If I don't come back, then I guess you'll visit me in prison one day with my kids," I told Bianka.

"I love you," she said, as tears dropped from her gorgeous eyes.

"I love you," I said, as blood covered my sight, and I drove away.

I was mentally ready to go to jail; I thought about God's training camp; I was suffering and crying for my family as I was driving to Mr. Robert Rubenstein's law office. And I thought, "I can't believe I will have to separate myself from my loved ones, once again."

"You're going to jail," said The True Voice.

"I can't believe that I've caused all this mess."

"You'll be fine in jail."

"I'll follow You!" hurting because of my family, I shouted to The True Voice in the midst of the storm. Suddenly, I arrived at the law office.

I arrived in my new 15-year-old *Toyota Avalon* I had just purchased to re-sell and to help sustain my family. As I stood in the elevator I asked, "Is this what you want from me, truly?"

"Just ask for Mr. Soto."

"Good morning."

"Good morning! How may I assist you?"

"Well, I'm looking for Mr. Soto."

"He is currently out of the office, but let me see if I can get you someone else in charge today."

"I'd like to speak with him only."

"Allow her to help you," said The Voice of Truth.

"Are you sure?" she said.

"You know what? Whoever can help me is fine."

"Ok, let me get someone for you."

"Sure."

"Lord, is this what you want from me?"

"Be ready."

"Marcial!"

"Yes, sir."

"I'm Robert Rubenstein, please follow me."

"Sure."

"We finally meet after almost two years of fighting this case for you."

"Thank God we did, sir."

"Come on in and have a seat, please."

He soon received a phone call and initiated a conversation. I was sitting in his sky office, seeing most building surrounding us, and suddenly, I said to The True Voice, "I don't have the strength."

"Open up your Bible."

"Where do I go?" I asked hoping Mr. Rubenstein would never hang up.

"The page divider."

"This one?"

"Read it."

"Finally, my brethren, be strong in the Lord and in the power of His might. Put on the whole armor of God, that you may be able to stand against the wiles of the devil. For we do not wrestle against flesh and blood, but against principalities, against powers, against the rulers of the darkness of this age, against spiritual *hosts* of wickedness in the heavenly *places*. Therefore take up the whole armor of God, that you may be able to withstand in the evil day, and having done all, to stand.

Stand therefore, having girded your waist with truth, having put on the breastplate of righteousness, and having shod your feet with the preparation of the gospel of peace; above all, taking the shield of faith with which you will be able to quench all the fiery darts of the wicked one. And take the helmet of salvation, and the sword of the Spirit, which is the word of God" (Ephesians 6:10-17).

"Remember these scriptures, they are another sign, My son."
"Another sign?"
"Yes, and don't be afraid, for I am with you."
"I apologize for the inconvenience, Mr. Ferreira."
"No problem sir; perfect timing!"
"Listen, we would have been able to get you much more money for your case, but since you had two surgeries, and you returned to play football, at this point, the defendant is willing to give us about $25,000 to $30,000. What do you think?"
"Mr. Rubenstein, what I'm about to tell you I really wanted to share it with Mr. Soto today because he has been there with me in this process..."
"We're partners; it's the same thing, please continue."
"...well, I slipped and fell on purpose, sir."
"Are you suuure?"
"I'm 100% percent sure, sir?"
"Are you really sure?"

"Take me to jail if needed, sir, but I'm sure, sir."

"No, no I won't take you to jail. Does Mr. Soto knows about this?"

"The purpose of my visit today was to see him personally and inform him."

"Maybe it was a good thing that we met instead; I'll prepare a letter, and we'll call you when it's ready, and we'll simply cancel all this."

"Sir, please forgive me for all the trouble."

"I forgive you."

"Thank you so much, sir. Please have Mr. Soto call me, please, at his convenience; I'd like to ask him for forgiveness as well."

"Will do, Mr. Ferreira."

"You have a blessed day, sir," and I left.

And suddenly, The Voice of Truth appeared and said, "You're not going to jail."

"Is it you?"

"Yes son, you had to learn a lesson."

"A lesson?"

"Why would you lie to me, and allow me to suffer throughout these months?"

"I never did, I just illustrated to you what you faced, and then, I delivered you from it as you follow My Voice."

"Couldn't You just tell me?"

"I discipline My children."

I was filled by Him as I was driving back home, and I shouted, "Thank you O Lord! For your mercy; for Your Love endures forever!"

## Psalm 148: Praise to the LORD from Creation

And I continued:

Praise the LORD!

Praise the LORD from the heavens;
Praise Him in the heights!
Praise Him, all His angels;

Praise Him, all His hosts!
Praise Him, sun and moon;
Praise Him, all you stars of light!
Praise Him, you heavens of heavens,
And you waters above the heavens!

Let them praise the name of the LORD,
For He commanded and they were created.
He also established them forever and ever;
He made a decree which shall not pass away.

Praise the LORD from the earth,
You great sea creatures and all the depths;
Fire and hail, snow and clouds;
Stormy wind, fulfilling His word;
Mountains and all hills;
Fruitful trees and all cedars;
Beasts and all cattle;
Creeping things and flying fowl;
Kings of the earth and all peoples;
Princes and all judges of the earth;
Both young men and maidens;
Old men and children.

Let them praise the name of the LORD,
For His name alone is exalted;
His glory *is* above the earth and heaven.
And He has exalted the horn of His people,
The praise of all His saints—
Of the children of Israel,
A people near to Him.

Praise the LORD!

# Chapter 33

# Back To
# The Boxing Gym

"**N**ow fast, and seek Me until I tell you to stop."
And three days later, in my tiny apartment, I began to sense His presence, and He said, "Ask your wife to anoint your head with My olive oil."

"Can you please pour some of that oil on my head?"

"Are you ok?"

"I'm fine."

"Ok."

"Thank you."

About an hour passed by, and I quickly began to feel peculiar. And suddenly, "Get up from your bed, and jump up and down," He said.

"But I can't even do a squat without having pain?"

"Do you trust Me?" I heard intensely, and I quickly raised up and jumped. Then, I jumped higher and higher, and I just couldn't believe what was taking place. He whispered again and said, "Now do push-ups until I tell you to stop." And I quickly got on the floor and began to do push-ups, non-stop. And as I was miraculously feeling no pain, He said, "Now do clap push-ups." And somehow, I was able to. And quickly, I was filled with His Spirit and began to shout joyfully,

"Praise The Lord. Hallelujah! O JHWH! Thank You, Yeshua!"

My wife was staring at me not fully comprehending that I had just been healed. And then He whispered, "I love you, My son, now go to Coach McKency tomorrow and tell him you want to do boxing, again."

"Oh, glory to God! Praise The Lord!"

## Back to the Boxing Gym

"I have to see Coach McKency, tomorrow," I said to Bianka.

"Again?"

"It's what The Lord wants."

"Are you sure?"

"I'm following Him."

"OK.  I guess."

## The Next Day

"Coach, how are you?" I said to Coach McKency.

"Oh, God; is that you?" he said, as I approached him, and we hugged.

"Coach, I just got back from North Dakota."

"Oh, it's cold up there, son."

"Yes it is, and I'm thinking about getting back into the ring."

"Really, son?"

"I believe God is directing me."

"God? Really?"

"I believe so, coach."

"I missed you so much, son.  Listen, I'm training Glen at the place tomorrow at around 10am; you're welcome to come, son."

"Really, coach?"

"I can't wait to see you tomorrow, son."

"I'll be there, God willing."

"But wait; where are you living by, now?"

"In West Park."

"Son, that's a 50-minute drive; are you working now?"

"The Lord will provide, coach."

"Ok, I'll see you tomorrow."

"I'll be there, God willing," and I left from the *Cadillac* Dealership where he also worked.

## Boxing at Thump Gym Again

"Son, remember Coach Jose?" said Coach McKency.

"Hey, coach; how you are?"

"I'm good, doctor." said Coach Jose

"Hey Marcial," said Glen, while hitting the heavy bag, "welcome back."

"Thanks, champ."

"Hey Marcial, I want you to train with Coach Jose this time so that we can get you fighting quickly," said Coach Mckency.

"Follow me, doctor," said Coach Jose and the training began.

I was attending *Thump Boxing Gym* from Monday through Saturday, consistently, and getting better and better, daily. And one day, during training, Coach Jose said, "Listen, boxing is not of Jehovah, doctor."

"Coach, I've been brought to this place, trust me, it has to be from God."

"Listen to me, I'm a *Jehovah Witness*, and my cousin turned pro, fought professionally, and decided to leave the boxing gym because he realized it wasn't from JEHOVAH."

"I get it brother, but listen, I evangelize everywhere I go, and He showed me this for a reason, coach."

"I'm just saying, doctor."

"I get you, coach."

"You know something: I'm here 'doing me,' but I know this [ain't] from JEHOVAH."

"I guess time will tell, coach."

"Come on let's get back to work."

"Yes, coach."

"You're going to hurt some people; keep training that way."

"I'm just following His will, coach."

"Ok, if you say so, doctor."

### The Next Day

We just finished training, and Coach Jose said, "Hey, doctor!"

"Yes, coach."

"Follow me.

"You see that bus stop over there?"

"Yes, coach."

"Start from there, and go around three times—that's just three miles."

And I was running and The Voice of Truth whispered, "Look up!" And I noticed a street sign that read, *El Camino Way*, and I kept on jogging. I began to hear distantly The Voice telling me to stop, but nothing happened yet, and suddenly, He said, "Soon you will see a staff; be alert!"

"I see one over there?"

"That's it! Pick it up once you're there."

"Are you going to turn it into a serpent? Or something else?"

"Pick it up, and don't be afraid."

"Ok, now what?"

"Keep jogging, and look at it."

"Yes, Lord."

"Remember the street sign?"

"Yes, Lord."

"It means what it reads in English and Spanish; keep following 'The Way.'"

"OK, and how about this wooden rod?"

"I want you to take it home, sand it down. And through you, I will write scriptures on it with a permanent marker."

"Are you serious?"

"Yes, son."

"Isn't this a little crazy?

"What seems crazy to the world, it's perfectly fine with Me."

"What am I going to do with it?"

"Soon, a time will come when many will need many real leaders to lead them—in the midst of an out-of-this-world, never-seen-before chaos. I will direct My servants in this world-wide event, and some will lead My sheep unto a hiding place."

"Is this You talking?"

"Yes, son; I will provide for those faithful servants, and I will extend My hand."

"Will people die?"

"Follow Me, son, and don't forget these signs."

"But wait. Wait. How about the stick?"

"Remember Moses, in My Holy Word?"

"Yes, Lord."

"He was My true servant, My Father gave to him *The Ten Commandments*, and He listened to Him and led My little children through a crucial era."

"The Exodus?"

"And much more, My son; for countless books could have been written to demonstrate all things fully."

"And what does that has to do with the stick?"

"Picture yourself leading a nation back to God."

"But how?"

"Remember what I showed you about Abraham at *The University of Miami*?"

"Yes, Lord."

"Store these moments in your long-term memory, and remain in Me; follow Me, My son."

"Coach, I lost count, but it was all worth it," I said to Coach Jose as I arrived at the boxing gym.

"OK, doctor! You're good for the day."

# Chapter 34
## *I'm Sick*

### Three Months Later

I was sparring with Elijah, another amateur boxer, and I noticed that I couldn't breathe. For about ten days I had the flu. I continued to show up for two more days with a fever, and finally, I realized that it was time to visit the hospital.

"You need to go to the hospital," said Bianka.

"I think you're right."

"I'm glad you're here, do you even feel?" said the physician.

"I believe so, sir?"

"Well, make sure he takes these, once-a-day, and no running at night for a week." And we left, and I called Coach Jose.

"Coach, forgive me, please."

"For what?"

"I'm going to have to miss for a couple of days."

"Hey doctor, you do what you have to do, and I'll be here waiting for you—get better soon."

"Thank you, coach."

"Thank you, doc."

### The Funds Are Low Again

"You need to leave boxing again," said The Voice of Truth.

"Are You serious?"

"You have to, son."

"But why?"

"You must find a job, and support your family financially—and now."

"But can I just continue with boxing and work in the morning?"

"You must work only."

"Why did you give me these talents: football, boxing, and the other sports, and now, not allow me to use them?"

"Quitting for a season does not mean you're out of the real race."

"I truly don't understand?"

"But you will at the appointed time."

"Yes, Lord."

"Remember this moment, and store it in your long-term memory."

"Yes, Lord."

## The Next Day

I was sitting in bed with my wife, and I initiated a conversation: "You know what I noticed?"

"What?" she said.

"Most great fighters end up in rough shape, financially or physically. For instance, look at Muhammad Ali, Macho Camacho, Julio Cesar Chavez... Isn't this crazy?"

"I guess."

"I don't understand why God has asked me to go to the boxing gym three times to quit soon after every-single-time?"

"Maybe it's you?"

"I can hear Him when he speaks to me: have you forgotten all the revelations already?"

"No, but I'm just saying, that maybe, you're misinterpreting them."

"I'm not misinterpreting or interpreting a thing—I just listen when He speaks."

"But maybe you're losing it?"

"I know I'm not crazy, and I'm being very careful in following Him."

"Well, I don't know."

"But you know what I noticed?"

"What's that?"

"Every time He sends me somewhere, I receive a sign that connects with a previously given sign."

"And what is He telling you?"

"I don't fully comprehend yet, but I know that if I continue to follow Him, I'll arrive at my final destination at some point."

"You are truly losing it."

"In fact, I know I'm finding it."

"Finding what?"

"The next key."

Macho Camacho was shot just hours after I had just mentioned him. I could not believe how I was just mentioning him, and there he was, on a stretcher, on TV. And a few days later, he physically died (May the True Counselor guide those family members in all their ways).

"Why does it have to be this way? I asked The Voice of Truth.

"Man is like a breath; His days are like a passing shadow" (Psalm 144:4).

"And that's it?"

"Know that it's just a season."

"And when does it begin? When does it end?"

"Follow Me, and you'll see."

# Chapter 35

# A Few
# Job Offers

## The Interstate Batteries Job Offer

"**H**ey, you know what?"

"What's that?"

"They called me from *Interstate Batteries* and offered me to come in for an interview."

"Really?"

"They want me to go tomorrow."

"Great! I hope this is God's will."

"I hope so, we'll see when the time comes."

## The Following Day

"You must be Marcial," said the manager.

"Yes, sir."

"Great! Come on in, young man."

"Thank you, sir."

"Have a seat."

"Yes, sir."

"I tell you what; this is very simple: we'll go for a ride together in one of our trucks; you'll help me deliver all the new batteries, and at the end of the day, you tell me what you think. And I'll tell you what I think about you. How does that sound?"

"Sounds good to me, sir."

"Oh, by the way, we'll pay you for this day, regardless of the outcome."

"Thank you, sir."

"You're ready?"

"I'm ready!"

"Let's go."

"Nice truck!"

"Get used to her, you'll be driving one of these if everything goes well!"

"Good!" And we headed for our journey in the truck filled with batteries. And after about a few hours, he asked, "What do you think so far; do you like it?"

"I can do this every day, sir."

"You see, so far we've delivered many batteries to different types of businesses—that's what it's all about! You will maintain and grow your own route. What do you think?"

"So far, so good, sir."

"Hey let's take a lunch break, do you want something specific?"

"I came prepared, sir."

"Oh, I see; boiled eggs and sweet potatoes; you must be on a diet?"

"It's just what I habitually eat, sir."

"See this belly?"

"I can see, sir!"

"That stuff is not coming in here, man," he said as he grabbed his belly.

"I can see, sir."

"You should give it a shot; it won't hurt you. Just try a piece. Here!" he said as he attempted to share a piece of his honey bun.

"Nah, nah; I'll be fine."

"Ok. Listen, let's get going and we'll finish soon."

"Yes, sir."

We were driving and delivering more batteries, and The Voice of Truth whispered while I was sitting on the passenger side, "Be ready! Another sign is coming."

"Really? What's this all about now?"

"Be ready."

"Yes, Lord."

"What do you think so far?" the driver asked.

"So far, so good, sir."

"You see, all you have to do is to pick up the old batteries and drop off the new ones—we're almost done."

"Yes, sir." And we just arrived at the office, and he said, "Have a seat; I'll be back."

"Be ready," The Voice of Truth said.

"I like this job; it's perfect: Do I take it?" I asked The True Voice.

"Be ready, a sign is coming."

"Hey, Marcial."

"Yes, sir."

"Follow me to this other office, better."

"Yes, sir."

"Have a seat; I'll be back quickly."

"Thank you, sir."

"Do I take the job, or not? I asked The True Voice, again.

"Read the sign in front of you."

"Which sign?"

"Right in front of you."

*Many of Life's failures are people who did not realize how close they were to success when they gave up*—Thomas A. Edison.

"Now think about it."

"I don't get it."

"Think about it some more."

"I'm confused.   What does this sign has to do with this job, and the decision I have to make soon?"

"Quickly! Reach your back pocket and open up your Bible."

"Ok, ok...where do I go?"

"Just open it."

"Ah, here?" And the first words I saw, read, "And you shall know the truth, and the truth shall set you free"—John 8:32.

"You're complicating things please help me decide."

"Focus."

"I'm trying."

"Just say the whole truth when the manager returns."

"Yes, Lord."

"I'm sorry for the delay," said the manager as he walked in.

"Oh, don't you worry, sir—perfect timing!"

"Good. Well, I spoke with my partner, and I explained to him how I like your attitude, and how you may fit adequately in our company. I want to offer you a job; what do you think...?"

"Oh, thank you, sir."

"...but first, my partner has to interview you, just to make sure we're on the same boat."

"Yes, sir."

"Follow me."

As I was walking into his partner's office, I realized that there was a signed Mike Tyson's glove, and a signed Muhammad Ali's glove portrayed along other sports collections. And the manager quickly said, "Marcial, this is my partner."

"It's a great thing to meet you, sir."

"Say the whole truth," The Voice of Truth whispered.

"Please have a seat," said his partner.

"Well, I see you soon," said the other manager as he walked away from the office.

"Well, Marcial; why should I hire you?"

"I'll show up every day, sir. And I'll give you all I have."

"Sounds good to me!"

"Are you planning on staying here for a long time, or are you planning on leaving soon?"

"Say the whole truth and do not sell yourself."

"But I need the job, I only have $70 to my name, and I have to provide for my family?"

"Don't be afraid, My son."

"Sir, I live day by day, one day, I can be here giving you my all, and the next day my Lord may ask me to go to China. I cannot promise you that I'll be here for three years or three days. But one thing I can promise is that I'll be here as long as The Lord wills."

"Oh, I like you Marcial, but I cannot afford to hire you, then train you for almost a year, and then, suddenly, you leave."

"I comprehend, sir, perfectly."

"Well, thank you for your time."

"Sir, this moment is just another sign for me."

"A sign?"

"You see those signed boxing gloves you have decorated there?"

"Yes."

"The Almighty God brought me to this place just to experience what I had to experience today, and to speak to me through those gloves, and other things I've seen around today."

"Really?"

"Yes, sir."

"Well, I'm a believer myself."

"It's a good thing to know, sir."

"You have a good day."

"Likewise, sir," I said and walked out.

"So are you ready to start," said the other manager as I walked out.

"Not really, sir, but I do want to let you know that God used you to show me a good thing today."

"God shows you things?"

"To all people."

"How's that?"

"Some are watching, and some are not."

"Watching for what?"

"All things."

"All things?"

"Yes, all things."

"He shows you things? Some are watching, and some are not? So you're watching?"

"As He is watching me."

"He watches you too?"

"He watches us all. For the eyes of the LORD run to and fro throughout the whole earth, to show Himself strong on behalf of those whose heart is loyal to Him" (2 Chronicles 16:9).

"Wow!"

189

"It's a good thing to meet you, sir."

"Oh! My pleasure."

And I walked out feeling as if I was just hired. I shouted, "Oh Truth, You set me free! Oh God, You are my strength! O Lord, you saved me!" And I arrived at my rented apartment quickly after, and my wife said, "How did it go?"

"Fantastic!"

"Oh good, I knew you'll get hired."

"I didn't; something better than that happened."

"Really?"

"Yes. The Lord spoke to me and showed me a fight again—boxing."

"But what are we going to do for work?"

"Don't you worry, He will make our paths straight as long as we continue to submit to Him" (Proverbs 3:6).

"Ok. I love you."

"A man without a job?"

"I just changed my mind..." she said and smiled.

"I love you too."

## The Other Job Offer

"Guess what?"

"I'm listening."

"I have an interview with a huge insurance company."

"Really?"

"Thank God."

"Well, may His Will be done."

"God is with us."

## The Following Day

"Hey listen, Jonah is not feeling too well. Can you rush to the pharmacy and drop off this prescription for me, please; before you leave for your interview?"

"Sure; let me hurry up."

"Just bring it when you come back from the interview."

"Ok."

I rushed to the pharmacy because the interview was nearing, and I had to be there on time.

## At The Pharmacy

"Good morning!"

"Good morning! How may I help you, sir?"

"Just dropping off this prescription."

"Will you like to wait for it?"

"How long will it take?"

"About 20 minutes." And The Voice of Truth came unexpectedly and said, "What's more important, the job, or your son, Jonah?"

"Are you serious?"

"He needs the medicine."

"Can't he wait till I return from the interview?"

"What's more important, My son?"

"Jonah, my Lord—my son."

"Now do what you think is righteous in My eyes."

"I'll wait for it ma'am."

"Ok, no problem."

"Thank you."

Time was ticking, and I didn't want to miss this appointment. I thought about leaving and returning, but that would have taken about two hours. I desperately needed to find a job, and I felt that I could not afford to let this opportunity pass. When suddenly, He said "You won't make it in time, My son, but I will provide."

"Are you serious?"

"But seek first the kingdom of God and His righteousness, and all these things shall be added to you" (Matthew 6:33).

"What's that supposed to mean?"

"I AM first, and your family is second, by placing Me first, your family will never lack—as, on Earth, they are first."

"But how will I provide without a job?"

"Look at the birds of the air, for they neither sow or reap nor gather into barns; yet your heavenly Father feeds them. Are you not of more value than they?" (Matthew 6:26).

"Yes, Lord."

"Jonah's medicine is ready.  Now go back to the pharmacist, and return to your wife and bless your son."

"Now?"

"Do not fear, My son?"

## At Home Again

"Hey."

"Is that a ghost?"

"Look again."

"What happened at the interview?"

"What's more important, Jonah or the interview?"

"I know, but he could have waited."

"That's what I believed as well, but God had another plan."

"If you say so."

"Wait, wait, He's..."

"Because you have done this and obeyed my Voice, I will reward you."

"Really?"

"Go to *Craigslist.org*, and you will find a job in the sales section."

"This one?"

"No."

"This one."

"Call right now."

## At Florida Fine Cars

"When can you start?" said Farzin, the human resources director.

"I'm available now."

"How does tomorrow; 9 o'clock sounds?"

"I'll be here, sir."

"See you then."

"Thanks a lot, sir."

# Chapter 36
## *Moving In With The Kids*

N
ow Yosi (Bianka's cousin) was about to serve her time in jail, for something that 90% of real estate agencies were doing. And she said to Bianka, "I can't trust anyone else: can you and Marcial move in, and help me with Jack and Sven while I'm gone?"

"We'll be there, don't you worry."

"Listen the rent is not much, and my mom will also help with what she can."

"Don't you worry."

"Also, I will be getting some income tax money, please keep that to pay some bills, or for whatever."

"Don't worry, Yosi; God is with you: this is your wilderness time."

She looked at her sons, and crying she said, "I'm so sorry: I promise you both that I'll never leave you again."

"I Love you, mom," Jack and Sven said as they cried.

"I love you," said Isabel, her mother, soaked in tears.

"If you have to sell my car, sell it. And I'll be fine when I come out," said Yosi, crying.

Suddenly, the Voice of Truth interfered and said, "For this is not a favor, but your duty, treat those kids as you treat your sons."

"Yes, Lord."

And a group of family members drove away with her to the jail camp, four plus hours away—to drop her off. And a new beginning initiated for her, and for us all, in our new temporary residence. Soon after, Bianka's mother received her visa to travel abroad and she also moved in with us.

And by then, I started to work as a sales consultant at *Florida Fine Cars*, and I was making $7000 to $13000 a month by telling the whole truth to clients. The people there are fabulous, especially, my good friend, Tyrone. I also trained every-single-day just in case The Voice of Truth would surprise me again. And I was spending more time with my son, Brandon, and everything seemed to be working according to God's will. And suddenly, The Voice of Truth reappeared and said,

# Chapter 37
## The Radio Station:
## "Welcome to Knockout!"

"**R**emember the letter you sent to multiple radio stations about six months ago?"

"Yes, I remember, and no one called me."

"Go to *Goggle* and search for *Almavision Radio, 87.7FM*, and call: Tell them you want to start a show there."

"But how I'm I going to pay for it?"

"Are not you producing now?"

"Yes."

"They will have a spot available after 7pm every Friday, which will be your spot."

"What am I going to do?"

"You will share *My Good News*."

"Isn't this a Spanish radio station?"

"Yes."

"I know I'm bilingual, but I don't think I can share Your *Good News* in Spanish, yet."

"You can, but instead, you will share it speaking in English; call now!"

I called the station, gathered some information, and we arranged an appointment for the following day.

"I provide," said The True Voice. And immediately after, I received a call, and the caller ID read: Ardell Lund—a great friend from Bottineau, North Dakota.

"Hey Marcial, I was just thinking of you and decided to call you; is it a good time now?"

"Oh, yeah brother, I'm just here at work taking a break."

"Good, so tell me what's new?"

"Well, I have an appointment tomorrow at a radio station, and I will try to start a show there."

"Really?"

"I'm hoping so."

"How much will this cost you?"

"Well, it's close to $800 for the whole month."

"Please send me your address and I want to support you in this new thing you're doing."

"Oh, no brother, this is truly not necessary. You already helped me with the new tires and the oil change before I came back to Florida; this is not..."

"Marcial, I'd like to help."

"...please brother, you surely don't have to."

"I know, but I'd like to. Don't forget to send me your address to mail to you my help."

"Thanks a lot, brother; this means a lot to me," and we disconnected.

## The Following Day

The next day, I met with Carlos Navas, and I signed a contract to begin a show called, *Knockout*, which aired every Friday at 7:30pm. It covered from Jupiter, Florida to the Florida Keys, through 87.7fm; it covered Cuba, and certain parts of the Caribbean through 1500am. It was available to almost the whole world through *almavision.tv*.

Many people called and shared much of their personal struggles with me. I did my best to guide then to "The Way, The Truth, and The Life—Yeshua" (John 14:6). Many times, I prepared my notes prior to the show, but most of the times, He would surprise me and say, "Go, I'll tell you what to say." And soon, I noticed that the best shows were always the shows I never planned—the shows He prepared in Heaven. Once, a lady called and said,

"Listen, I was stranded, walking on the streets, and afraid. And then, someone gave me a ride back to my car to attempt to jump the battery. And when the guy helped me, you were there speaking through a radio station I never listen to..."

"Really?"

"...I don't know, but I never felt like this before."

Soon, I realized that God truly knew about this—about what He said to me, previously. And during another show, I spoke about the: FEMA CONCENTRATION CAMPS; THE THOUSANDS OF NEWLY PURCHASED GUILLOTINES BY THE U.S GOVERNMENT; ALL THE EXECUTIVE ORDERS SIGNED BY OBAMA, AND OTHER PREVIOUS PRESIDENTS AGAINST OUR U.S CONSTITUTION; THE THOUSANDS OF TROOPS, FROM OTHER COUNTRIES, ALREADY TRAINING IN AMERICAN SOIL; THE LUCIFER'S TELESCOPE PROJECT FROM THE VATICAN; MARSHALL LAW, AND THE MILITARIZED POLICE; THE CURRENT WORSHIP OF LUCIFER AT THE VATICAN, AND INFILTRATION TO THE CATHOLIC CHURCH AND 'THE CHURCH OF TODAY;' THE NEW JESUIT AND FINAL POPE OF THIS AGE; THE 'INCOME TAX' FRAUD; 'THE MICROCHIP' IN THE OBAMACARE; THE SOON-TO-COME WORLD-WIDE DECEPTION DIRECTED BY THE ROMAN EMPIRE, THE U.S, AND THE WORLD'S ELITE—THE JESUITS AND THEIR BRANCHES; A SOON TO COME WORLD-WIDE FINANCIAL COLLAPSE THAT WILL AFFECT ALL MANKIND; A SOON TO COME PERSECUTION OF BIBLE DOERS IN AMERICA, AND WORLD WIDE; CERN (THE EUROPEAN ORGANIZATION FOR NUCLEAR RESEARCH—THE NEW TOWER OF BABEL, GEN. 11); THE NEW WORLD ORDER WITH THE ONE WORLD RELIGION AND ONE WORLD CURRENCY...

And specifically, I explained to the people about the real reason for the establishment of these multiple FEMA CONCENTRATION CAMPS throughout American soil. And Lazaro, my great friend who always helped me with the show's programing, said, "Is this really happening?"

"Yes, brother?"

"Here in America; in the U.S?"

"Yes. Not only that I can now see it with my own eyes, but I know because God has been showing to me some stuff, and the dots are beginning to connect."

"Really?"

"I can't quite put the puzzle together yet, but for years, I've been having visions, and I've been having dreams. I write them down to later interpret them. I've been on this roller coaster with God, that, to be honest, I still do not fully comprehend.

"Is this Biblical?"

"Yes, Lazaro. So far, I've been matching case by case, and it looks like all cases could be encapsulated in an aftermarket capsule, and the capsule it's about to burst soon."

"What are we going to do?"

"Listen, brother, you do what you can, and I'll do what I can."

"How?"

"Remember the Constitution?"

"Yeah, but what about it?"

"Remember the first three words?"

"Not really?"

"WE THE PEOPLE."

"Ok."

"Those that consider themselves righteous must unite unlike never before in world history."

"How?"

"In love, but with courage; to fight the good fight of righteousness, and to bring back YHWH (God) to this country and the world before it's too late."

"But how can we stop all this?"

"I don't know yet, but in following The Spirit of Truth—I guess He'll tell us when the time comes."

"Oh, God."

"We can't be afraid, brother."

"Thank you so much, brother—Hallelujah!"

"God is with us, brother."

"Hallelujah!" we shouted mutually, inspired by The Voice of Truth.

## Three Months Later
## At the Radio Station with Lazaro

"Hey, Marcial!" Lazaro said.

"Hey, brother."

"Listen to me carefully."

"What's going on?"

"Hey, you know the guy that makes us the business cards, and works with our magazine; the one that sits back there who is in charge of the media and public relations?"

"Oh yeah, I met him when I signed the contract for the show."

"Pay close attention."

"I am, brother."

"He recently told me that FEMA, just had a secretly held meeting with most well-known pastors here in Florida."

"Seriously?"

"Seriously."

"How did he hear about it?"

"Remember, he is in charge of our magazine, and deals with the media, and all that stuff. And you know that all those 'big time pastors' come here all the time to record, and he deals with them constantly."

"Did he tell you anything about it?"

"Well, he said not to worry, that it was all about helping the people. But listen, he's back there now; why don't you ask him yourself?"

"Good idea brother."

## The Media Man

"Hey, how are you, brother?"

"I'm blessed brother!"

"Good to hear that brother. Hey listen, would you mind sharing with me what you've heard about this secretly held meeting that just took place with FEMA, and most well-known pastors here in Miami?"

"Oh, FEMA is just trying to help us 'the believers'; aren't we blessed brother?"

"Of course, all faithful servants are. But can you tell me a little bit more about it."

"Yeah, all the 'big time pastors' were there, and FEMA just stressed that, 'If something like a food shortage, or a natural disaster, or a potential war, or a potential financial collapse were to occur—to not worry. And to just lead their flock to the FEMA CAMPS where we will all be provided—with all of our needs.'"

"Oh, I see."

"Isn't this wonderful that a secret meeting has taken place, here in Miami, recently, just to put the Christians first?"

"Thanks a lot, brother; I won't take much more of your time."

"Thank you, Marcial."

The Voice of Truth quickly surrounds me and says:

"Why didn't they televise this meeting if it is to help Christians, truly? Why has FEMA not used all media to inform all people? Why just a meeting with the 'big time pastors?'"

"Is this a setup?" I asked Him.

"My son, remember the Holocaust?"

"Yes, Lord."

"Many were warned and not too many warned before reality arrived. My true servants sounded the trumpets constantly till it was too late to react. But the grand majority had a Normalcy Bias."

"What's a Normalcy Bias?"

"It's nothing more than believing that just because everything seems normal today—because we eat, drink, and sleep; and have peace, love, and security—it will be perfectly normal tomorrow."

"So they had this?"

"Not only that they had this; it was worse."

"Really?"

"Yes, they did not believe all my faithful servants whom I raised to deliver them from the sword."

"But why did You not stop all this?"

"My son, it will take too much time to explain this now, but know this: 'I have given men the will to choose good or evil, and at My appointed time, I judge in righteousness."

"How's that?"

"For I am perfect, and wickedness shall not hover over the surface forever."

"And the FEMA CAMPS?"

"THEY ARE SIMPLY MODERN DAY CONCENTRATION CAMPS."

"How will they get the people there?"

"It can all be found in one scripture in My Holy Word."

"Really?"

"Study; seek Me and prove all things for yourself, and you shall find the Word."

"But can't You just tell me now?"

"Follow Me, and you'll see."

# Chapter 38

# *Two Men In Black*

I was following up with my clients from my desk by calling and emailing, and doing everything I could to ensure client satisfaction. Suddenly, I saw two men—dressed in all black from head to toe—walking into the dealership. And from far away, I realized that one of them was the same black guy I met at *The University of Miami* last year while I trained at the wellness center— my first UM friend. He was next to a tall white guy as they walked in together.

"Hey, brother how are you?"

"Oh, I noticed that you guys have lots of good deals here, and we're just looking for something cheap."

"You don't remember me?"

"You?"

"I know I lost about 40lbs of muscle, but it has only been about a year; you really can't remember?"

"Uh..."

"From UM; the first or second day of school at the wellness center."

"Oh man! I didn't even recognize you: You work here?"

"Yes, brother."

"I haven't seen you around on campus?"

"God had other plans for me, and I had to withdraw."

"I'm sorry to hear that, man."

"Don't be, brother, His ways are not men's ways. But let me show you what I have, brother; I'm glad you're here! Please follow me. Is that ok with you, both?"

"Sure."

"We follow. You lead us."

"Fantastic! This way please."

Suddenly, while speaking with my only formally introduced UM friend, The Voice of Truth approaches me and whispers as He secretly joins our conversation, "I sent them both to reveal to you what's coming next."

"Oh, Lord what's next?

"Don't be afraid."

"Can I just have a normal life already?"

"You must finish the race, and fight the good fight of faith, My son, for you are capable, and I AM with you" (1 Timothy 6:12).

"Yes, Lord."

"Listen carefully to everything they say; for they will not buy a car, but they will hand you over a key."

"Really?"

"Listen carefully."

## Speaking with the Two Men in Black

"What do think of this one?"

"Oh, I'm not so sure."

"That's ok, brother."

"Hey, this is a little off-topic, but have you thought about going back to UM?"

"Well, I sent my application again earlier this year just in case God sends me back for some reason."

"Good! I hope it works out for you, and that, maybe I can see you on campus again."

"If The Lord sends me back; I'll see you there."

"God willing," my friend said as they were both driving out.

"God willing brother; God, is with you both," I shouted.

I tried to make sense of this encounter and rapidly came The True Voice, and said, "How far is UM from here?

"About a 40-minute drive now."

"How many salesmen are in this dealership?"

"About thirty-five."

"How many dealerships exist from here to UM?"

"Hundreds, thousands, countless... I assume?"

"They, the two men in black, were the key; I brought them to you. Now, remain still and in seven seconds look to your right, and listen carefully."

And after seven seconds exactly, by my count, suddenly, "Hey Marcial!"

"Hey Disney, how are you?"

"Hey listen; didn't you play football, and boxed for a while?"

"Something like that, brother."

"Were you at UM and then left it or something?"

"Something like that, brother."

"I don't know, but I think you should go back."

"Really?"

"Hey, have you had your lunch already?"

"I brought my own, you know, my wife always fixes something for me."

"Just eat that later; I think this is important: how about some *Subway*?"

"Are you sure?"

"It's on me; I got you, brother."

"Ok. Good."


## At Subway Subs

I'm having lunch with Disney, and suddenly, The Voice of Truth came and voiced, "A third sign is coming your way; be ready!" and quickly, "Hey Marcial, long time no see, brother."

"Hey Disney, this is Daniel; I call him 'the street disciple.'"

"Hey Daniel, it's my pleasure."

"Are you still holding the sign with the Ten Commandments on Countyline Road?" I asked Daniel.

"Sometimes brother; how are you doing?"

"Well Disney and I are here talking about the possibilities of maybe going back to school: what do you think?"

"Man, I just went back to school! Just go back, brother! I'm telling you; just go back."

"This is your third sign," said The True Voice.

"Hey, brothers; I guess this is 'a day of signs' for me."

"Just do it," they both said.

## Preparing The FFC Business Plan
## & Leaving for the First Time

For a whole week, I had been allocating an hour of the day and creating a business plan to increase the dealership's sales. I figured, "As a sales consultant I can only help myself and the company partially, but as a leader, I may help the entire sales staff and the company." For this reason, I knocked at the general manager's office, and said, "Hey Chase! Do you have a minute for me?"

"For you? Come on in, Marcial."

"I prepared this plan for the company, and I believe that if we do this we'll all win."

"Great, I'm glad you've taken your time to produce something like this: I tell you what; leave me a copy and I'll let you know what I think."

"That's your copy, sir."

"It's a pleasure doing business with you, Marcial."

"Thank you, sir," I said and I walked out of his office.

## The Voice of Truth

"You will leave this Company soon, but you will train in this territory for your soon-to-come fight."

"Is it You again?"

"In three days—beginning from today—you will go back to Chase and you will speak these words: 'Hey Chase, I know that this may be too much to ask, but I was wondering if I can borrow that huge four-story building next door, just to train?'"

"What's this all about?"

"I need to train you for the fight of your life?"

"You need to train me?"

"Yes, My son."

"Why in an empty four-story warehouse?"

"You will bring your tractor tire, your pushing sled with all your weights, your sledgehammer, your resistant bands, your punching bag, your weighted vest, your boxing gloves... and everything else, I will remind you when that hour comes."

"But Chase hasn't even allowed me to train there yet?"

"I have opened their hearts for this petition, My son."

"Really?"

"Why just me in an empty warehouse?"

"You won't be alone."

"And why do I have to leave from this job, but I must stay here to train?"

"Don't be afraid."

"I thought this job was Your gift?"

"It was, and the hour will come when you will have to move to your following territory, and find another gift."

"But isn't the warehouse here?"

"My son, follow Me, and you will see."

## Three Days Later

"Hey, Chase do you have a minute?"

"Just a minute?"

"A Cuban minute."

"Come on in, Marcial."

"Hey Chase, I know that this may be too much to ask, but I was wondering if I can borrow that huge four-story building next door, just to train?"

"To train?"

"Yes, just to train; I won't bother anyone, no one will know I'm there, and I will just come early in the morning to train."

"To train?"

"Yes, to train."

"In an empty warehouse?"

"Yes, sir."

"I tell you what; it's a good thing to have you around here, Marcial. Allow me speak with the owners, and I'm sure it won't be a problem, but let me just double check with them. Is that ok?"

"Sounds perfect to me, sir."

"Good enough."

"Thanks a lot, this is worth more than a million dollars to me, sir."

"I'll be waiting for my check," joking he said.

"It's in the business plan."

"I can't believe I almost forgot to tell you," he said, "I shared your business plan with the owners, and they like it a lot actually. Please take it to Farzin, and to Jamie. And we're trying to see where to place you in the company."

"Thanks much, sir."

"My pleasure," and I walked away.

## Leaving from Florida Fine Cars: The First Time.
### *The Following Week*

"Your time is coming."

"For what?"

"Another test."

"Can I just stay in one job, do good, help others, provide for my family, and still follow You?"

"Yes."

"Good! We finally agree."

"But it won't be My perfect will for you, son."

"Oh Lord, please, allow me to stay here and just provide for my family...please?"

"You may, My son."

"Are You sure?"

"Yes."

"Thank you, my Lord."

"Look up."

"Yes."

"What do you see?"

"Not much?"

"Think."

"The sky and the clouds?"

"Can you see anything else?"

"Not really."

"Does this mean you've reached your limit?"

"Oh, Lord please just tell me already."

"*Florida Fine Cars* is a simple tool to lead you to your next key—the following sign."

"But I'm happy here."

"By conforming yourself, you're neglecting your gifts; by pressing on the brakes, you're ceasing to accelerate; without acceleration, you'll never reach your final destination."

"Yes, Lord."

"Be ready!"

### Three Days Later

"Hey, Farzin; do you have a minute?"

"Sure, come on in."

"I'm sorry, but I'm giving you my two weeks' notice, today."

"I don't understand."

"I'm sorry."

"Why?"

"This is what God prefers for me."

"God wants you to leave your job?"

"In this moment and time: yes sir."

"But I have your new pay plan for your new management position?"

"Please forgive me, sir; I must do this."

"Well, I'm glad we met, you know that the doors will always remain open here for you, Marcial."

"Thanks a lot, sir."

"Have you talked to Chase about this, and the other managers?"

"I decided to come to you first since you were the one that gave me an opportunity when you hired me, but now, they will know as well."

"The doors are wide open for you, Marcial."

"Thank you, sir."

# Chapter 39
## God's Training
## And Revelations

I managed to arrange everything on the third floor of the warehouse—as The Lord commanded—on my final day at *Florida Fine Cars*. Quickly, The Voice of Truth approached me and said:

"First: From Monday through Friday, you will ride your bike to the warehouse, train as I command you, finish the training before the dealership opens and return at My ordered time.

"Second: On Sundays, visit *Point of Grace Church* in West Park, with your family, and take Brandon every time you have him with you.

"Third: At night, you will run over the bridge by the strip club, and I will be with you always...."

"But how do I pay bills?"

"...Fourth: Don't be afraid."

### Day 1: In the Morning

It was 4:21 am, and The Voice of Truth said, "Wake up! For you are late." And I rushed, got on my knees quickly, grabbed two bananas, and out the door I went. I was pedaling my bike over the bridge, and suddenly, I sensed Him coming, and He declared:

"You're training for My fight."

"What fight?"

"Look to your left," He said as I was pedaling down the bridge.

"I'm looking."

"Do you see the amount of cars at the strip club's parking lot?"

"Yes, Lord."

"These are My little children."

"Really?"

"But they are a result of multiple generations that departed from My ways. Focus as you pedal, for you must protect your body as it is your temple" (1 Corinthians 6:19).

"Yes, Lord, but which ways are You referring to?"

"My son, they are all in My Holy Word—the Holy Bible."

"But almost no one wants to read nowadays; most just desire to party, and have a good time, and have much sex with different partners, and just... I don't know."

"My son, it is not their fault entirely."

"How's that?"

"For the most part, their fathers, their grandparents, and multiple generations prior to their existence departed from My Word."

"But can't they just choose to follow You? Can't You just call them as You called me? Can't they just live righteously according to Your will?"

"You were once there."

"And what does that mean?"

"You listened to Me at your appointed time, and you answered the call, finally."

"I don't comprehend?"

"I'm this final call; I'm pouring out My power, My Holy Spirit, unto My servants."

"But what do we do?"

"It is no longer an obligation of just sharing salvation for those who are lost, only. Instead, it is the true church's duty to share a soon-to-come judgment for all nations, especially, for America—the United States of America."

"Why?"

"Follow Me, and you will see."

"But how can I help, now?"

"Remember the number 16?"

"From the revelation? From the lawyer?"

"Keep it in your long-term memory."

"But people won't believe me; they're too busy enjoying their lives?"

"You will blow the trumpets, sound the alarm, ring the bell—and those that have ears to hear will hear the warning and truly repent."

"But I'm just a man without political power, without influences, without money; I just don't have what it takes?"

"All you need is within you."

"How is that possible?"

"For My Spirit of Truth is in you."

"Since the beginning of times people have been talking about You, and for some reason, most prefer to live without You. Why is this?"

"My son, deeply in their hearts, they all long to be with Me, but deception has frozen their hearts."

"How can I do my part?"

"Remember, focus on My soon-to-come judgment, and this will guide you."

"Can we prevent this?"

"You just arrived at the warehouse."

"Can we prevent this?"

"Do 30 rounds of 3 minutes at 90% intensity."

"Of what?"

"Alternate each round with exercises of your choice, and hit the bag for the final 16 rounds."

"But can we prevent all this? The Judgment?"

"Follow Me, and you will see."

"Yes, Lord."

## Day 1: The Afternoon with the Health Issue

"Hey," I said to my wife, "I'm sorry that I can't satisfy you, or provide for your conjugal needs as God mandates me."

"Listen, I understand."

"I know, but it has been over a year, and I have not been able to provide for your needs."

"Don't worry; God is with us."

"I don't understand, God mandates me to satisfy you, but my penis can't stay hard for long enough anymore—I'm only 29 you know."

"Listen, I don't care anymore, I'm used to it already."

"Please, don't deceive yourself; haven't you realized that perhaps this may be the main reason for our countless arguments each day?"

"This is not the reason."

"Bianka, we've been arguing for over a year now, consistently, and our peace has faded away."

"Is that we've been on this roller coaster, and you say that God tells you to do this and that...but doesn't God want you to have a normal life?"

"Don't you think I desire one?"

"You always put God first, even before us, so I don't know."

"We've talked about this, hundreds of times..."

"Yeah, but we're always last."

"...if we put Him first, then all things will fall into place, including the well-being of our marriage."

"I'm just tired of living like this."

"How?"

"Bouncing from place to place."

"Look up."

"I'm looking... Marcial."

"Is that a roof over your head?"

"Yes, but you know what I mean."

"Listen, I receive God's love every day and share it with you, but we must continue to follow Him—the One, Who knows all things."

"So, I'm not following Him?"

"Just follow Me as I follow Him."

"You always say the same thing. But don't you see me here next to you always?"

"Yes, but we can be using this time to encourage each other, to equip each other, to embrace each other, instead of allowing the father of deception into our lives."

"I'm just tired of all this. One day, you're training to be a world champion; the next day, you're at a job; the following day, you're not there; the next one, God is talking to you... I don't know, I don't know what to do anymore?"

"I'm so sorry I can't satisfy you due to this low testosterone thing, and who knows, maybe a combination of these revelations and this low T thing."

"You know I'm used to it already."

"That's what The Voice of Lies wants you to believe so that you give up and no longer search for a cure."

"Why don't you take testosterone then?"

"You know that's only going to shut down what I have left, and eventually destroy me."

"You don't know that; you're not a doctor."

"Bianka, don't you think I researched this, experienced this, and done this for long enough to know the ultimate result. Plus, I've been asking God to heal me with His methods—His ways."

"I know, but you've tried everything."

"And with faith in Him we must continue to work."

"Don't worry about me; I just want you to find healing."

"So you don't care whether we become intimate again or not?"

"I mean, I do, but it is not a priority anymore; I'm used to it already."

"I recommend that you follow me, or otherwise, you will stay so behind, that one day, it will become almost impossible for me to return to you or for you to reach me."

"You want me to follow you; that's all you always say."

"That's all you need to do, you see, as you follow me I follow The Voice of Truth, and as I learn from Him you learn from me and Him. If, for any reason, I fail to follow Him, you will recognize it immediately, and then, you must continue His path and carry me through my pain."

"I'm just tired of all this."

"I love you."

"But you don't show it."

"Could it be that you can't see it due to our current distance?"

"I've always been here next to you, but I don't feel this love that we once had."

"If you're waiting for a feeling, you'll never choose to love, but the day you choose to love you'll discover all your feelings."

"Look, I just want our marriage to work."

"Follow me and you'll see."

## Day 1: The Evening

It was 8:03pm and The Voice of Truth showed up and said:

"Hurry! Get ready! For you must go for a jog."

"Yes, Lord."

I was running over the bridge on Miami Gardens Drive, and I knew not where to go. Suddenly, I realized that He was right next to me. He said, "Turn right on 2nd Avenue and run until I tell you to stop."

"And when do I stop?"

"Just run, My son."

"1 mile, 2 miles, and I just passed the dealership; 3 miles, and He's nowhere to be found; 4 miles, 5 miles... when do I stop?"

"Be ready!"

"Do I go to the *Hard Rock Casino*? To the boxing gym by there? Is it not too late for that?"

Suddenly, I felt a sharp pain in my right knee, and it caused me to slow down, and I quickly said, "I thought I was completely healed?"

"You are healed, My son."

"Why this pain suddenly?"

"Look up!"

"I don't see anything."

"The traffic light!"

"The traffic light?"

"Read."

"Hollywood Boulevard."

"Yes. Stop. Now focus!"

"I'm trying; can I catch a breath first?"

"Focus, there's not much time for that in a real fight."

"Yes, Lord."

"Evil men have brainwashed Mankind through the media, and especially through Hollywood."

"How?"

"The lamp of the body is the eye. If therefore your eye is good, your whole body will be full of light. But if your eye is bad, your whole body will be full of darkness. If therefore the light that is in you is darkness, how great is that darkness!" (Matthew 6:22-23).

"But most people like violent movies, and the shows filled with drama, and the media, and mostly everything that has nothing to do with You. Why is this?"

"My son, the answer is infinite, but know this: My Judgment is coming!"

"Can't You just speak from heaven so that all people hear You, and truly repent from their wicked ways?"

"I am the Alpha and the Omega, the Beginning and the End, the First and the Last" (Revelation 22:13).

"Is that a yes?"

"I declared everything in the beginning and all was done according to My will."

"Then how do people believe in You in the midst of their deception-filled lives?"

"How did you believe?"

"I don't know; I guess I just knew?"

"All people know."

"But that's impossible."

"My Grace is sufficient."

"Yeah, but; don't they have to know your rules and regulations to follow You according to Your will?"

"You mean My Law of liberty? The Law that sets Mankind free?"

"I guess?"

"My Commandments are in the Bible, and My Word also—which I inspired men like you and many others to write according to My will."

"The Ten Commandments?"

"That's part of it?"

"But isn't every 'big time pastor' saying that we no longer need them—that 'we're saved by grace.' And that, Jesus the Christ paid for all our sins at the cross?"

"My son, this will take some time to explain now, but follow Me, and you will see."

"And what about Hollywood? How can I help people understand that darkness is entering through their eyes?"

"I will take you there."

"Me?"

"Don't be afraid."

"Why? How?"

"It is late, call your wife and tell her to pick you up."

"Yes, Lord."

## Day 2: In the Afternoon (John 3:16)

"I'm ready now."

"You will push your pickup truck until you arrive at the park."

"Yes, Lord."

"No, disruptions."

"No, breaks?"

"Perfect."

"And who will steer it?"

"I gave you a helper."

"Yes, Lord.

"Bianka, can you help me with this workout today?"

"Sure, don't I always?"

"Wait, wait; not yet," said The True Voice as I intended to start, "look into your license plate."

"Yes, Lord."

"Never take your eyes off it."

"But how can I focus?"

"How can you not focus?"

"Yes, Lord."

I was pushing the truck and I was seeing was JOHN 3:16. And The Voice of Truth returned and said, "Remember, I have chosen you."

"Can I take a break?"

"You don't have time for breaks in a fight, My son—for the Enemy hits you endlessly while you rest."

"My legs are giving up, please?"

"All you need remains in your sight, remember? The lamp of the body is the eye."

"Do I stop?" shouted my lovely wife.

"No, not yet," I screamed somehow.

"Can we stop, Lord?"

"For you have need of endurance, so that after you have done the will of God, you may receive the promise" (Hebrews 10:36).

"Can I just take a break?"

"The promises."

"The promises? What about them?"

"Remember the number 16."

"It never leaves my presence for some reason."

"Focus, you're almost there."

"At the park?"

"Receiving your next key."

"Another one?"

"Each key opens a new door revealing your next step to My perfect will."

"Your perfect will?"

"Yes, and My Message to Mankind through you."

"Can't You just use more people?"

"I am, but you must sound the trumpet louder than ever."

"Why louder?"

"16."

"What about it?"

"2016!"

"2016?"

"A very important Key."

"Is all this Biblical?"

"Follow Me, and you will see."

"A dead end! I'm not crashing into a school," shouted Bianka.

"Can I, now?"

"Listen to your wife."

## Chapter 40

# *Before Returning To The University of Miami*

I was at *Dr. Michael Krop Senior High School* picking up Yosi's son, Jack, because he had a fever. Suddenly, a man walked into the office, and the young student, helping at the counter, said, "May I have your name, sir?"

"Sure, I'm Wilfredo Duran." And quickly, I thought, "Manos de Piedra Duran, the well-known boxer." And I approached him and asked, "Are you related to the boxer?"

"Oh, yes, he's my cousin."

"Do you train?"

"I'm training some amateur girls, and I'm preparing a tournament for them."

"Good!"

"Hey, take my number, you never know."

"You're right, you never know."

"Hey Marcial," says Jack as he walked in, "thanks for coming."

"You don't look too good."

"I know."

"Let's go home."

### Driving Toward the House
### With The Voice of Truth

"Are you going to take me back to boxing?"

"The fight has not ended, My son."

"Is that a yes?"

"You must fight the good fight."

"Which is?"

"Remember what Coach Jose said about UM?"

"About their boxing team?"

"Yes, My son."

"Ok?"

"You will receive the scholarship once again, but this time, you will stay longer."

"Ok?"

"But how can I support myself and my family?"

"Just continue to buy, and resell cars locally."

"But that's not steady?"

"I will provide."

"Are you asking me to remain as a full-time student; train twice-a-day; continue with the radio station program; father my kids and be a husband—well, at least partially—and be great in all areas?"

"Yes, I'm suggesting you to fulfill My will for you."

"But I'm broke, I need to support my family?"

"Yet not completely broken."

"Are You going to break me more?"

"The sacrifices of God are a broken spirit, A broken and a contrite heart—These, I will not despise" (Psalm 51:17).

"Are You going to hurt me?"

"In brokenness, you will find the next key."

"Why boxing again for the fourth time? Why *The University of Miami*, again? Why not a job, or establishing an organization? Why not help many through another method?"

"For My thoughts are not your thoughts,

Nor are your ways My ways," says the Lord.

"For as the heavens are higher than the earth,

So are My ways higher than your ways,

And My thoughts than your thoughts" (Isaiah 55:8-9).

"Yes, Lord."

"Don't be afraid. For I am preparing you for the real fight."

"And how about 2016?"

"Follow Me and you'll see."

"Is something big happening in 2016?"

"Big is small."

"I thought big was big?"

"Follow Me and you will see."

## Point of Grace Church Events
## & Selling Cars

It was Sunday, and I was sitting at *Point of Grace Church* with my family, listening to the sermon, and simultaneously asking The Voice of Truth for guidance: "How am I going to pay for tuition?"

"Will you trust Me?"

"But I need $10,000 by tomorrow?"

"Don't be afraid, and just go."

"Where?"

"You know."

"To UM?"

"Don't be afraid."

"But I don't want to waste people's time?"

"I will provide."

"But it's too late already; I don't have the books, I haven't picked my classes, and I can't just show up unprepared?"

"Why not?"

"I don't know; You tell me."

"Sell the two cars you own and ride the train."

"But that takes time."

"Sell them to *CarMax*."

"And how will I get around, and get to school?"

"Take the bus and the train."

"Is this what you really want from me?"

"It's just a step toward the next key."

"A step, selling all I have left?"

"What's more valuable to you: those two cars and a job, or receiving a revelation from My Kingdom?"

"A revelation?"

"Follow Me and you will see."

"Why can't You just tell me now?"

"For you are not prepared to receive this wisdom, My son."

"But why all these crazy decisions?"

"I've chosen you."

"Please give me a sign; I need to know for sure."

"Be ready!"

"For what?"

And suddenly, I felt someone touching me on my shoulder from behind, and I turned around and said, "Hey, Tony! You caught me by surprise."

"Hey brother, I don't know, but I feel a heaviness in my heart that wants me to tell you something."

"What is it, brother?"

"I feel that God is telling me to tell you just to go, and to not be afraid," he said, "and that He has something huge for your life."

"Really?"

"I felt it strongly, brother."

"Is this the sign?" I asked The Voice of Truth.

"Listen to him."

"Brother, I feel you should just go wherever God is telling you to go."

By then, I was trembling on the inside, and all people were beginning to exit from the church's edifice. I said to my wife and the kids, "Please wait for me in the car, something significant is happening right now."

"Hey, Marcial! How are you?" said Pastor John Perdue

"Hey brother, I'm just here with Tony trying to make sense of all this."

"And what's that?"

"For some reason, I keep hearing The Voice of Truth telling me to go back to *The University of Miami*, but I'm not 100% sure, yet."

"Pastor," said Tony, "I don't know, but I felt this strong heaviness in my heart right when you finished the sermon. And I just couldn't hold it—I had to tell brother Marcial."

"Let us pray," he said and we formed a men's triangle as we held our hands.

He was praying, and I began to feel an uncontrollable shaking in my body. I was crying, and The Voice of Truth revealed Himself through this manifestation and said:

"Go, just go."

"IN JESUS' NAME. AMEN," said brother John."

"AMEN," Tony and I repeated.

Then Tony prayed, and then I prayed, and by the time we were finished, I knew it was time to go find the next key in God's chosen territory—*The University of Miami.*

Chapter 41

# *Back to UM*

## The First Day: Again

I was sitting inside of my first class—the Sociology of Sports, taught by Dr. Jomills H. Braddock II—with two car titles in my backpack, and The Voice of Truth whispered: "Remember boxing and football?"

"Yes, Lord."

"You are at *The University of Miami*—in a sport's class."

"Ok?"

"Learn—it will help you understand better a soon-to-come decision."

"Another decision?"

"And many more to come."

"And how am I going to pay for classes, I'm still $10,000 short, and everyone is telling me that there are no more funds?"

"After the third day, after class, I will direct you to an office."

"But I've been in all offices?"

"I will choose the people this time."

## The Third Day After Classes

"Number seven!" said the lady as my turn came up.

"I'm here!"

"Please follow me."

"I'm right behind you," I said.

"How may I help you?" she said as we both sat down.

"Well, I'm just about $10,000 short from the tuition."

"Have you tried a personal loan?"

"I can't borrow a cent anymore; unfortunately, my credit score was divided by two."

"Can a family member help you?"

"I have to help my family."

"All options have been exhausted already, and there's nothing else we can do."

"What I don't comprehend is how last year, I was given these funds, but this year, they don't exist?"

"Sir that was last year."

"I comprehend, but can't you make it happen this year?"

"Sorry, there's nothing we can do," she said. But The Voice of Truth came silently and said, "Look at the brochure."

"Which one?"

"That one that says: 'Need help? Can't pay for tuition? We can help!' Take it, thank the lady for her help and visit that office."

"Yes, Lord."

"Thanks for your help. May I take this brochure?"

"Sure."

## At The Other Office

I was knocking, and no one answered. I knocked harder and harder, but still, no one opened the door. I walked away, and as I was almost nearby the admissions office The True Voice said, "Go back!"

"But I was just there, and no one opened?"

"Go back, and knock again."

"Yes Lord."

I knocked once, and immediately, a nice lady answered and said, "Hello! Welcome! Please come on in."

"I was just knocking very hard a few minutes ago."

"Oh, it's just that it's very hard to hear the knocks from back there."

"Oh, ok."

"How may I help you?"

"Well, this is the situation..."

"I understand. Although it seems like you have received all your funds, allow me to speak with some people in the admissions department. And, I'll inform by tomorrow if I'm able to get, maybe

$500 or $1000 additionally.  I will try my best to help you.  How does that sounds?"

"Wonderful!"

"It's my pleasure to help you, Marcial."

"Thank you so much," and I walked away.

## Speaking with The Voice of Truth again

"Now what am I going to do?"

"Ask your wife to help you drive both cars to *CarMax*, today, and just sell them."

"Both?"

"Go, My son."

"Yes, Lord."

## The Trip to CarMax

"Can you follow me to *CarMax*, today, please?"

"But we can't afford a new car."

"We have to sell ours instead."

"But how are we going to get around?"

"The Lord will provide."

"OK, if you say so."

"Thank you; I love you."

"I love you too."

## At CarMax with the Sales Representative

"I have wonderful results for you, Mr. Ferreira."

"Great!"

"For your 2002 *Ford Explorer*, we can give you a check today! For the excellent amount of $1,500!  What do you think?"

"It's worth around $2,500 wholesale, $3,000 private, and $4,000 to $5,000 if you retail it."

"Oh no, because..."

"Ok, no problem.  And how about the *Land Rover*?"

"For that one we can offer $3000, today!"

"This isn't fair. What do I do, Lord?" I ask The True Voice.

"Sell the *Land Rover*."

"We'll give away the *Land Rover*," I said to the sales rep.

"OK, no problem; I'll be back with the paperwork. May I have the title, please?"

"Here you go."

"Thanks."

## She Returns in 15 minutes

"Mr. Ferreira, unfortunately, we won't be able to purchase this car in this very moment."

"Why?"

"Because the title is less than 30 days old."

"What do I do now?" I asked The True Voice.

"Just go home and I'll tell you."

"I understand ma'am; thanks for your help anyhow."

## Driving Home with The Voice of Truth

"Can you explain this, please?"

"You must be tested in all areas."

"I don't understand?"

"I have to test your heart."

"I'm still lost."

"I had to see if you were willing to sell all for Me."

"But you know what I will or will not do. Why am I even tested?

"Tests make you strong through Me, My son."

"So, do I sell the cars? Do I sell one car? Do I not sell them at all?"

"Put a for-sale sign on the *Land Rover*, and list it for $4,500."

"And how about the *Explorer*?"

"It is my gift to you and your family."

"But we owned it all along?"

"For you brought nothing into this world, and you can carry nothing out of it" (1 Timothy 6:7).

227

"Yes, Lord."

"Look at the American flag," He said as I drove by the tiny park by the house.

"I'm looking."

"This is a vital key, My son."

"Yes, Lord," and Bianka and I arrived.

The next day someone called me as I was driving to the auto parts shop to purchase coolant. And that night, I sold the *Land Rover* for $4,500. I was still short by $5,500, but The Voice of Truth came to comfort me, and said, "Do not fear My little sheep." But I was still concerned because the balance was due in two days, or else, I would have had to withdraw once again.

## The Next Day at Home:
## Reading my UM's Sent Emails

"I don't know how this was possible, but somehow, they gave you an additional $8000 scholarship..." And suddenly, I was crying, confused by all the continuous events, and filled with the Spirit of Truth. I shouted within me, "O thank You, Father!

"Thank You for all things and this miracle." But suddenly, I sensed a confusion and asked, "Why me? Why can't it just be all in order; everyone tells me you're a God of order?"

"Most are too busy dictating other's lives, 'Let them alone. They are blind leaders of the blind. And if the blind leads the blind, both will fall into a ditch'" (Matthew 15:14).

"Yes, Lord."

## The Next Day

"Pay all the house bills, and the balance of your tuition."

"But what about the books; I won't have sufficient funds?"

"Follow me, and I will provide."

"Shouldn't I pay for tuition, and then pay some bills slowly?"

"Will you trust Me?"

228

"Yes, Lord."

## The Next Day on my Way to UM

"Follow that minivan," The True Voice said.

"I'm going to pass the university."

"Follow the minivan."

"Yes, Lord.

"I'm almost by my PO box."

"Stop at the PO box, and search for all the letters."

And as I was opening every letter—mostly all from student loans, and debt collectors— suddenly,  I noticed a letter from Ardell.  I quickly opened it, and it read:

*Hello, Marcial & Family! I'm praying that all is good with your family. Thank you for your love and prayers,*
*Sincerely,*
*Ardell & Joan Lund.*

And the letter came with a $1000 check.

I was packed with emotions, I couldn't comprehend, and I didn't know what to do.  And suddenly, He came again and said, "Buy your books."

"I promised myself that I'll never touch this money, except for the radio station, and the ministry?"

"My son, you are the ministry.  And you paid this month's bill already, just inform Ardell, and he will understand and support you."

"Yes, Lord."

# Chapter 42

## *Boxing On*
## *The Sabbath*

D uring these times, I was training with Coach Mickey, and I was a part of the *UM's Boxing Team*. Regularly, I attended to class and shared the Good News of God's Kingdom through *Almavision Radio*. I was also buying and selling cars as I drove back and forth to school. However, insufficient time remained in my day for my family. And The Voice of Truth said, "Go to *Florida Fine Cars* again and ask for work."

"When will I have time?"

"They will work around your schedule."

"But I'm up by 4:03 every morning; I'm swimming at the wellness center before class; I'm in class till 12:30pm; I buy the cars from 2pm to 5pm; then I'm training with the boxing team from 7pm to 9pm; then I'm running over the bridge at night; I'm recording the show on Thursdays; I'm in church on Sundays...I'm not even spending enough time with You or my family?"

"From now on Coach Mickey will train you and CJ—the champ—right after class. And then you may work at *Florida Fine Cars* right after this."

"And when will I study?"

"In between classes."

"And when will I read the Bible?"

"Listen to My Word as you drive everywhere. On your way to UM, on your way to the boxing gym, on the way to work..."

"When will I worship you?"

"Do the same while you drive."

"But aren't you getting the leftovers?"

"Soon, you will have the time you desire for Me."

"And my family?"

"They will see the fruit of your labor at My appointed time."

"Why all this?"

"You are My warrior."

"Are you taking me to the 2016 Olympics as you've shown me forever?"

"It's no longer just about you and a handful, My son."

"You mean?"

"The Era is near."

"An Era?"

"A horrible Era."

"Please explain this."

"16."

"So I'm going to the Olympics? Am I making it to the *NFL*?

"Think big!"

"How much bigger can this get? The *NFL* and a professional boxing career; sharing You and Your Word—after winning every fight—to millions. And helping millions with the funds you bless me with."

"Too small."

"Too small?"

"Bigger."

"I can't see bigger," I shouted, confused by this dilemma.

"Yes, you can!"

"From where?"

"Up here."

"I can't see it."

"Let Me show you..."

## The Sabbath: A Vital Key

It was Saturday, and right before I entered into the boxing gym to spar with some boxers from other gyms, a group of *Jehovah Witnesses* approached me and handed me a brochure. I asked The Voice of Truth, "Shouldn't I be doing the same?"

"At the appointed time you will."

"And don't the Jews worship you on Saturdays or Fridays?"

"My son, it is all in the Sabbath."

"So it's all about Sundays?"

"Go to your Bible app quickly, and enter Genesis 2:1-3."

"Thus the heavens and the earth were finished, and all the host of them. And on the seventh day God finished his work that he had done, and he rested on the seventh day from all his work that he had done. So God blessed the seventh day and made it holy, because on it God rested from all his work that he had done in creation", (Genesis 2:1-3, ESV).

"Now go to Exodus 20:8-11."

"Remember the Sabbath day, to keep it holy. Six days you shall labor and do all your work, but the seventh day is the Sabbath of the Lord your God. In it you shall do no work: you, nor your son, nor your daughter, nor your male servant, nor your female servant, nor your cattle, nor your stranger who is within your gates. For in six days the Lord made the heavens and the earth, the sea, and all that is in them, and rested the seventh day. Therefore the Lord blessed the Sabbath day and hallowed it" (Exodus 20:8-11).

"Why is this important?"

"Because it is all in the Sabbath."

"All things regarding life?"

"All things concerning a soon-to-come event."

"On a Sunday?"

"On *The Sabbath, My Shabbat, Mi Sábado, The Seventh Day*—from sunset on Friday, to sunset on Saturday."

"So I've been wrong all along? So what am I doing in this boxing gym on a Saturday?"

"You will soon honor Me on the Sabbath, but you must receive the key first."

"The Sabbath is a huge key?"

"Yes, but I must train you for the huge *Sabbath Fight*?"

"When will it be?"

"Soon, be ready! Now go! And train hard."

"I'm lost."

"Soon you will be found."

## Driving Home

"Spend the rest of this Sabbath with me, and I will show you something."

"Yes, Lord."

"Now when you arrive at the house open your Bible, and write scriptures on your boxing gloves until the sun sets."

"On my gloves?"

"You must fight with My Word."

"I'm lost."

"Blessed be the Lord my Rock,

Who trains my hands for war,

And my fingers for battle" (Psalm 144:1).

"But why will I fight if You're all about love?"

"Greater love has no one than this, than to lay down one's life for his friends," (John 15:13).

"But You laid down Your life, You didn't jab your opponents?"

"You're getting somewhere."

"Then why am I boxing?"

"Follow Me, and you will see."

# Chapter 43
## *The Radio Station And Florida Fine Cars*

By then I was working at *Florida Fine Cars*; training two to three times per day; attending to UM; sharing God's Kingdom through the radio show, and throughout all places; spending a little time with my family; studying in between classes; listening to the Word while driving, and I was arguing with my wife every-single-day as I was labeled 'crazy' and 'different' by her. Plus, I was dealing with a low testosterone level issue due to my wrongly-made past decisions, and perhaps because of this revelation—causing me to become erectile dysfunctional. In other words, not being able to provide for my wife's conjugal needs completely.

### A Different Course

I'm suffering,
but I'm fighting back.
I don't fully understand,
but I realize I don't have to.
Too much is happening,
and I'm starting to see that too much will be revealed.
I'm seeking to just satisfy my wife,
but The Lord longs to show me something else.
I'm praying for all things, including my healing
even while in the midst of intercourse,
but The Lord keeps showing me a different course.

And suddenly, The Voice of Truth said: "Take your olive oil to church tomorrow, and I will tell you what to do."
"Would you heal me Oh Lord, please?"
"Be ready for what pleases Me."

## The Next Day at Point of Grace Church

"Watch, they're going to talk about healing today," I told my wife and the kids as we were walking in. And now we were sitting inside, and Pastor John Perdue was actually speaking about something else. I asked The Voice of Truth: "What happened?"

"Be still, and know that I am God;

I will be exalted among the nations,

I will be exalted in the earth!" (Psalm 46:10).

"Really?"

"Be still."

"Yes Lord." And I was beginning to sense an uncontrollable force pulling me as brother John gathered his final words, and suddenly, The Voice of Truth declared: "Go to James 5:13-16."

"I'm searching, I'm searching; here it is:

"Is anyone among you suffering? Let him pray. Is anyone cheerful? Let him sing psalms. Is anyone among you sick? Let him call for the elders of the church, and let them pray over him, anointing him with oil in the name of the Lord. And the prayer of faith will save the sick, and the Lord will raise him up. And if he has committed sins, he will be forgiven. Confess your trespasses to one another, and pray for one another, that you may be healed. The effective, fervent prayer of a righteous man avails much" (James 5:13-16).

"Are you sick?"

"Yes, Lord," I shouted within me attempting to retain discretion in the church.

"Now get up! And tell brother John that you want to speak to the congregation and that you want to do exactly as My Word suggest."

"In front of all people?"

"Would you like to be healed, My son?"

"Yes, yes; please!" again I shouted within me, but silence remained around me.

"Now is the time!" The Voice of Truth shouted.

"If anyone needs prayer, please come to the altar," said John.

"Now is the time!" The Voice of Truth said again.

And I was trying to hold these accumulations of all things stirring within me, but it was fully grown already. The pain was bursting out of my chest, and I approached Brother John and said, "Brother John, may I speak to the Body—it's from The Lord."

"The altar is yours, brother," he said.

And I turned around to face all servants and my wife and family, and filled by The Voice of Truth I shouted in tears, "The Lord sent me to stand here, today! To speak the truth found in James 5:13-16, and God declares:

"Is anyone among you suffering? Let him pray. Is anyone cheerful? Let him sing psalms. Is anyone among you sick? Let him call for the elders of the church, and let them pray over him, anointing him with oil in the name of the Lord. And the prayer of faith will save the sick, and the Lord will raise him up. And if he has committed sins, he will be forgiven. Confess your trespasses to one another, and pray for one another, that you may be healed. The effective, fervent prayer of a righteous man avails much" (James 5:13-16).

And I kept shouting:

"Are you suffering? Are you sick? Have you committed sins? Are we willing to pray together? Will you like to be forgiven? If your answer is yes, please come. And let's receive this promise right now. But right now! Please come."

And I continued speaking and said, "My beautiful wife, would you bring me the oil you have next to you, please?"

She quickly got up, walked to the altar, handed it to me, and returned to her spot. The Voice of Truth quickly said, "I long for her to stay with you up here, but leave her alone, and pour out the oil to all my little children who willingly come."

"I need the healing," said a nice lady as she walked up.

"Me too," another one.

"Lord, forgive us!" said an old man desperately

"Me! Please! Don't forget me!" the school principal shouted.

And Brother John began to pour out the oil to all enjoying the experience, and then I poured out "half a bottle" to him and his wife, on their heads, and everything was intensifying. The glory of The Almighty covered the atmosphere, and I was standing and staring at my wife, and I quickly asked The Voice of Truth, "Why is she still there sitting?"

"I only knock in all doors, but some have developed secret codes."

"Please bring my wife and family up here."

"At the appointed time she will hand Me her secret code."

"Please give me her code now?"

"Keep following Me and you will see."

And then I was walking out with my wife and the kids from the heavenly edifice, and unexpectedly, Jack said, "Everything changed from today."

"Those are my words, store them in your long-term memory," The True Voice said right after.

"God spoke through you, Jack," I said and we departed.

# Chapter 44
## *The Boxing Dream*

I t was a week before my first fight, and The Lord revealed me this dream:

I'm tossing and turning in my bed, and it feels like a fight—a boxing match. And all I can see is that I'm hitting the opponent with jabs, rights, body shots, and I'm blocking almost everything. By now it's clear that I'm winning the fight. Who's the opponent? I don't know, but I know I'm winning. Boom! An upper right hand, and he's on the canvas. He can't get up. He stumbles. But he's a true fighter and returns. And again, a left hook to the body, but this time he's out; out for the day. And suddenly, The Voice of Truth stands as the referee, next to both, to call out the winner, and He shouts,

"And the winner is...," and He lifts the arm of the boxer I just knocked out twice. I'm blown away by the results; the outcome is hard to swallow, and it was clear that I won the fight. Suddenly, I wake up confused, and The Voice of Truth said clearly, "You lost."

"But it was clear that I won."

"You won the boxing match, you gained fans, you appeared to be strong and talented, but you lost in My eyes."

"How's this possible?"

"You will find out tomorrow."

"Yes, Lord."

### The Next Day: Leaving the Boxing Gym Again

I was in my Monotheism class seating and surrounded by over 300 hundred students, and suddenly Dr. Michelle G. Maldonado, said, "Let's watch a clip from the movie, *The Apostle* by Robert Duvall."

First, she played a section that showed the Apostle praying for a young man as the young man had just crashed his car, and the young lady that appeared to be the young man's girlfriend, was physically dying. And then, Dr. Maldonado said, "Let's watch this other clip." And suddenly, bursting out of the screen multiple people shouted: "HOLY GHOST POWER! HOLY GHOST POWER!"

And I was beginning to feel it. I wanted to get up and shout, but I was holding Him back with all my strength; It was growing within me, but I was jabbing Him back with my limited strength.

"HOLY GHOST POWER! HOLY GHOST POWER!" and I was almost shouting with the actors out of joy.

"HOLY GHOST POWER! HOLY GHOST POWER!" and the class ended.

And soon after, I was walking to my car desiring to shout, and as soon as I turned it on, I heard the voice of a radio-evangelist shouting through the same radio station—through where I shared the Good News:

"For we do not wrestle against flesh and blood, but against principalities, against powers, against the rulers of the darkness of this age, against spiritual hosts of wickedness in the heavenly places" (Ephesians 6:12).

And I shouted: "Hallelujah! I'm all Yours JHWH! I'm all yours Yeshua! Just take me where you want me to go now!"

And I was driving north on I-95 toward the boxing gym to spar against CJ—the UM 152lbs champion—to prepare for my first official amateur fight happening within a week. And in the midst of the supernatural event The Voice of Truth shouted, "Stop."

"On I-95?"

"Pull over."

"This is the highway."

"Pull over!"

And He visited me and manifested His power in an incomprehensible way, and He said, "Follow My Voice."

"Yes, Lord," I said as I was driving again.

"Exit now."

"Here?"

"Yes."

And I was driving through the streets of Downtown Miami, and He shouted again, "Read the signs."

"The one that says, 'Worry less live more?'"

"Yes."

And another one, "I'm here for you," on the bus as it passed by me.

"Look up!"

"777 on an edifice?"

"Ahead of you!"

"A statue of a man with a historic weapon?"

"The street sign," He shouted.

"4th Street?"

"Listen to the radio station; now!"

"You're more than a prophet," a Spanish song playing.

"To your left."

"Unity is our strength," a huge sign.

"Now go to the boxing gym."

"Yes, Lord."

"If you desire to follow My perfect will, then you must leave boxing once again."

"Oh, Lord, please not again; why all this? Why all the turmoil? Why coming and going? Why have You taken me to the boxing gym four times to then ask me to leave? Why?"

"It is My perfect will."

"This?

"My first fight is within a week; you've shown me boxing and sports forever; You brought me to this place, and I could make history at 30 years-of-age—once I win the Intercollegiate Championship in April. At this rhythm, I may turn pro by 2016. Why now?"

"You don't have to, but now you know My perfect will."

"To quit?"

"Quitting is a stage in life that initiates another one."

"I'm not a quitter and You know this."

"2016."

"I won't make it anymore!" I shouted.

"2016!"

"What do You want from me?"

"2016 will be the year of *The Event*."

"You've shown me Boxing at the Olympics, and the NFL."

"O you of little faith."

"Little faith!"

"2016 will be the beginning of a world without Me."

"But that's impossible?"

"The world, and exclusively, the United States of America has removed Me from all places—from the public square. This evil generation will receive the Evil One as they've longed for."

"O no, ABBA! Please protect us."

"You."

"Me?"

"You are My boxer, My warrior, My fighter."

"Then why are You asking me to quit from boxing?"

"You will lead many as I lead you."

"How?"

"In the fight against principalities, against powers, against spiritual hosts of wickedness in the heavenly places."

"Me?"

"You are My chosen one, My son."

"Me?"

"One of many, but, unfortunately, not many are willing to fight."

"But I'm not in the Armed Forces?"

"For you daydream with My Forces."

"Day dream?"

"For you are armed with My Forces."

"And do I really have to quit from boxing, today?"

"You must pick your fight."

"Pick my fight?"

"Of flesh and blood; or against principalities, against powers, against spiritual hosts of wickedness in the heavenly places, against the wicked

Governments—against all the schemes of the prince of the power of the air, Satan."

"Me?"

"Do you want to win all the championships, collect all the belts, even share My Testimony after every fight, or do you prefer to fight for Me, wholeheartedly? And blow the trumpet so that all can hear and fight back to restore a nation, and a dying world?"

"But you're the Only One that can fix this world."

"I agree, and I will make it perfect soon. But you can blast the trumpets so that all can hear and repent from their wicked ways. You can proclaim this soon-to-come Great Tribulation to all those remaining lost; you can sound the alarm to wake up all; you can lead them, instead of just telling them; you can act, instead of just watching it all unfold; you can fight the good fight of faith through Love."

"Me, someone who doesn't have a Ph.D. in Theology? Someone, who is not legally ordained by men?"

"Therefore take up the whole armor of God, that you may be able to withstand in the evil day, and having done all, to stand.

Stand therefore, having girded your waist with truth, having put on the breastplate of righteousness, and having shod your feet with the preparation of the gospel of peace; above all, taking the shield of faith with which you will be able to quench all the fiery darts of the wicked one. And take the helmet of salvation, and the sword of the Spirit, which is the word of God; praying always with all prayer and supplication in the Spirit, being watchful to this end with all perseverance and supplication for all the saints" (Ephesians 6:13-18).

"And what do I do with this Word?"

"Live it."

"How do I tell Coach Mickey?"

"Write the message on paper, spar with CJ as you promised, and then hand it over to him—he will accept."

"But You're telling me not to fight anymore."

"Focus on the Real Fight, My son."

"Yes, Lord."

## Sparring with CJ

I wanted to dodge the punches, but I couldn't; I wanted to punch back, but I couldn't. All I kept hearing was 2016 over and over. I was hitting him back, but my fire was gone. He hit me back even more, and I just didn't understand why. All my power vanished, from one day to another. All my speed disappeared in a flash. And suddenly, The Voice of Truth said: "I'm holding you back because this is your last day."

"At least allow me to enjoy it."

"If you do; they will come back."

"They will come back?"

"Yes, remember yesterday at the gathering in the congregation?"

"Yes."

"The spirits of a boxer were cast out from you."

"But I thought you healed me from my penis problem, and I was getting ready to perform my duties after this?"

"I replaced your flesh and blood fighting spirits and placed within you a spiritual warrior."

"This means I won't be able to satisfy my wife as I planned?"

"At the appointed time you will."

"And when will that be?"

"At the appointed hour."

"Can we make an appointment now for the next hour?"

"Listen to My words found in John 5:5-9:

Now a certain man was there who had an infirmity thirty-eight years. When Jesus saw him lying there, and knew that he already had been in that condition a long time, He said to him, "Do you want to be made well?"

The sick man answered Him, "Sir, I have no man to put me into the pool when the water is stirred up; but while I am coming, another steps down before me."

Jesus said to him, "Rise, take up your bed and walk." And immediately the man was made well, took up his bed, and walked.

And that day was the Sabbath" (John 5:5-9).

"I will heal you at the appointed hour, My son."
"Yes, Lord."
"Coach, please read this:

*This is it.  I have accomplished what The Lord wanted me to accomplish.  This is my last day.  Thank you so much, coach, for everything.  One day, you will understand fully when I share my story,*
*God Bless you!*
*Marcial,*
*11/12/13.*

He remained mute for a moment, and then he said, "At least, let's finish the workout."  And every second after that was painful; not because of physical pain, but because the bigger part of me was passing away at that very moment.  I didn't comprehend why all the back and forth, all the crazy decisions, all the different trips, all the signs and revelations, all the personal issues, all the listening of The Voice of Truth, and the entire lifetime journey...to then quit in a breakthrough and pivotal moment.  The Voice of Truth said:
"I gave you the talent to be a world boxing champion, and a gift to make it professionally in many Sports.  And because you've walked away from all things, I will show you a new way, and I will make you My warrior.  And I will train you for the *Real Fight*—be ready!"
I said to my sparring partner, "CJ, this is my last day brother, I must leave," with much pain in my heart.  And he was mute as well and shook my hand as a good friend.  I walked out leaving all that was left from my Boxing Spirit at *Biscayne Boxing Gym*.

## Driving away from *Biscayne Boxing Gym*:
## UM Boxing Team's Gym

2016! 2016! It was all I could hear; it was all I could see; all I could smell; all I could daydream. Osvaldo Gacet, a friend and client from *Florida Fine Cars*, called me and filled by The Spirit of Truth, I shared with him the glory of God.

Ahead, suddenly, I remember seeing three white birds flying by, and The Voice of Truth said, "Make a U-turn and pray for an impaired lady you just drove by." And I did just that: I parked, followed her, and I asked her, "Ma'am, may I pray for you?"

She shouted, "Go away!"

Once again, I said filled with The Spirit of Truth, "Ma'am, would you please allow me to pray for you; God wants me to pray for you?"

She quickly shouted, "No! Leave me alone!"

"Walk away," The True Voice said, "she ran away from her healing."

"Can I have her healing then?"

"At the appointed time you will have it, My son."

And I was shouting out the window, "JESUS LOVES YOU!" while driving north on 6th Street. And suddenly, The True Voice said, "The horse riders on the bus." And I kept driving and praising The Almighty, and He pointed toward a gas station sign, and it read on the sign: *Food Mart.*

## At Home

I looked at my phone, and the date revealed: 11/12/13. And the time revealed was 3:49pm as I knelt down to pray. I showered quickly and drove away again, to work. And as soon as I entered the premises, I remembered that I had borrowed Kiko's *Hess* fuel card—a sales manager—from the past Saturday, and I handed it to him as soon as I walked in. He immediately said, "Hey, do you think you can help us with the management team as we planned before you left last time?"

"Sure brother," I said, and I worked until late that day.

# Chapter 45
## On My Way Home Again:
## The Signs Interpreted

"Remember the signs?" asked The True Voice.

"Please refresh my memory."

"HOLY GHOST POWER! HOLY GHOST POWER!"

"From the movie?"

"Yes. I will pour out My Spirit unto all my servants, and they will discover themselves."

"And what else?"

"The radio-evangelist from the radio station."

"What about him?"

"He used My Word and said:

'For we do not wrestle against flesh and blood, but against principalities, against powers, against the rulers of the darkness of this age, against spiritual hosts of wickedness in the heavenly places.'"

"And why is this word important?"

"It will continue to appear in your life, and it is a vital word for the plan of attack.

"Remember, when I touched you, and asked you to pull over on I-95?"

"Yes, Lord."

"This is how it will feel when all are touched, but with much more power. Now think about the time when you drove, and I showed you much."

"The 'worry less live more' sign?"

"Do just that and I will show you a plan of attack."

"The 'I'm here for you' sign?"

"It is just a reminder, that 'I'll never leave you nor forsake you,' My son"(Hebrews 13:5).

"And the '777,' on an edifice?"

"My Father and I just like 7's.  Remember the Sabbath?"
"Yes."
"It's on the 7th day."
"And how about the other two 7's?"
"Just want to make sure you don't forget the Sabbath Day."
"And that's it?"
"No, keep them in your long term memory; you will see them again soon."
"The two 7's?"
"Yes."
"And the statue of the man with the historic weapon?"
"World War Z has already begun."
"But I don't see any soldiers, or tanks by the house?"
"Soon you will see."
"In 2016?"
"Just wait and see."
"On American soil?"
"I highly recommend that all repent."
"Repent?"
"From their wicked ways."
"And will You pull away Your sword?"
"I've done it before."
"When?"
"Read the Book of Jonah."
"Which one, Jonah has many books?"
"Not your son's books, but from My Holy Word."
"And how about the '4th Street,' sign?
"It represents the season."
"Which season?"
"2016."
"How is that?"
"Because I'm telling you."
"And the Spanish song that said, 'You're more than a prophet'?"
"You'll see why later."

"And the huge sign that read, 'Unity is our strength'?"

"I chose a huge advertising board for you to comprehend fully, that *uniting with others for the same cause will be one of the most vital components in the attempt to blow the trumpets.*"

"But how do we do this when most have jobs and are busy with their daily routines?"

"I will explain later, but know this..."

"And what's that?"

"...that if they comprehend that their lives are at risk, most of them will react."

"And if they don't?"

"You can only do your part, My son."

"Will we all die?"

"Focus on your job, My son."

"And will 2016 really be the beginning of a world without You?"

"Focus on your job My son, and I can pull way the sword. 'If My people who are called by My name will humble themselves, and pray and seek My face, and turn from their wicked ways, then I will hear from heaven, and will forgive their sin and heal their land'" (2 Chronicles 7:14).

"And just the land?"

"For I made Adam from dust, and dust is born from the land."

"Will we all be healed?"

"The word 'if' remains as a vital component."

"Can you heal my penis issue now?"

"It is the best example I can find to explain and to illustrate to you my pain for a wicked generation."

"My penis issue?"

"As you long to receive your healing to restore your marriage, I long to see a restored humanity to bless My Bride."

"But you're The Son of the Living God, The King of kings; The Lord of lords: why can't you just restore all things now?"

"All must be fulfilled, My son."

"And why am I writing a book if all must be fulfilled? What's the point?"

"Because you're fulfilling your purpose."

"Which is?"

"Just blow the trumpet as loud as you can. And those who are called by My name will humble themselves, and pray and seek My face, and turn from their wicked ways. Then, I will hear from heaven and forgive their sin, and heal their land."

"Really?"

"It's in the short, but powerful Book of Jonah."

"But people won't care; they won't listen."

"If the trumpet is blown by the ones that truly care; by the ones that truly long to see the nations and the United States of America restored; by those that are sick and tired of living in the midst of unrighteousness day-by-day; by those whom truly believe in The Name above all names; if it's blown by those that see these things unfolding, and if it's blown until all things return to My Word, then, it shall make history on Earth as it is in Heaven."

"How do we do this?"

"Follow Me and you'll see."

"And what about 'the three birds' that flew by as I was driving home?"

"These represented the angels whom I sent to redirect you."

"To pray for the lady?"

"Yes, My son."

"And the 'horse riders' on the bus sign?"

"And I saw heaven opened, and behold a white horse; and he that sat upon him was called Faithful and True, and in righteousness he doth judge and make war" (Revelation 19:11, KJV).

"This is You?"

"I'm on My way back, My son."

"And the sign at the gas station reading, *Food Mart*?"

"Be 'food smart.'"

"Food smart?"

"Go to Matthew 24:45-47."

"Who then is a faithful and wise servant, whom his master made ruler over his household, to give them food in due season? Blessed is that servant whom his master, when he comes, will find so doing. Assuredly, I say to you that he will make him ruler over all his goods" (Matthew 24:45-47).

"And this means?"

"Did you noticed that it is in the same chapter where I speak of the End of this Age?"

"Yes."

"This passage was written in an earlier Era, but most importantly, it is mainly for a soon-to-come Era."

"You're the Master?

"Correct. And the food it's not just food, but my Word—the Bible."

"And what do we do?"

"Think of a time when people will kill for a slice of bread."

"But what do I do?"

"Go to Genesis 41:29-41."

"Indeed seven years of great plenty will come throughout all the land of Egypt; but after them seven years of famine will arise, and all the plenty will be forgotten in the land of Egypt; and the famine will deplete the land. So the plenty will not be known in the land because of the famine following, for it will be very severe" (Genesis 41:29-31).

"Do you comprehend?"

"I'm lost."

"Remember the '777' sign?"

"From the edifice in downtown?"

"Yes. And do you remember when I told you to keep the other two sevens in your long-term memory?"

"Yes, Lord."

"I prepared you to comprehend this passage, mentioned above, in the Book of Genesis—for this Era."

"How's that?"

"Instead of seven years of great plenty coming through the land, which, in this case, represents the whole world, the world shall receive three and one-half years of plenty."

"What do you mean?"

"And instead of seven years of famine, which in this case I'm also referring to the whole world, the world shall receive three and one-half years of famine."

"And will this be...?"

"Deadly."

"Deadly?"

"Your imagination is not capable of fully comprehending it, My son."

"And when shall this be?"

"Before the year 2016 ends, the final three and one-half years could begin."

"And what do I tell the people?"

"To follow Joseph's example."

"Individually, or together?"

"United you shall stand strong, but individually, you'll cause limitations."

"In a nutshell?"

"Matthew 24:45-47, gives you the answer, but those whom I've called to help the needy will attempt, wholeheartedly, to follow Joseph's example."

"Thank you, my Lord."

"I'm here for you, My son."

# Chapter 46
## *The Mark of the Beast Revelation*

"And how about 'the date' of the day You asked me to leave boxing for the fourth and final time?"

"11/12/13?"

"I believe so."

"What's 1 x 1 x 1?"

"I believe it's one."

"And 1+2+3?"

"6."

"Just put the 1 in front of the 6."

"16?"

"2016, in My language."

"But people won't believe me for this isn't biblical?"

"It is biblical."

"Is it?"

"Most must comprehend the revelation to comprehend, then, the next part."

"The Biblical part?"

"Yes."

"Can I just get to that part already; people must be tired of reading all these stories?"

"If you don't explain the revelation completely, some will not believe. And My will is for My sheep to believe this soon-to-come worldwide event."

"Yes, Lord."

"Look at the date again."

"I'm staring at it."

"1+1+1=3, correct?"

"Yes, Lord."

252

"1+2+3=6, correct?"

"Yes, Lord."

"Unite 3 and 6."

"36?"

"Can you think of anything related?"

"Oh, no! Oh no, Lord! 3 and 6, 6 and 3, 666, THE MARK OF THE BEAST?"

"Now do you remember the time when you knelt down to pray?"

"3:49pm?"

"3+4+9=16. Correct?"

"I agree."

"Before the year 2016 ends, The Whole World may clearly see 'THE MARK OF THE BEAST.'"

"But some of us see it already?"

"Those who are not watching will see it all, vividly, by then."

"Before 2016 ends, The Antichrist on his temporary throne?"

"Sound The Trumpets now, My son—before it's too late."

"Yes, Lord."

## Chapter 47
# *Leaving The University of Miami Again*

I had just arrived for class and parked. And I was walking toward my Spanish class, when suddenly, The Voice of Truth said, "No, not that way; turn this way today," and I followed His instructions. I was almost there, and The True Voice said, "Sit on the nearby bench and wait; for you are early for class," and I followed His instructions. And as soon as I sat down, I saw a thick red paper right in front of me, placed on the floor, and held by multiple smooth and round stones, and written with a silver ink marker were the capitalized words, declaring:

*THE FUTURE IS UNCERTAIN AND THE END IS ALWAYS HERE.*

And at the bottom right corner, I noticed words written in another language. The Voice of Truth quickly came and said, "Go to class, and I'll show you something else." I entered the classroom desperate to receive the revelation, and suddenly, He said, "Look down."

"What is it?"

"Your book cover."

And I saw a picture of two worlds side by side, and right under, the words: 'Technology' and 'Community,' written in Spanish. He said, "Soon, I will remove this world that has replaced community for technology, and restore all communities.

"Really?"

"I promise you."

"How soon?"

"Remember, understand the events happening now, the events that will soon take place, but most importantly, focus on the 'plan of action' to sound the trumpets as loud as possible."

Dr. Fiorella Cotrina, initiated her lesson, and The True Voice returned and said, "Remember the sign?"

"Which one?"

*"THE FUTURE IS UNCERTAIN AND THE END IS ALWAYS HERE."*

"Is this a coincidence?"

"Out of all places in the entire campus, I sent one of My servants to place this sign in that precise spot."

"Really?"

"The red paper, and the silver coloring to ensure you would not miss it."

"And how about the smooth stones?"

"To prevent the vital message written in the paper from flying away.

"And remember the story of David and Goliath?"

"I do."

"You must be David, but Love is in your stone."

"So don't kill?"

"Love instead, for it's your best weapon."

"And why a red paper?"

"Blood!"

"Blood?"

"Much blood."

"Is this related to 2016?"

"And to most events unfolding now, and all events beginning in 2016 and following after."

"Please just do something to stop this?"

"I am."

"And what's that?"

"The people."

"Which people?"

"You and My endless friends and servants."

"But I can't stop this, or fix this, or even solve this on my own?"

"You're on track."

"And how is that going to help?"

"Unite the true saints; My sheep shall prevail."

"The saints?"

"But are not they dead, and buried in Saint Peter Square?"

"You need to read your Bible a little bit more."

"Really?"

"My servants; those who follow Me are My true saints."

"So unite Your servants?"

"ASAP."

"How?"

"Keep following Me, and you'll see."

"And what must we do?"

"First you must learn how to unite all, and then, I will instruct you, My son."

"Yes, Lord."

"A Diós" Professor Cotrina said, and the Spanish class was over.

## Three Weeks Later
## In the Midst of Final Exams

My little but taller brother, Marcos, was with me that day, as he was also living with me, and as I had to take him to *Miami-Dade College* after finishing with the finals. And during the entire semester, I attempted countless times to finish a final paper for my Arab-Israeli conflict class with Dr. Omer-Sherman. But for some strange reason, I never had the time or made time for it: this was unusual because I habitually did everything when it involved schoolwork—from the very moment the work was assigned.

I said to Marcos, "Hey, do me a favor," as we were walking into UM, and he was unknowingly wearing a UM sweater in the summer time.

"What's that?" he said.

"Would you type the rest of this final paper for me while I take my other final?"

"To type?"

"Here's my notebook; all the info is there."

"Ok, sure."

"Just wait for me here, and I'll come after class."

"Fine."

"Thanks, Marcos."

"You're welcome," he said, and I rushed to my Spanish class.

## Seeing Marcos Again After Class

"Hey, how was it?"

"Oh, it's fine."

"Good, just save it and let's go to the library, where it's quiet, to edit it."

"Oh! What happened?" he said surprised.

"Oh, no, this can't be happening," I said shocked.

"Wait, wait, maybe we can recover this."

"Let me go to the help desk, maybe that guy knows how to recover it."

"Ok."

"Sir!"

"Yes, how may I help you?"

"Well, the computer just turned off out of nowhere, and I can't recover my final paper."

"Oh, I'm sorry, but I truly wouldn't know how to help you there."

"Seriously?"

"Yes, sir."

"I understand," I said and united with my brother again.

"Marcos, let's go to the library, and I'll try to re-type the whole thing."

"But will you have enough time?"

"I have about an hour, I guess I'll find out."

"Ok."

I was typing as fast as I could but I began to sense strongly The Spirit of Truth in the atmosphere. And as I was typing, my very own written words began to speak to me through the final research paper. And I was beginning to receive The Voice of Truth's message, but my common sense was not connecting. Suddenly, He said, "You must leave." But not truly comprehending due to the pressure of having to turn in a final paper, I continued typing as fast and carefully as possible.

"You must leave," repeated over and over as I typed rapidly.

For you to somewhat comprehend what took place, I feel obligated to show you a part of the unedited final paper: this is the beginning section of the paper:

*Marcial J. Ferreira*
*December 1, 2013*
*Dr. Omer-Sherman*
*English 397-D*
*Arab-Israeli Conflict Paper*

*Prior to my first day in this class I had a narrow understanding of the Arab-Israeli Conflict. I remembered how I always watched the news' broadcast to try to learn something from it. But, for the most part, I could not figure out a way to set aside some time to study the Arab-Israeli Conflict—at least not sufficiently from a worldly viewpoint. I always wondered, "Why so much fighting, hatred, murdering, and confusion?" I always had many questions in my heart, and I remained curious most of the time and did not find myself wanting to study this conflict until my life changed forever. Of course, all of us have a story to tell, and the uniqueness of the story is what separates us—it makes us completely different from each other. To fully expand on this experience, I feel obligated to share with you a short version of a story:*

*Since I got saved, by the way, the truth, and the life—Jesus the Christ (John 14:6), I began to consider the Holy Bible, seriously. And I began to apply The Words of God to my life. Everything began to change rapidly in all areas of my life. I started to think differently, to act differently; I began to desire different things... All of the sudden, I began to experience a transformation. I was*

*able to save my brother's life by simply listening to the Voice of*
*God one day—through the Holy Spirit...*

"It is 'I' again," He said, as I typed the last sentence above.

"Is this really You?"

"You listened to the same Voice the day you rushed to your brother's apartment; the day you took the red light; the day I kept you up all night—you listened."

"And are You really asking me to leave now from one of the best universities in the world; when I only have three finals remaining in a few days?"

"Yes, My son."

"And damage my transcripts, when instead I can try keeping the 4.0 GPA?"

"Yes."

"Can I just think about this over the winter break?"

"You must close the door, My son."

"Why?"

"For it will remain as a strong temptation for you."

"Getting a Ph.D. one day, and defending others with a law and a religion degree through the U.S Constitution is a temptation?"

"The U.S Constitution is collecting dust in the White House, My son."

"I don't understand."

"If we were living in a different Era, I would have allowed you to accomplish all things I placed in your heart."

"But why not now?"

"The time is near, My son. And if my real servants don't all leave all things for this world-changing cause, then it shall remain impossible to overcome evil with Love before I return to establish true world-wide peace."

"You took me out of football four times; out of the boxing gym four times; moved me to Miami when I was ranked 8th in swimming in The Dominican Republic, and when I was becoming better and better in baseball, basketball, soccer, and cycling. You also dragged me away from my last business; You orchestrated the loss of multiple jobs; you gave me countless scholarships, including to *Ivy League* Schools; You gave me the 4.0 GPA, the discipline in all things, the countless talents, a mind to develop water from thin air; You've taken me everywhere, and now, you want me to leave, in this very moment, at this very hour, from the place where You, and only You, blessed me with a scholarship to attend?"

"My son, for the cause is greater than what your eyes can see, greater than your GPA, wider than your talents, and it's coming faster than your jab."

"Why me?"

"Remember, I brought you to this place to show you what most dream to attain; to show you what most wish to learn through books, and I simply chose you..."

"But why me?"

"...you are My servant, and you may choose to work for something that will soon perish, or instead, you may choose to work relentlessly for My soon-to-come Kingdom, on Earth, in this final hour."

"This final hour?"

"Let's put your GPA to the test.

"What comes to your mind when you think of all the signs, all the encounters, all the moments, all My divine appointments, all the people, all the Scripture I've shown you, simply all things?"

"Please don't tell me."

"I won't."

"I don't know."

"Be honest with yourself."

"This is too hard."

"But not impossible."

"Please, just let me be a father and a husband at least."

"Go back to the day you were born; what I had to do; the many people that stopped their daily routine and came to donate blood; the radio stations that willingly sounded their trumpets in the attempt to save a few; your 300-plus-pounds grandmother crushing her own knees as she knelt down, seeking and begging me, and the endless events that for the sake of time I won't explain—all for you to simply come out of your mother's wound and live."

"But you do this every day?"

"I do, and I have allowed all the other events in your life to prepare you for a time as such."

"Anyone will think I'm crazy."

"Crazy are those refusing to listen to Me."

"Please just sound Your Trumpets from Heaven."

"You're still in a test, what's in your heart when you look at *The Big Picture*?"

"You know the answer."

"I do, but this is your test, not mine."

"2016."

"Why is this?"

"Can this be multiple choice only?"

"I'm testing your earthly 4.0, and I'd like to see if you're ready for a heavenly upgrade."

"My life is the best explanation I can give, Lord."

"Very good."

"Now what?"

"The ball is on your hands, My son."

"I hate balls already; can I have my boxing gloves, and a punching bag for a moment?"

"The Big Picture, My son! The Big Picture."

"Are you ok?" said my brother, Marcos, sitting next to me.

"Let's go," and I got up and walked away, and he followed.

"Did you finish?"

"Remember this moment."

"But don't you have to turn in the paper soon?"

"This divine moment is my final paper."

"Which one?"

"You won't comprehend now."

"Why not?"

"This is my final day in this place, Marcos."

"But don't you have finals?"

"A final chance, is what we all have."

"A final chance?"

"Don't worry; I'll tell you someday."

"Temptation is coming," said The True Voice.

"Here is free magazine!" said a young lady as she attempted to hand me the UM's magazine titled: *IT'S ALL ABOUT SPORTS.*

"That's a temptation," I said to Marcos as The Voice of Truth confirmed it.

"Really?"

"We must go."

"I don't get it."

"But soon, you will."

God spoke to me, and that was my last day at *The University of Miami.*

# Chapter 48

# Leaving Florida Fine Cars: The Second Time

D uring these times, I was working as a sales manager for *Florida Fine Cars*, and, for the most part, all things seemed to operate fine. Helping clients was an everyday thing, and helping the sales consultants I enjoyed very much, but working with the other sales manager, Rafael Espalliat, was a challenge. On one occasion, he raised his voice at me, and I allowed time to pass, and then approached him right before we closed the store. We made peace, and I forgave him for sinning against me. I remember thinking about hitting him with a quick combo, but The Voice of Truth stopped me quicker. And time passed, and he disrespected me a second time. I went to The Lord, and He said: "My son, it's all about the Sabbath."

"And what does the Sabbath have to do with Rafael disrespecting me?"

"It's all in the Sabbath."

"He's going to get Your wrath this coming Sabbath."

"Love, My son."

"I can't take it anymore! I'm closing most deals, but only the sales consultants see it; I'm giving them my all, but some of the sales managers remain blind?"

"It's all in the Sabbath."

"In the Sabbath?"

"Yes, I'm preparing you for the next step."

"The next step?"

"Be ready!"

"Yes, Lord."

Suddenly, in the midst of a car-deal Rafael interfered, and stuck out his middle finger under the table, and pointed it at me, while I was speaking with a client. I was trying to get up to let him have his

'Sabbath blessing,' but The Voice of Truth came rapidly and said, "You will go to jail today if you hit him."

"I'm ok with that; I can't take this disrespect anymore!"

"My son, will you not do this for Me?"

"He needs to learn a lesson; he can't continue to just disrespect all consultants, and disrespect me just because he thinks he owns this place."

"Lead by example."

"Let me just set an example; just some body shots, please?"

"Boxing is not the way, My son."

And Rafael got up quickly and walked over to the office of Chris, our general sales manager, to fake cry and make up another story. I saw the whole thing unfolding as I sat at the sales podium. I could read their bodies as they move. And suddenly, The True Voice returned and said, "Go to the four story building warehouse, behind it, by the trees and the lake, and seek Me in prayer."

"Yes, Lord."

Now I rushed toward one of my secret places because I needed the healing, or else I was going to explode. And I knelt before The God of Abraham, Isaac, and Jacob—YHWH; The only True and Everlasting God, and I said:

"Please take this cup away from me," and time passed and the silence remained as my best companion. One minute, three minutes, and suddenly, a cat appeared...just a cat. But soon after, He said, "Go back to the sales podium, My son."

"Yes, Lord."

"Write My Words on paper."

"I'm ready."

"In two days, all things will change, My son," and I wrote the date and time, but not the message since I thought it wasn't important.

"Really?"

"In two days."

And immediately after He said this, Mike Williams, a sales consultant, passed by, and I said with a smile on my face, "Hey, Mike!"

"What's good family!?"

"In two days all things will change for me."

"Family, you scare me when you talk like that. I already have enough with your radio show; talk to me, talk to me: what do you mean?

"In two days, Mike."

"Alright then!" Mike said and he walked away.

### The Following Day

The following day, I was called to Chris' office. Mr. Farzin, the human resources director, was there, and he said, "Marcial, I'm here because I feel that I must be part of this."

"Yes, sir, I understand," I said knowing that he was surprised by the upper management decision. And after listening to all they had to say, I pulled out the crumbled piece of paper, where I believed I had written the message, but noticed that I had not written The Voice of Truth's message. And that I had written the date and time only. Regardless, I said:

"I was told that—in two days—all things would change, so I guess tomorrow will be a new day for me." And In two days I was a sales consultant again, instead of a sales manager. But my peace wasn't complete, and suddenly, The Voice of Truth appeared while I was walking around the car lot, and said: "Son, it's all about the Sabbath."

"That's a big statement."

"You must leave to understand."

"From *Florida Fine Cars,* again?"

"Yes."

"And the bills?"

"You saved $30,000 in four months, with this you shall have enough to complete the next mission."

"Do You think I can save up some funds, and maybe use my skills to do something for myself, my family, and others?"

"You will, My son. But remember that true security only resides in Me—not in money."

"I understand, but can I just help many honest and needy people by using money?"

## Give Your Time

"You will help much more by giving Me your time, My son."

"My time?"

"What is time?"

"Money."

"That's one of the biggest lies of all times, created by *the father of lies, the master of deception*—Satan."

"Really?"

"Can you buy a house with money?"

"Yes, Lord."

"A car?"

"Sure, I can."

"Food?"

"Yes."

"All the goods for sale, or even not for sale for the most part—in the whole world?"

"Correct."

"Now buy me a century of My time."

"Well, that's impossible."

"A decade."

"No one can."

"A second."

"I can't do it."

"You can unite all the riches of the world, and attempt to buy a single second of My time, but you won't be successful. My time is not for sale, for I have been, 'Declaring the end from the beginning, and from ancient times the things that are not yet done, saying, My counsel shall stand, and I will do all my pleasure'"(Isaiah 46:10, KJV).

"Then this means that I may find *The End of this Age* in Your Word—in the Holy Bible?"

"This means what it says, and you may also search Me and My Word to find the treasures of My Kingdom."

"The Kingdom of Heaven?"

"Soon coming to Earth."

"But we've been told about this since the beginning of times?"

"This means all should be prepared, right?"

"I suppose."

"But they're not prepared, My son."

"And can you just put all this together for me already?"

"At the appointed time."

"And what does 'time' has to do with quitting again from *Florida Fine Cars*?"

"It's time for you to leave, My son."

"Yes Lord."

"Remember this: *Time, 2016, and The Sabbath*."

"Yes, Lord."

"This will help you comprehend *the message*."

# Chapter 49
## *Revelations At The Park: Obadiah The Prophet*

I t was late at night, and an argument had just erupted, between my wife and me—due to all the pressure coming from all angles. She was in fear, due to all my revelations revealed to her. I felt a heavy burden, due to the disastrous times to come soon, and the millions of lives at stake. And suddenly, The Voice of Truth said: "Go for a walk."

"Yes, Lord."

I was walking toward the tiny park where I usually take my kids to play. And as I was arriving, The True Voice said, "Stop!"

"Here?"

"Yes."

"Now what?"

"Look! To your left." And suddenly, I was filled with The Spirit of Truth as I saw the American flag in a divinely appointed time, all over again.

And immediately, He said: "This is our fight, My son."

"Our fight?"

"You need to gird up your loins! Hold on to My Word! And act now!—according to My will."

"How?"

"Get on top of the playground slides and sit."

"Now what?"

"Remember, when I placed you in the basketball arena at *The University of Miami*, and I showed you the UM flag, and next to it, the American flag?"

"Yes, Lord."

"This is another reminder."

"But You show me these all the time."

"I do, but sometimes, we have moments, and these are special moments—moments that help cultivate the seed I planted in you."

"How's that?"

"Walk away now, and worship Me in spirit, and I will show you My majesty again."

I started worshiping Him, and I was walking toward the house again, and as I was approaching the house, He whispered, "Continue and follow Me."

"Where to?"

"Just follow."

"Yes, Lord."

"Stop!"

"Stop?"

"Now!"

And I was stunned by the rapidly delivered command, and quickly, once again He stated, "To your left again." And, unexpectedly, I saw another American flag hanging in between the City of North Miami Beach's flag and a Florida flag.

"Have you noticed something?" He asked in the midst of my amazement.

"O Lord, is this what it seems like?"

"Yes, My son."

"Please confirm it."

"The American flag does not fly because the Eagle is dying."

"I need more than this."

"Obadiah 1:2-4."

## The Predictions of Judgment on Edom

"·Soon [Look; Behold] I will make you ·the smallest of [or weak among the] nations.
You will be greatly ·hated [despised] by everyone.
Your pride has ·fooled [deceived] you,
you who live in the ·hollow places of the cliff [clefts of the rock].

Your home is ·up high [on the heights],
you who say to yourself,
'·No one can [Who can...?] bring me down to the ground.'
Even if you ·fly high [soar] like the eagle
and make your nest among the stars,
I will bring you down from there," says the Lord"
(Obadiah 1:2-4, EXB).


"Is this really happening? Will this really happen again?"
"Keep reading."
"Where?"
"Obadiah 1:7.
"All ·the people who are your friends [your allies; the people
of your covenant/treaty]
will force you ·out of the land [to the border].
The people ·who are at peace with you [or who promised
you peace; of your peace]
will ·trick [deceive] you and ·defeat [overpower] you.
Those who eat your bread [indicating fellowship and
friendship] with you now
are planning a trap for you,
and you will ·not notice it [be taken by surprise; have no
understanding]" (Obadiah 1:7, EXB).


"Please deliver us all from all evil; please just find another way."

"My son, I just brought you to this place, in My Spirit of Truth, to
reveal the truth through My majesty."

"And why is the wind shaking the two other flags, and bonding with
them?"

"For it is My Hand that still carries these little ones."

"I'm lost."

"My children still have hope, but only if 'they unite all' according to
My will."

"Can You be specific, Lord?"

"Keep walking, and watch all things carefully."

"Yes, Lord."

"Turn right!"

"I'm following."

"Do not fear."

"Why should I?"

And suddenly, a pit bull rushed out of the darkness, barking. And The Voice of Truth whispered, "Be still, and stare at his eyes; The One, who abides in you, has authority over all creatures," and the pit-bull left quickly.

"Is this important?"

"Most have ran away from many crucial, life-changing turning points due to fear, and they've have lost many battles. But the day My people stand still without fear, without excuses, with My Word in My Spirit of Truth, united all for one cause, in front of the rulers of this wicked generation, on that day, real change will come."

"How do we do it?"

"Face-to-face."

"But, it's not so easy."

"But if all will just make an effort to understand the reality to unfold soon, which will affect the whole world, then all, will forget quickly about their differences and privileges. And most will work diligently to establish My Law on Earth as it was in the beginning."

"Can I get a to-do-list for this?"

"Remember the pit bull?"

"Yes, Lord."

"Almost the whole world is being controlled by one pit bull."

"Really?"

"Most of My children, are following all things except My Word and Sprit of Truth."

"But most don't know any better."

"You're correct to a certain extent."

"And that is?"

"It's too complex to explain now. But know this: if more people will just rise in this *final hour*, then humanity, still has a chance to prepare the true Church for My soon-to-come arrival."

"YESHUA MINETZEREF?"

"The King of kings."

"On Earth?"

"As it is in Heaven, My son."

"My King?"

"To rule with a Rod of Iron."

"Yeshua Ha Mashiach?"

"Be ready!"

# Chapter 50

## *Yosi is Back!*

After being away in jail for almost two years, Yosi returned home. Thank God that her family, my wife and I, her mother, Jack and Sven, and the rest finally reunited again. The time came for us to find a new temporary place again, and quickly, The Voice of Truth said, "Go to The Dominican Republic."

"Alone, or with my family?"

"Just go, My son."

And for almost two weeks, I desperately searched for the specific order. Part of me wanted to go by myself to focus on His plans, and the other side wanted to take my family. I said to my wife right before going to bed, "Hey, I was getting ready to buy this ticket to leave soon, by myself, but the Voice of Truth said, 'Wait till tomorrow, and I will show you something.'

"I think I'll do just that instead."

"Are you sure you must go by yourself only?"

"I don't know, but I know that the time is near, and I will know soon."

"Ok, fine."

"Please pray, as I will be making this important decision soon."

"I will."

### The Next Day at 6:10 am

"Hey did you buy the ticket already?" Bianka asked.

"No, I haven't, but I'm a click away from the purchase."

"I think we should go together."

"Why?"

"I don't know how it feels when God speaks, but I believe, He spoke to me through a dream."

"Really."

"I think so."
"Ok, if you say so."

## The Voice of Truth Speaks

"Did you notice the time?"

"Yes, Lord."

"How often Bianka rises so early in the morning?"

"Not often at all."

"Go with your family."

"And what's the purpose of this trip?"

"I will show you more."

"More?"

"The keys to unlocking My Message for Humanity."

"In The Dominican Republic?"

"Yes, where you were born."

"But don't You think I'm low in funds, and that I need to find myself a job?"

"I've given you one."

"Really? And when do I start?"

"Effective immediately."

"Yes Lord, I'll follow You."

# Chapter 51
## The Trip To
## The Dominican Republic

We arrived at, *El Aeropuerto Las Américas*, in Santo Domingo. And Bianka, Bandon and Jonah, and I departed with my mother to the *City of Santiago*. And my mother in law, *Doña* Juana, enjoyed the ride with her brother, Polin, to his residence in Santo Domingo. After three days had passed, my family and I departed to Polin's house in Santo Domingo. Polin said to us all, speaking in Spanish, "Hey, who wants to go to the farmhouse?" And we all agreed.

### In *Jobo Claro*, "The Farmhouse."

We had just arrived at *Jobo Claro*. And all I had in my mind were all those things I saw on the way to this place: the amazing sights, the beaches, the mountains filled with nature, the animals declaring God's glory, and the farm life as it was in the old biblical days. Suddenly, as we were trailing uphill in Polin's truck, the neighbors waved their hands at us and some shouted:

"Welcome back!"

"Wey!" it's a Dominican thing.

And others just stared.

### That Night

Suddenly, the electric power was gone, and The Spirit of Truth led me by announcing, "Go to the neighbor's house, and I will show you something."

"Now?"

"In this very moment."

And soon after I was walking downhill, away from the house that sits on a rock—on a hill. And The True Voice said, "Be ready." And, I entered into the old wooden little house, and suddenly, I received a message. He said, "Open up your heart to the poor, and they shall prophesy in My Name."

"To these people?"

"I'll tell you when."

And I was sitting in the neighbor's living room with the neighbors. And a lantern shined through the darkness and enabled us to see our faces, partially. And the old lady, which prepares home remedies from herbs said, "Tell us what you do for a living?" I looked at them one by one as I held on to my words, and quickly, He visited again and said through me, "I serve The Voice of Truth."

"The Voice of Truth?" Sonia, the other lady, that sat in front of me asked.

"Yes. I serve Him," I said as I pointed toward the Heavens, "and for this reason I'm here now."

"Really?"

"Be ready!" I said.

"For what?" Berroa said, one the farmhouse's watchmen and farmers.

"For all things to come soon."

They all looked at me, thirsting for more truth, and I continued and said, "If all choose to repent The Lord will open up His ears to all."

"But what's coming?"

"What's important is that we act now; all of us, all people. And God will listen once we act truthfully."

"Please be specific," the lady that prepares the healing bottles said.

And suddenly, Sonia countered and said, "Listen to him, for this young man has wisdom, not of this world." And quickly after, The Voice of Truth visited again and said through me addressing to Sonia, "For you did not speak from your own, but He spoke through you— The Voice of Truth." And the remedy lady was filled instantly and said,

"Say more! Say more!" And Sonia replied, "Listen to him, all of you; for what comes out of his mouth comes from God."

"Darkness unlike never seen before lies ahead. The Final War has begun. Those that label themselves 'Christians' will be tested beyond the unthinkable. People will soon kill each other for a cup of contaminated water, for a rotten banana. Many in the Armed Forces, and the local militarized police, will think that they will be serving their government and God, but instead, they will serve Satan—the father of deceptions. Most will say, 'Where is God?' but God will say, 'Where were you when I kept knocking at the door of your heart? Where were you when I asked you to feed the hungry? Where were you when I asked you to visit the prisoner? Where were you when I asked you to forgive others? Where were you when I asked you to follow Me wholeheartedly? Where were all My little children? Where were you all?'"

"Is this really going to happen?"

"For it is written, THE WORD OF GOD IS PERFECT"(Proverbs 30:5).

"Then why even try?" said the healing lady.

"You'll know soon, allow me to continue, please."

"Listen to him," Sonia said.

"It is all in the Holy Bible. Although, men have tried to remove and corrupt the wording of it, we must comprehend that The Spirit of Truth reveals all things, including, this very thing in the hearts of an evil generation. I don't want to take up much time because I understand that you must all rest."

"No, no please continue?"

"Ok. Be ready now, because before the year of 2016 ends, the world will receive what it has been seeking for."

"Are you referring to the Second Coming of The Savior—The Messiah?"

"Not specifically. Instead, I'm referring to the events that are soon to take place, here on Earth, prior to the return of The King of kings— Yeshua Ha Mashiach."

"And how do we know this is true?"

"If you're in tuned with The Voice of Truth, through His Word and Spirit, then you, and all who desire to follow Him in humility, in spirit, and in truth may also know."

"And how can we do this now?"

"United in The Spirit of Truth and in The Word of our Master."

"But is not that easy to do this?"

"But it has been easy to remain in our comfort zone."

"And what do you suggest?"

"For those who consider themselves servants of The Lord of The Armies to rise unlike never before. Not in violence, but with a relentless spirit, and demanding The Law of Liberty of The Living God in all atmosphere—in every place where there is breath."

"And who can help?"

"Servants of The Lord, disciples, apostles, pastors, deacons, youth ministers, Sunday school teachers, women leaders... But not just in the church, also, those that see and believe, or believe and see that this is Humanity's final moments and that all must create a righteous unity, rapidly, to perhaps change such a catastrophic worldwide outcome."

"But if it is written, then how can we change this?"

"It is also written that we must sound the trumpets when we see the sword coming."

"Will that change anything?"

"It may change a lot of things."

"How so?"

"What if God sees our humility, our willingness to serve Him, our effort to repent from our wicked ways, our desires to seek His Face, but most importantly: our righteous deeds. Don't you think that the sword may flee from the territory of the humble?"

"Maybe."

"He can allow it, and He can remove it."

"Thank God I'm saved," said the old lady.

"Don't be fooled by the Enemy."

"How so?"

"If you were saved yesterday, are you guaranteed salvation tomorrow?"

"Of course!"

"So if you decide to sit back and relax as a useless servant, do you think you will enter into soon-to-come Kingdom of Heaven, here on Earth, governed by The King of kings?"

"Once saved, you're always saved!"

"Write this down."

"I'm ready."

"Read: 2 Thessalonians 2:3; Matthew 24:24; Luke 14:34; John 15:6; Romans 11:21-22; 1 Corinthians 3:16-17; 1 Corinthians 10:12; Hebrews 10:38; and Revelation 3:5. Got them?"

"Yes."

"Study these and you will comprehend the truth about your salvation as long as you remain in The Spirit that gives it."

"The salvation?"

"And the truth."

"And when will this all take place?"

"Work now like never before, because before 2016 ends this whole world will initiate a journey as the false messiah/false god/Antichrist rises. And those not watching will finally see him for what he truly is— you will clearly see *The Mark of The Beast* spoken of in the *Book of Revelation*."

"Can you show us where you found this in The Bible; where we may seek?"

"I can, but I have to write a book so that you comprehend to the best of your abilities."

"At least some scriptures?"

"Don't worry, just begin with what you have, and God himself, will give you the rest."

"And the book?"

"You'll get it soon; God willing."

We prayed, I got up and walked uphill to the house sitting on a rock.

## That Night at the Farmhouse

I had just finished a Bible study with my wife, and for some reason, soon after, I felt as if I had to speak to the remedy lady. Or even better, to an old man named, Galfo, who finds the herbs for the remedy lady for the preparation of the healing bottles. I shared this with my wife, and we both got on our knees and went to bed right after.

## The Next Day

"It is a little bit embarrassing to share this with others," I said to Bianka.

"Who cares? Just do it, and don't be afraid."

"Are you sure? You know this is a small farm town, and all will probably know soon."

"Do you want to be healed?"

"I can't wait just to do my job as a husband."

"Then act now!"

"Ok."

## Speaking with Galfo at His House

"Hey Galfo, I have a situation."

"Talk to me," he said as the sheep played in his backyard.

"You know, I lost my strength, my physical power, and, unfortunately, even my penis' power."

"I understand," attempting to counsel me he said.

"I can't satisfy my wife anymore," I said as I held a river of tears.

"It's ok," he said and tapped me on my recovered shoulder.

"Please, help me."

"Listen. Today, I will search for the herbs, and by tomorrow, I will hand them over to our neighbor, and she will prepare the bottles according to my directions."

"Thanks a lot, brother."

"I'm here for you."

## The Following Day

The following day I purchased a gallon, instead of a bottle, from the healing lady. And we all returned to Polin's house in Santo Domingo.

## Claiming My Father's Inheritance

I decided to take a trip to *La Romana*, without my family, on a bus, to see my other family members. But most importantly, to visit my father's tomb, and to investigate about my father's inheritance. He deceased temporarily on, July 22nd of 2004. And since we were living in Miami when this unfortunate moment occurred, my brothers and I, signed a power of attorney giving legal power to our aunt, Mati—to handle all things necessary regarding his will. In 2004, I was told by my mother and brothers that I had inherited my father's old car. All three of us: Angel, Miguel, and I, thought that perhaps this was my father's will, surely. We figured, "He knew what he was doing when he prepared his will for us." And we also assumed, "Maybe they're just working on it." After a decade plus, The Voice of Truth said, "This is one of the reasons for this trip; for you must see."

I spent three days walking around *La Romana*, in search of my father's attorney. I visited the attorney I used to visit with my father when I lived with him as a child, and he sent me to another lawyer. Then, I visited the one in charge of the case, and he gave me his story. Then, I visited another lawyer involved, and he was extremely polite. By the third day, I had spoken with four attorneys, and conversed with three of these four. I also visited my father's apartment home, and Lilian, my father's widow, greeted me through the apartment's window after not seeing me for over ten years. I departed, then met an old lady while walking down the main avenue, and she handed me a flyer about a revival campaign happening at a local church. Therefore, I went to the local church called, *El Sinai*, and just listened to The Voice of Truth while I sat there. And holding on to my earthly father's will, and additional paperwork, I listened. The Voice of Truth said clearly, "Read your father's will when you arrive at aunt Mati's house."

I didn't know what this was all about, but I continued to worship Him. Soon after, I departed and traveled across the city in a *carrito concho,* (a cab).

## At Tia Mati's House

And I was sitting in a rocking chair on aunt Mati's front porch, and The Voice of Truth said, "Read your father's testament now." Thus, I quickly grabbed the manila folder and slowly read it. And quickly, I noticed that my father had left me and my brothers, as an inheritance, his building, and the personal charge of collecting the monthly rent from all tenants with his wife. And that he had left us his personal belongings. I also noticed that he had assigned me other responsibilities. Then The Voice of Truth said, "Now read the other document, not the testament, but the one your father prepared prior to his final marriage."

So I was reading it, and I saw: "20000 *tareas,* (About 3108 acres), and another land of *8000 tareas, (about 1243 acres).* It mentioned a house in Puerto Rico and another piece of land."

And I paused, and just sat there for a moment in awe—blown away by the whole truth. I couldn't believe how no one had brought this information to my attention—it wasn't sinking in. I was told that he had left me as an inheritance an old car, but that was just part of the truth—the whole truth remained incomplete. *Tio* Domingo (my uncle), quickly said to me, "You know, your father wrote a letter stating that, 'If something were to happen to him, to please investigate his wife, Lilian.'"

"Really?"

"He also consulted with me the possibility of lending about 400,000 US$ to some man, that considered himself a businessman, and I told him not to do it."

"I see uncle."

"I don't know, but this whole thing has been a mess. You and your brothers had to be here."

"I agree, but we were trusting in our mother, and in aunt Mati."

"Your aunt did what she could, but you all had to be here to face this."

"I agree uncle, but why weren't we informed of this?"

"Didn't your mom tell you?"

"Not really; this is the first time I read my father's testament."

"Listen, go to your uncle, Fari—you know he has been a well-known lawyer forever, and his daughter is a judge in *The City of San Pedro* also—maybe they can help you."

"Thank you, uncle."

"Just don't give up on you father's inheritance, son."

"I won't."

## The Voice of Truth Speaks

I was shocked by the whole thing. And I almost physically fought against one of the lawyers called, Pedro de la Rosa, because he couldn't simply make me copies of my father's testament. I was surprised by the additional information provided by my uncle and aunt. I truly didn't know what else to expect anymore. Suddenly, my uncle walked away and left me alone on the front porch. And The Voice of Truth came, sat in the rocking chair next to me, and said,

"Are you shocked?"

But the silence hovering over the front porch was even more shocking. I was in a peculiar state that words cannot to explain.

"I believe I am," I respond after a moment of silence.

"Remember the dream you had before your son Jonah was born?"

"Yes."

"Clearly?"

"How You showed me his face, and how You told me that he would be born in the same month and day of my father's earthly death?"

"And did he look like the picture I showed you in the dream when he was born?"

"Identical."

"And was he born on the same day and month of your father's death; despite the doctor informing you otherwise?"

"Yes."

"Remember how Bianka, herself, didn't even realize when her water had broken, and how you remembered the date I had given you, and then asked her to come to the hospital because you knew that you were going to see Jonah's face the following day?"

"I remember."

"Now listen to Me; pay close attention."

"Yes, Lord."

"Are you ready?"

"I think so."

"How many of my children, live and die each day, and never get to see My Testament?'"

I sat there on the *shocking* chair thinking about this question while my father's testament situation kept flying through my finite mind.

"I guess too many," I replied with my guard up for some reason.

"And why is that?"

"I wish I had the perfect answer, my Lord."

"I am the answer."

"You?"

"I desire for you to inform all people that, 'I am the way, the truth, and the life... (John 14:6)."

"And why did You remind me of Jonah's story?"

"For many reasons."

"Which are?"

"For you to remember that when I speak you must consider it done—and the whole world as well."

"Yes, Lord."

"And I named him Jonah to remind you of the Book of Jonah in the Bible."

"The Book of Jonah?"

"When he finally went to Nineveh, and all repented when he preached My Word to all!"

"And what do I do with my father's testament?"

"Whose Testament is more important?"

284

"I'm lost."

"If you fight for your earthly father's testament, and his will for you and your brothers, you will miss the opportunity to act like Jonah in this final hour. But if you fight to bring my 'Old and New Testament' back into the lives of all, and into this sinful world; you shall truly receive your reward—your inheritance."

"So forget about my father's testament?"

"Remember, 2016?"

"Yes."

"If you engage yourself in your father's testament, and with that legal case, then you will disqualify yourself due to the limited time."

"And can't I just sound the trumpets later?"

"Later will be too late; for the time is now!"

"Now?"

"You have been trained for this moment, My son."

"And just let all of them that are stealing continue to steal, and dishonor my father's testament."

"Think about how many more are stealing, corrupting, disintegrating, and dishonoring My Testaments."

"But my father's inheritance could be worth: thousands, or millions, or more, I don't know. And what about the many things that are priceless?"

"My son, for I have chosen you to sound this trumpet in this final hour; most people remain in bed glued to their TVs as the remote controller controls them and their cell phones shower them."

"What else are You going to ask me to leave behind?"

"You're dying to live, My son—truly."

"And what do I do tomorrow?"

"You will know when I bless you with it."

### The Following Day

"Go to your father's tomb."

"Yes, Lord."

## At My Father's Tomb

"But there's nothing here, I can't find it."

"Keep searching," He said. And I searched and searched and no success, and He visited me again, and said, "Nothing?"

"Nothing; I just can't find it?"

"Don't worry, return to aunt Mati's house and ask her to come with you."

"Yes, Lord."

## At Aunt Mati's House

"*Tia* (Aunt), do you think you can come with me to visit my father's tomb?"

"Sure darling, I'm the only one that truly visits him; I'll show you everything."

"Thank you, *Tia* (aunt)."

"You're always welcome."

## At the Cemetery Again

"This is it," said aunt Mati.

"But this reads, *Juez* (Judge) Miguel Gomez, and not Marcial Eloy Ferreira Vargas?"

"I know, it's sad."

"And where is my father's tomb?"

"Unfortunately, my son, they probably eliminated him and used this space since he did not have a sign on his tomb."

"So his wife never placed a sign on his tomb when we buried him—after we returned to Miami?"

"I believe she didn't, my son."

"I see; don't worry aunt, it's not your fault."

"Just come back in the morning and ask the man in charge—they usually help."

"I see," I said, and we drove away to her house.

# The Voice of Truth Speaks

"I know you are in pain," He said and I kept quiet for a while. And He returned after a while and said, "My son, listen to Me."

"Yes Lord, and what do I do now?" as my heart was broken I replied.

"This may be tough for you to grasp fully, My son. But you had to live this moment to comprehend better what I'm about to explain."

"This moment?"

"Yes, this moment."

"I'm listening, but please don't hurt me."

"You couldn't find your father's tomb, correct?"

"And why you asked me to keep searching for it when you knew about this all along?"

"My son, allow Me to show you something."

"Yes Lord," in much pain I said.

"Most have removed Me from My place on Earth as they removed your father from his tomb."

"And I have to live through this to comprehend this issue?"

"To comprehend it wholeheartedly, yes."

"And why?"

"Because you need to feel what I feel to act how I act."

"And how must I act now? What do you want me to do?"

"Your life is your tool, My son."

"My life; a life filled with drastic decisions?"

"And the wisdom you shall receive from those decisions, and from Me directly."

"And what do I do with it?"

"Share it."

"How?"

"Catch a bus to *Santo Domingo*, and return to *La Romana* with your wife and kids in a few days. And enjoy those moments while you are there."

"And what's next?"

"I'll tell you when the time comes."

"And how about 2016, and all the events to soon occur, how do I tell people about all things?"

"Enjoy this time with your family, and I'll visit you in Miami once again."

## In Miami Again

"My son."

"Yes, Lord."

"Move out of Yosi's house as you already completed the word you promised to her, and find a new place to live in."

"But I'm low in funds?"

"You still have a little bit left."

"And then what?"

"Then you will write a book."

"A book?"

"First, you must write about My revelations and your life's experiences. And then, you must write about the things I will reveal to you when the hour comes."

"And is not this a very long book?"

"I will summarize all things for you, My son."

"Can I just talk about 2016, and the events to come, and not proclaim my privacy and the privacy of others to the whole world?"

"All things must be combined for most to comprehend and act quickly. And then, some will comprehend the events to-soon-unfold beginning in 2016."

"And why not just the facts without all this drama?"

"Do you believe in Me in the same way you did when you first met Me?"

"No."

"Why not?"

"I don't know."

"Because our relationship, our encounters, My revelations, My miracles, My majesty, My glory, My blessings, and much more...did not just occur when you found Me at the Christian football camp."

"And this is important because?"

"Because those that thirst for the truth need to foretaste—at least to a certain extent through the book—what you have experienced; to better comprehend what I will soon reveal."

"And what must I do now?"

"Go back to the Dominican Republic, alone this time, and write a book."

"Write a book?"

"Yes."

## In The Dominican Republic at the Hotel

"I don't think I can do this."

"Yes you can; don't be afraid."

"Are you sure about this?"

"The whole truth must come out now; for now is the final hour."

"Me?"

"Yes. Just do it."

"Like Nike?"

"No, like 2016."

"I can't. I don't know enough."

"Don't worry, My son; I'll take over from here."

"But I thought You had taken over from the beginning?"

"Yes, from the very first word."

"So what do You mean?"

"The upcoming section is for those desiring a true and biblical explanation."

"Biblical?"

"My Word."

"Your Word?"

"The time has come."

"For what?"

"For My Bride to wake up!"

"Wake up?"

"Rise!"

# THE OMEGA

## THE BOOK: A REVELATION, A STORY, AND THE TRUTH

# Chapter 52

# Matthew 24:36 Deception

I am The Voice of Truth. And I have allowed My servant to share with you visions and supernatural encounters, yet some of you remain in a state of unbelief. Could it be that some of you remain caught up in your personal lives, and, therefore, cannot see clearly? Could it be that some of you know or feel that something catastrophic is about to unfold on Earth, but remain too afraid to sound the trumpets? This is My conclusion: 'Fear has captivated the hearts of all flesh, and only a few have managed to escape.'"

"Really?"

"Just listen, My son. And allow me to open the Book of Daniel again."

"Daniel?"

"Yes, remember?

'But you, Daniel, shut up the words, and seal the book until the time of the end; many shall run to and fro, and knowledge shall increase'" (Daniel 12:4).

"Knowledge shall increase regarding prophecy?"

"In all things; in all people. Some will use it for good, but some for evil."

"And why now?"

"Daniel 12:9."

"Daniel 12:9?"

"And he said, "Go your way, Daniel, for the words are closed up and sealed till the time of the end" (Daniel 12:9).

"If the words were closed and sealed till the time of the end...?"

"You're close."

"...then, You will unseal the Book—what humanity could have not been able to see throughout all history?"

"How?"

"I don't know, but it looks like it."

"Read Matthew 24:36."

"But concerning that day and hour no one knows, not even the angels of heaven, nor the Son, but the Father only" (Matthew 24:36).

"I know the hour!" He said as soon as I finished reading the scripture found in Matthew 24:36.

"How can You when it says that not even the Son knows?" I responded puzzled by the statement of The Voice.

"I know the hour, and I am the Son!" He repeated.

"But the Bible—Your Living Word—says that You do not know?"

"I know the hour!" again, I heard clearly as I was in the dining room holding on to the Bible.

"I need a break," I said in the midst of this contradiction.

"Take it and rise early."

## The Next Day

"Go deep, My son."

"Deep?"

"I will share with you different kinds of translations, and in the end, I will ask you questions.  Fair enough?"

"You are, always."

"Read these older translations referring to Matthew 24:36:

## Matthew 24:36 (Older Versions)

"But of that day and hour no one knows, not even the angels of the heavens, but [my] Father alone" (Darby's Translation, DBY 1890).

"But of that day and hour no one knoweth: no, not the angels of heaven, but the Father alone" (Douay-Rheims Challoner Revision, DR 1750).

"But of that day and houre knoweth no man, no, not the Angels of heauen, but my Father onely" (Original King James Bible, AV 1611).

"BUT concerning that day and concerning that hour, no man knoweth; neither the angels of heaven, but the Father only" (John Etheridge Peshitta-Aramaic NT, 1849).

"But of that day and of that hour, knoweth no man, nor even the angels of heaven, but the Father only" (James Murdock Peshitta-Aramaic NT, 1852)

"But of that day and hour knoweth no man, no not the Angels of heaven, but my father only" (Geneva Bible, GNV).

"But of that day and hour knoweth no man, no, not the angels of heaven, but my Father only" (King James Version, KJV).

"Now read these newer translations referring to Matthew 24:36:

## Matthew 24:36 (Newer Versions)

"But about that day or hour no one knows, not even the angels in heaven, nor the Son, but only the Father" (New International Version, NIV).

"However, no one knows the day or hour when these things will happen, not even the angels in heaven or the Son himself. Only the Father knows" (New Living Translation, NLT).

"But concerning that day and hour no one knows, not even the angels of heaven, nor the Son, but the Father only" (English Standard Version, ESV).

"But of that day and hour no one knows, not even the angels of heaven, nor the Son, but the Father alone" (New American Standard Bible, NASB).

"Now concerning that day and hour no one knows--neither the angels in heaven, nor the Son--except the Father only" (Holman Christian Standard Bible).

"No one knows when that day or hour will come —not the angels in heaven, nor the Son, but only the Father" (International Standard Version).

"No one knows when that day or hour will come. Even the angels in heaven and the Son don't know. Only the Father knows" (GOD'S WORD® Translation).

"But of that day and hour knoweth no one, not even the angels of heaven, neither the Son, but the Father only" (American Standard Version).

"But of that day and hour knoweth no one, not even the angels of heaven, neither the Son, but the Father only" (English Revised Version).

"What stands out? What are the differences?"

"The older translations do not mention anything about the Son, yet the newer translations state, 'nor or neither the Son'—The Son is not in the picture."

"Why?"

"I don't know; I have no clue?"

"Think."

"I can't think of anything."

"Revelation 22:18, 19."

"For I testify to everyone who hears the words of the prophecy of this book: If anyone adds to these things, God will add to him the plagues that are written in this book; and if anyone takes away from the words of the book of this prophecy, God shall take away his part from the Book of Life, from the holy city, and from the things which are written in this book" (Rev. 22: 18, 19).

"So men have been adding and taking away from Your Original Word."

"I inspired my servant John to write this, because I knew that, at some point, men would get too creative."

"So which translation is correct? Are not all these Your Word?"

"My Word is the Voice speaking to you now..."

"And the Bible?"

"Also, My Word, but what you have is not 100% authentic."

"So how can I trust in it?"

"You trust in it through The Voice of Truth, and whenever there is a minor transliteration that leads to a major misinterpretation the trumpets will sound from heaven, and you'll be notified."

"So do I trust in the Bible?"

"Yes, but always remember that you must remain in Me to unseal the treasures of heaven on Earth."

"In You?"

"Without Me the Bible is just a book.   But with Me, it's a Book that breathes and sends signals throughout the Universe, and to all those who are willing to receive and eat from it."

"And Matthew 24:36?"

"Go to the Young's 'Literal' Translation."

"'And concerning that day and the hour no one hath known -- not even the messengers of the heavens -- except my Father only" (YLT).

"Keep in mind; this is the 'literal translation.'"

"Ok."

"What do you see?"

"Matthew 24:36, again and again."

"Deeper."

"Deeper?"

"No one hath known..."

"The same thing all over; what's this all about?"

"This is all about opening your eyes so that you have the tools to blow the trumpets, now."

"How?"

"Let us read the words of Matthew 24:36, from the Greek scrolls,

Περὶ δὲ τῆς ἡμέρας ἐκείνης καὶ τῆς ὥρας οὐδεὶς οἶδεν οὐδὲ οἱ ἄγγελοι τῶν οὐρανῶν εἰ μὴ ὁ πατὴρ μου μόνος (Stephanus Textus Receptus, 1550).

"What's this?"

"But concerning that day and hour no one "οἶδεν," neither the angels of the heavens, except my father only."

"English or Spanish, please?"

"The tense of οἶδεν (oiden) is *perfect active indicative*, which can best be rendered in English as 'has known', or to better comprehend, 'no one has known yet.'"

"Seriously?"

"I am The Voice of Truth."

"I'm lost."

"This is how it was originally written, and how it must be written, today, as the literal translation in your modern English Bibles,

'And concerning that day and the hour no one 'has known'—not even the messengers of the heavens—except my Father only'"


"So no one has known, or no one knows yet the time or the hour, but at some point in time some will know?"

"Exactly."

"This can't be true."

"Why not?"

"Because throughout history all have failed to predict The Day of Your Coming, or the day of the False Messiah/Antichrist, or something as incredible as this."

"The information was always there, but knowledge had not yet increased because The Book was sealed."

"How's this...?"

"Daniel 12:4."

"So to better comprehend, you are saying that from generation to generation, for centuries, people have failed to see this truth about Matthew 24:36?"

"They have not failed; the book was sealed, and for this final hour, I have selected you and some of My servants to view a minor section of it."

"Why me?"

"Why not you?"

"I don't know."

"Now, you know."

"What do I know, I dropped out of college?"

"You knew enough to listen to Me then, and you know enough to listen to Me now."

"And now what? What do we do?"

"But made Himself of no reputation, taking the form of a bondservant, and coming in the likeness of men" (Philippians 2:7).

"So You were like us?"

"I was like you; you are made in My image. And when I said 'no one has known,' or 'no one knows yet' the day and the hour, I was walking with men as you walk with men today."

"Ok?"

"Did my disciples believe I knew, or if, at some point I will know, or if, at some point you will know?

"I'm not sure."

"They knew—to some extent—who I was and My identity as I walked with them on Earth in those days.   Therefore, they comprehended when I said, 'No one has known, or no one knows yet the day or the hour...'"

"Really?"

"Read Revelation 12:9."

"So the great dragon was cast out, that serpent of old, called the Devil and Satan, who deceives *the whole world*; he was cast to the earth, and his angels were cast out with him" (Rev. 12:9).

"He has deceived the whole world as you can see, but 'truth shall spring out of the earth; and righteousness shall look down from heaven' to wake up My Church—My Body." (Psalm 85:11).

"How do I know I'm not being deceive as I write this book?"

"Keep listening, and you'll see.

"My people are destroyed for lack of knowledge.

Because you have rejected knowledge,

I also will reject you from being priest for Me;

Because you have forgotten the law of your God,

I also will forget your children" (Hosea 4:6).

"Lack of knowledge?"

"The follower of today's knowledge finds unconditional stupidity."

"Unconditional stupidity?"

"Unlimited wisdom is what I have to give to those willing to follow Me."

"To follow You?"

"Yes, 'And you shall know the truth, and the truth shall make you free'" (John 8:32).

"Make me free?"

"From all things."

"I'm still doubting this whole Matthew 24:36 thing."

"I will guide you through My Word and you shall know the whole truth."

"Now?"

"No, next year!"

"Next year?"

"No, now.  Just kidding."

"Really!"

"Yes, let's go to work."

"Where?"

"There.

"But you, brethren, are not in darkness, so that this Day should overtake you as a thief.  You are all sons of light and sons of the day. We are not of the night nor of darkness" (1 Thessalonians 5:4, 5).

"So if I'm not living in darkness, the Day of Your Return to establish your soon-to-come Kingdom on Earth will not overtake me as a thief?"

"Correct.  Now there,

"Remember therefore how you have received and heard; hold fast and repent. Therefore **if you will not watch**, I will come upon you as a thief, and you will not know what hour I will come upon you" (Revelation 3:3).

"So for those that are watching you will not come as a thief, and, therefore, we will know the hour at the appointed time?"

"**...if you do not wake up**, I will come like a thief..." (Revelation 3:3, NASB).

"And how are people supposed to wake up if they have been deceived by the Devil?" (Revelation 12:9)

"And it shall come to pass afterward

That I will pour out My Spirit on all flesh;

Your sons and your daughters shall prophesy,

Your old men shall dream dreams,

Your young men shall see visions.

And also on My menservants and on My maidservants

I will pour out My Spirit in those days" (Joel 2:28, 29).


"But was not this fulfilled in the Book of Acts in the 2$^{nd}$ chapter?"

"History repeats itself, My son—a twofold prophecy."

"And is this what will happen?"

"This is what's happening now, and this is what will happen with much more intensity as we approach The Day of My Return."

"And how about 2016? Will the Antichrist truly reveal himself before 2016 ends as You have been showing to me for all these years?"

"For nothing is hidden that will not become evident, nor anything secret that will not be known" (Luke 8:17).

"So this is real?"

"Watch therefore, and pray always that you may be counted worthy to escape all these things that will come to pass, and to stand before the Son of Man" (Luke 21:36).

"So some will escape?"

"And some will not."

"And why not?"

"Read:

"And they overcame him by the blood of the Lamb and by the word of their testimony, and they did not love their lives to the death (Revelation 12:9).

"And I saw thrones, and they sat on them, and judgment was committed to them. Then I saw the souls of those who had been beheaded for their witness to Jesus and for the word of God, who had not worshiped the beast or his image, and had not received his mark on their foreheads or on their hands. And they lived and reigned with Christ for a thousand years" (Revelation 20:4).

"But these are some of Your followers and they will be beheaded?"

"Yes, these are some of My warriors who will choose to live forever by not loving their lives, by not worshipping *the beast* and *his image*, and by not receiving *his mark* on their foreheads or on their hands."

"And how about those living their lives by their wicked ways; those who are not in tuned with The Voice of Truth?"

"I highly recommend a word."

"A word?"

"Repentance."

"Most will not believe these things."

"But some will rise and lead My sheep to their True Shepherd."

"But the veil is too thick for most, how can I better explain Mathew 24:36?"

"For what happens to the sons of men also happens to animals; one thing befalls them: as one dies, so dies the other. Surely, they all have one breath; man has no advantage over animals, for all is vanity" (Ecclesiastes 3:19).

"So men have no advantages over animals, and all is vanity?"

"If you isolate your vision only in that verse alone you will eventually believe that this is true, but if you study the entire Bible then you can learn the whole truth."

"For example?"

"You were made in God's image, you rule over animals, you named all animals, then how can you not have advantage over animals...?"

"I see."

"...and this is what has happened with Matthew 24:36. First: it was the mistranslation; second: it was men's corruption; and third: most remain confused because they are not listening to Me."

"I need more proof, please."

"And in the morning, 'It will be foul weather today, for the sky is red and threatening.' Hypocrites! You know how to discern the face of the sky, but you cannot discern the signs of the times" (Matthew 16:3).

"Anything else?"

"So teach us to number our days, that we may apply our hearts unto wisdom" (Psalm 90:12, KJV).

"More please, all people need to know now."

"And Jesus came and spoke to them, saying, "All authority has been given to Me in heaven and on earth" (Matthew 28:18).

"All authority in Heaven and on Earth?"

"Yes."

"But that's a significantly huge statement?"

"When did I say this?"

"I don't know, You tell me?"

"After My Resurrection, before I ascended to sit on the right hand of My Father."

"So You received all authority in Heaven and on Earth, and, therefore, You have the authority to know all things, including, The Day of Your Return and the Day of The Antichrist?"

"It is very simple: Mathew 28:18, was written after My Resurrection, and Matthew 24:36, before My Resurrection.  In Mathew 24:36, I was a bondservant, and in Matthew 28:18, I was glorified in My Father's image."

"And why is this whole Matthew 24:36 explanation so important?"

"Because of this misunderstanding and mistranslation almost the whole world has been fooled to believe that no one can know the time and the hour of My soon-to-come return."

"Is the Book really opening now?"

"So shall My word be that goes forth from My mouth;
It shall not return to Me void,
But it shall accomplish what I please,
And it shall prosper in the thing for which I sent it" (Isaiah 55:11).

Chapter 53

# Ezekiel 7:
# The End of This Age

"Ezekiel 7."

"Ezekiel?"

"The end has come upon the four corners of the land."

"The end! The end! Now?"

"Read it slowly:

## Ezekiel 7 (KJV)

"Moreover the word of the Lord came unto me, saying,

Also, thou son of man, thus saith the Lord God unto the land of Israel; An end, the end is come upon the four corners of the land.

Now is the end come upon thee, and I will send mine anger upon thee, and will judge thee according to thy ways, and will recompense upon thee all thine abominations.

And mine eye shall not spare thee, neither will I have pity: but I will recompense thy ways upon thee, and thine abominations shall be in the midst of thee: and ye shall know that I am the Lord.

Thus saith the Lord God; An evil, an only evil, behold, is come.

An end is come, the end is come: it watcheth for thee; behold, it is come.

The morning is come unto thee, O thou that dwellest in the land: the time is come, the day of trouble is near, and not the sounding again of the mountains.

Now will I shortly pour out my fury upon thee, and accomplish mine anger upon thee: and I will judge thee according to thy ways, and will recompense thee for all thine abominations.

And mine eye shall not spare, neither will I have pity: I will recompense thee according to thy ways and thine abominations that are in the midst of thee; and ye shall know that I am the Lord that smiteth.

Behold the day, behold, it is come: the morning is gone forth; the rod hath blossomed, pride hath budded.

Violence is risen up into a rod of wickedness: none of them shall remain, nor of their multitude, nor of any of their's: neither shall there be wailing for them.

The time is come, the day draweth near: let not the buyer rejoice, nor the seller mourn: for wrath is upon all the multitude thereof.

For the seller shall not return to that which is sold, although they were yet alive: for the vision is touching the whole multitude thereof, which shall not return; neither shall any strengthen himself in the iniquity of his life.

They have blown the trumpet, even to make all ready; but none goeth to the battle: for my wrath is upon all the multitude thereof.

The sword is without, and the pestilence and the famine within: he that is in the field shall die with the sword; and he that is in the city, famine and pestilence shall devour him.

But they that escape of them shall escape, and shall be on the mountains like doves of the valleys, all of them mourning, every one for his iniquity.

All hands shall be feeble, and all knees shall be weak as water.

They shall also gird themselves with sackcloth, and horror shall cover them; and shame shall be upon all faces, and baldness upon all their heads.

They shall cast their silver in the streets, and their gold shall be removed: their silver and their gold shall not be able to deliver them in the day of the wrath of the Lord: they shall not satisfy their souls, neither fill their bowels: because it is the stumbling block of their iniquity.

As for the beauty of his ornament, he set it in majesty: but they made the images of their abominations and of their detestable things therein: therefore have I set it far from them.

And I will give it into the hands of the strangers for a prey, and to the wicked of the earth for a spoil; and they shall pollute it.

My face will I turn also from them, and they shall pollute my secret place: for the robbers shall enter into it, and defile it.

Make a chain: for the land is full of bloody crimes, and the city is full of violence.

Wherefore I will bring the worst of the heathen, and they shall possess their houses: I will also make the pomp of the strong to cease; and their holy places shall be defiled.

Destruction cometh; and they shall seek peace, and there shall be none.

Mischief shall come upon mischief, and rumour shall be upon rumour; then shall they seek a vision of the prophet; but the law shall perish from the priest, and counsel from the ancients.

The king shall mourn, and the prince shall be clothed with desolation, and the hands of the people of the land shall be troubled: I will do unto them after their way, and according to their deserts will I judge them; and they shall know that I am the Lord"(Ezekiel 7, KJV).


"Is this real?"

"I allowed it before due to rebellion, and I will allow it again if My little children remain soaked in their wicked ways."

"But there has to be another way?"

"Any recommendations?"

"Shout from heaven, and we will listen."

"My son, the hour is at hand. And those that wholeheartedly desire to blow the trumpets may begin now—before they run out of air."

"Air?"

"Yes. Begin to jog now; all will need their maximum endurance."

"Jogging?"

"Some of My servants will lead many when the collapse strikes unexpectedly, and some will escape to the wilderness with their families—from the turmoil caused by my soon-to-come Judgment."

"The Collapse?"

"I'll tell you about it later, but for now, let me help you with Ezekiel 7."

"How?"

"Let's play a game, you tell Me the verse number and I'll tell you what it means in this hour—for this Era."

"Yes, Lord."

"Verse number two."

"The end is at hand."

"When?"

"Stick to the game plan."

"The fifth."

"Referring to the collapse of all things."

"Like the U.S dollar and all other world currencies?"

"If the dollar holds them?"

"Then they shall all fall?"

"Correct."

"Seventh."

"The trips, the vacations, the partying, the self-indulgence, the planning for college, the planning for self-growth, the business investments, even the planning for weddings ...must all cease. And the focus must be in Me, now, completely. And I shall consider acts of true repentance."

"And why not weddings, they are beautiful, and they are part of Your creation?"

"'For indeed the days are coming in which they will say, 'Blessed are the barren, wombs that never bore, and breasts which never nursed!'" (Luke 23:29). 'But woe to those who are pregnant and to those who are nursing babies in those days!'" (Mark 13:17).

"And this is in 2016?"

"Before 2016 ends, you will see."

"But this isn't fair?"

"Will you like to lead countless pregnant mothers in the midst of an all-out collapse...?

"...In the midst of worldwide confusion—with no food, no shelter, and blood covering the face of the Earth?"

"Not at all."

"Then why will you encourage a honeymoon in times as such?"

"And how about birth control?"

"You don't want Me to go there.   Now wake up! And sound the trumpets before it's too late!"

"But I'm trying to find healing for my penis to satisfy my wife soon?"

"My son."

"Yes, My Lord."

"Will you follow Me?"

"Will you heal me and only allow me to do the least a man ought to do for his divinely given wife?"

"At the appointed time you shall be healed?"

"When? When?" I shouted desperately.

"Will you follow Me, My son?"

"How about those that want to marry, but are willing to not have children because they comprehend what is coming?"

"I encourage union and marriage, even in these times if it is to prepare for what is coming.  But My son, how many marriages will remain united and not participate with their physical duties?"

"I know; the majority will have sex, but..."

"Will you follow Me, My son?"

"The twelfth verse."

"People will faint because they will not be able to buy or sell unless they accept the soon-to-come worldwide payment method implemented by the one-world-government."

"The fourteenth."

"Many have warned of the evil that's coming as My messengers did in biblical times. Many have blown the trumpets to this wicked generation—mirroring the Days of Noah—but almost the whole church remains asleep, and she takes naps during the day."

"Number fifteen."

"Long-suffering will come from all angles."

"16."

"Only a remnant will survive."

"The nineteenth verse."

"Silver and gold usually rise in an economic collapse—people have used it to trade throughout history. But this is the final hour. A worldwide payment method will be implemented as it has been already established in secrecy. I will 'literally' be the only True Salvation when reality strikes relentlessly."

"Twenty-one and twenty-two."

"The enemies are already on the inside: an antichrist and final Pope, Pope Francis, is one enemy, a Jesuit Order trained Pope. And another antichrist is your very own President, Barack H. Obama, the leader of the soon to fall nation. And these two leaders, along with their allies, shall lead a world size army, and defile even My holy places—like the congregations and synagogues—as My hand will be removed almost completely from the surface of the Earth."

"And will you not help us?"

"My hand will carry My true and faithful servants even during these Earth shaking moments."

"So one of these two is the Antichrist?"

"We'll cover this later, My son."

"And what about the extraterrestrial invasion? Could this be the Antichrist coming?"

"My son, I will show you something later."

"Twenty-third."

"'Can two walk together, unless they are agreed?' (Amos 3:3). In union and through Me you shall all stand, and deliverance shall embrace thee."

"The 26th."

"Most will thirst for a sign or a counsel due to the misery and calamity, but words of wisdom will evaporate."

"Twenty-seven."

"My Judgment has come!"

"And why is it written twice in the same chapter: 'Then you shall know that I am the LORD!' And once: 'Then you shall know that I am the LORD who strikes?'"

"Because all must comprehend that these are My trumpets sounding now from heaven. And all will seek Me in these soon-to-unfold horrifying events—even if they don't realize whom they're seeking for.

"Go to the Book of Lamentations."

"La...?"

"Yes."

# Chapter 54

# *The Rebirth Of Lamentations*

**"I**'m here."
"Read the whole book."
"The whole...?"
"It's just five chapters."
"But I'm tired, and..."
"Do you really want to know what's about to unfold?"
"Now?"
"The hour has come, My son."
"Yes, Lord."
"Ready?"
"Wait, wait; are we playing the same game?"
"Yes, but remember that this game can soon become a reality if My people remain dead spiritually."

## Lamentations 1: Jerusalem in Affliction

"How lonely sits the city
That was full of people!
How like a widow is she,
Who was great among the nations!
The princess among the provinces
Has become a slave!

2 She weeps bitterly in the night,
Her tears are on her cheeks;
Among all her lovers
She has none to comfort her.
All her friends have dealt treacherously with her;

They have become her enemies.

3 Judah has gone into captivity,
Under affliction and hard servitude;
She dwells among the nations,
She finds no rest;
All her persecutors overtake her in dire straits.

4 The roads to Zion mourn
Because no one comes to the set feasts.
All her gates are desolate;
Her priests sigh,
Her virgins are afflicted,
And she is in bitterness.

5 Her adversaries have become the master,
Her enemies prosper;
For the Lord has afflicted her
Because of the multitude of her transgressions.
Her children have gone into captivity before the enemy.

6 And from the daughter of Zion
All her splendor has departed.
Her princes have become like deer
That find no pasture,
That flee without strength
Before the pursuer.

7 In the days of her affliction and roaming,
Jerusalem remembers all her pleasant things
That she had in the days of old.
When her people fell into the hand of the enemy,
With no one to help her,
The adversaries saw her

And mocked at her downfall.

8 Jerusalem has sinned gravely,
Therefore she has become vile.
All who honored her despise her
Because they have seen her nakedness;
Yes, she sighs and turns away.

9 Her uncleanness is in her skirts;
She did not consider her destiny;
Therefore her collapse was awesome;
She had no comforter.
"O Lord, behold my affliction,
For the enemy is exalted!"

10 The adversary has spread his hand
Over all her pleasant things;
For she has seen the nations enter her sanctuary,
Those whom You commanded
Not to enter Your assembly.

11 All her people sigh,
They seek bread;
They have given their valuables for food to restore life.
"See, O Lord, and consider,
For I am scorned."

12 "Is it nothing to you, all you who pass by?
Behold and see
If there is any sorrow like my sorrow,
Which has been brought on me,
Which the Lord has inflicted
In the day of His fierce anger.

13 "From above He has sent fire into my bones,
And it overpowered them;
He has spread a net for my feet
And turned me back;
He has made me desolate
And faint all the day.

14 "The yoke of my transgressions was bound;
They were woven together by His hands,
And thrust upon my neck.
He made my strength fail;
The Lord delivered me into the hands of those whom I am not
able to withstand.

15 "The Lord has trampled underfoot all my mighty men in
my midst;
He has called an assembly against me
To crush my young men;
The Lord trampled as in a winepress
The virgin daughter of Judah.

16 "For these things I weep;
My eye, my eye overflows with water;
Because the comforter, who should restore my life,
Is far from me.
My children are desolate
Because the enemy prevailed."

17 Zion spreads out her hands,
But no one comforts her;
The Lord has commanded concerning Jacob
That those around him become his adversaries;
Jerusalem has become an unclean thing among them.

18 "The Lord is righteous,
For I rebelled against His commandment.
Hear now, all peoples,
And behold my sorrow;
My virgins and my young men
Have gone into captivity.

19 "I called for my lovers,
But they deceived me;
My priests and my elders
Breathed their last in the city,
While they sought food
To restore their life.

20 "See, O Lord, that I am in distress;
My soul is troubled;
My heart is overturned within me,
For I have been very rebellious.
Outside the sword bereaves,
At home it is like death.

21 "They have heard that I sigh,
But no one comforts me.
All my enemies have heard of my trouble;
They are glad that You have done it.
Bring on the day You have announced,
That they may become like me.

22 "Let all their wickedness come before You,
And do to them as You have done to me
For all my transgressions;
For my sighs are many,
And my heart is faint."

"This sounds like a horror movie."

"Horror may soon be the movie."

"Horror?"

"Truth delivers you out of horror."

"The first verse."

"Who has been great among the nations for a very long time?"

"America? The U.S?"

"Now the leaders that remain are slaves, and the cities remain desolate."

"Fourth."

"People will mourn because most have disregarded my Holy Days found in Leviticus the 23$^{rd}$ chapter. And rape and horrible crimes shall increase in the land."

"Fifth."

"Because of many with evil hearts, and because of their wicked ways most will end up in concentration camps—and even some of the saints."

"FEMA camps?"

"This is a worldwide Judgment, My son."

"But many are following You step by step: this isn't fair for those?"

"Sound the trumpets My son; for this book is for all who are willing to turn back—to repent with sincerity."

"The seventh verse."

"The fancy cars, the mansions, the extravagant vacations, the fine dining, the ballroom parties, the promiscuity, the excess of greed...will all remain."

"Remain?"

"Yes, but only in their imagination as they all kill each other for a rotten coconut."

"The eighth."

"Her sin has caused her death."

"America?"

"It will be a domino effect, My son."

"And will it affect the whole world?"

"The end.  The end has come, My son."

"In 2016?"

"It is the beginning of the most painful era Mankind shall see."

"And why 2016?"

"We'll get there at the appointed time, My son."

"Ninth."

"America has hidden her wicked actions, her sins.  And her pride will bring her to her knees because she abandoned My Law."

"How about the collapse?"

"It will be terrible."

"Why?"

"She must decrease for all to increase."

"The rest of the world?"

"Only temporarily."

"The New World Order?"

"The New *Fake* World Order."

"Fake?"

"Yes.  The New—Fake god, fake money, fake government, fake laws, fake security, fake peace, and fake everything—World Order."

"And when will we have a real one?"

"I'm coming quickly, My son."

"Number ten."

"Even most congregations and the synagogues will be destroyed."

"But how can You allow this?"

"You'll get the big picture soon, My son."

"The eleventh."

"A slice of bread will be traded for precious stones; a can of sardines for a bike; a can of corn for a gold chain..."

"Why?"

"Can you eat a gold chain and survive?"

"16."

"The tears of the people will create rivers in the desolate land."

"The eighteenth verse."

"My Commandments."

"Your Commandments?"

"Now! In all territory, or it will be too late very soon."

"Nineteen."

"It is written, clearly."

"But how can the priest and the elders, who serve You, die searching for food?"

"They may all wake up now and blow the trumpets as you are, or they may be cut off from The True Vine."

"But aren't they serving You?"

"They are not watching; they are not acting; they are not warning the people; they are not following; they are too busy talking about prosperity, tithing, and self-growth and have failed to blow the trumpets—for much blood is on their hands."

"But they are helping others."

"And they are missing a vital component."

"Which is...?"

"Time. The time of The End of This Age is at hand, and they must be all leading the True Church."

"Where to?"

"So that all focus on blowing the trumpets now. Now! Because the hour is at hand."

"Do I really have to continue writing about these horrific scenes?"

"Many were brave enough to write about it, then; many had no other choice but to live through it; some skim through these scriptures today, and only a remnant truly study and walk in My Word, today— to warn the people. For which category would you like to participate?"

"How much more will You ask me to write from this terror?"

"Word by word the end shall be described."

"Yes, Lord."

### Lamentations 2: God's Anger with Jerusalem

How the Lord has covered the daughter of Zion
With a cloud in His anger!
He cast down from heaven to the earth

The beauty of Israel,
And did not remember His footstool
In the day of His anger.

2 The Lord has swallowed up and has not pitied
All the dwelling places of Jacob.
He has thrown down in His wrath
The strongholds of the daughter of Judah;
He has brought them down to the ground;
He has profaned the kingdom and its princes.

3 He has cut off in fierce anger
Every horn of Israel;
He has drawn back His right hand
From before the enemy.
He has blazed against Jacob like a flaming fire
Devouring all around.

4 Standing like an enemy, He has bent His bow;
With His right hand, like an adversary,
He has slain all who were pleasing to His eye;
On the tent of the daughter of Zion,
He has poured out His fury like fire.

5 The Lord was like an enemy.
He has swallowed up Israel,
He has swallowed up all her palaces;
He has destroyed her strongholds,
And has increased mourning and lamentation
In the daughter of Judah.

6 He has done violence to His tabernacle,
As if it were a garden;
He has destroyed His place of assembly;

The Lord has caused
The appointed feasts and Sabbaths to be forgotten in Zion.
In His burning indignation He has spurned the king and the priest.

7 The Lord has spurned His altar,
He has abandoned His sanctuary;
He has given up the walls of her palaces
Into the hand of the enemy.
They have made a noise in the house of the Lord
As on the day of a set feast.

8 The Lord has purposed to destroy
The wall of the daughter of Zion.
He has stretched out a line;
He has not withdrawn His hand from destroying;
Therefore He has caused the rampart and wall to lament;
They languished together.

9 Her gates have sunk into the ground;
He has destroyed and broken her bars.
Her king and her princes are among the nations;
The Law is no more,
And her prophets find no vision from the Lord.

10 The elders of the daughter of Zion
Sit on the ground and keep silence;
They throw dust on their heads
And gird themselves with sackcloth.
The virgins of Jerusalem
Bow their heads to the ground.

11 My eyes fail with tears,
My heart is troubled;
My bile is poured on the ground

Because of the destruction of the daughter of my people,
Because the children and the infants
Faint in the streets of the city.

12 They say to their mothers,
"Where is grain and wine?"
As they swoon like the wounded
In the streets of the city,
As their life is poured out
In their mothers' bosom.

13 How shall I console you?
To what shall I liken you,
O daughter of Jerusalem?
What shall I compare with you, that I may comfort you,
O virgin daughter of Zion?
For your ruin is spread wide as the sea;
Who can heal you?

14 Your prophets have seen for you
False and deceptive visions;
They have not uncovered your iniquity,
To bring back your captives,
But have envisioned for you false prophecies and delusions.

15 All who pass by clap their hands at you;
They hiss and shake their heads
At the daughter of Jerusalem:
"Is this the city that rise
'The perfection of beauty,
The joy of the whole earth'?"

16 All your enemies have opened their mouth against you;
They hiss and gnash their teeth.

They say, "We have swallowed her up!
Surely this is the day we have waited for;
We have found it, we have seen it!"

17 The Lord has done what He purposed;
He has fulfilled His word
Which He commanded in days of old.
He has thrown down and has not pitied,
And He has caused an enemy to rejoice over you;
He has exalted the horn of your adversaries.

18 Their heart cried out to the Lord,
"O wall of the daughter of Zion,
Let tears run down like a river day and night;
Give yourself no relief;
Give your eyes no rest.

19 "Arise, cry out in the night,
At the beginning of the watches;
Pour out your heart like water before the face of the Lord.
Lift your hands toward Him
For the life of your young children,
Who faint from hunger at the head of every street."

20 "See, O Lord, and consider!
To whom have You done this?
Should the women eat their offspring,
The children they have cuddled?
Should the priest and prophet be slain
In the sanctuary of the Lord?

21 "Young and old lie
On the ground in the streets;
My virgins and my young men

Have fallen by the sword;
You have slain them in the day of Your anger,
You have slaughtered and not pitied.

22 "You have invited as to a feast day
The terrors that surround me.
In the day of the Lord's anger
There was no refugee or survivor.
Those whom I have borne and brought up
My enemies have destroyed."


"This book is too painful to read, My Lord."

"For what is better: For some to read and write the warnings so that many can wake up, or for most to remain in their comfort zones to soon see others lamenting once again?"

"But most do not care about this truth?"

"But the few that do will rise and blow the trumpets till I return."

"The ninth verse."

"For they will panic due to the unknown to soon unfold. Most will have no vision because they have removed My Law from their territory."

"The eleventh and the twelfth."

"Yes, many mothers will see the death of their children because of the famine."

"This is truly unfair."

"And where are the men and women and young adults who claim to serve Me? Where are My people? My little children? Will they rise to prevent this holocaust? Will they blow the trumpets, now, or will they all say, 'What's for lunch?' while their stomachs remain filled?"

"But You must stop all this?"

"Keep writing; you'll know what to do soon."

"Number fourteen."

"False prophets."

"False...?"

"Yes, those that keep talking about everything else but this."

"Are they not blowing the trumpet?"

"Not a whistle.  Not the horn in their cars.  Yet they shout to all, 'Prosperity is coming!'  These are those that call themselves, 'pastors.' And they are leading My sheep one step closer to the guillotine."

"The guillotine!"

"At the slaughter camps."

"But I thought they offered salvation through You, My Lord?"

"Some still do, but, unfortunately, most will beg for literal salvation in the soon to come world-wide persecution."

"The last 42 months?"

"Written in Revelation 13:5 and in the Book of Daniel."

"How can this be?"

"Follow Me and you'll see."

"The fifteenth."

"Is this the city that is called 'The perfection of beauty, the joy of the whole earth'?"

"New York?"

"Remember the book, *The Harbinger* by Jonathan Cahn?"

"The one that's blowing the trumpets and shaking the Earth through Your guidance?"

"Right."

"Isaiah 9:10! 9/11! The towers!?"

"Here:

'The bricks have fallen again."

"All over again?"

"But they will have no stones to rebuild."

"At all?"

"Whatever the people do; it will be temporary."

"And why New York?"

"And Vatican City also."

"The Vatican?"

"New York just represents men power, money, fame, and riches..."

"And?"

"...but the collapse will embrace all things."

"And how about the Vatican?"

"She is the head on Earth, of all deceptions, and she shall fall at her appointed time."

"Number seventeen."

"I also will do this to you: I will even appoint terror over you, wasting disease and fever which shall consume the eyes and cause sorrow of heart. And you shall sow your seed in vain, for your enemies shall eat it" (Leviticus 26:16).

"Why?"

"The Creator must judge His creation."

"Any alternatives?"

"Once again, the word is, 'Repentance.'"

"Verse nineteen."

"Now is the time to arise and shout, 'Hallelujah!' with all sincerity; now is time to seek Me wholeheartedly; today is the day to lift up all hands toward Me."

"And why are the women eating their very own children in the 20th verse?"

"For this reason you are writing as I lead you because no mother or person should eat My little children whom I have wonderfully made."

"Can this really happen, again?"

"Unfortunately, in times of confusion all things are possible, My son."

"Even this?"

"For it is not My will, but judgment is at hand."

"Do we have to do this for three more chapters?"

"Just read them as soon as you find strength, My son."

"Wait! Wait! What's this?

"The tongue of the infant clings
To the roof of its mouth for thirst;
The young children ask for bread,
But no one breaks it for them.

Those who ate delicacies
Are desolate in the streets;
Those who were brought up in scarlet
Embrace ash heaps.

The punishment of the iniquity of the daughter of my people
Is greater than the punishment of the sin of Sodom,
Which was overthrown in a moment,
With no hand to help her!"
(Lamentations 4:4-6, NKJV).

"All will take place in a flash, My son.
"Here:
"Those slain by the sword are better off
Than those who die of hunger;
For these pine away,
Stricken for lack of the fruits of the field.
The hands of the compassionate women
Have cooked their own children;
They became food for them
In the destruction of the daughter of my people"
(Lamentations 4:9, 10).

"I know you carry a heavy burden, My son, but this is what happens
when My people live through wickedness."
"How about this one?

The kings of the earth,
And all inhabitants of the world,
Would not have believed
That the adversary and the enemy
Could enter the gates of Jerusalem"
(Lamentations 4:12).

"These are the U.S borders; they will be destroyed."
"And how about the RFID chips and RFID tattoos?"
"Keep reading."
"They tracked our steps
So that we could not walk in our streets.
Our end was near;
Our days were over,
For our end had come" (Lamentations 4:18).
 "Can this really happen?"
"Keep reading, My son."

## Lamentations 5: A Prayer for Restoration

Remember, O Lord, what has come upon us;
Look, and behold our reproach!
2 Our inheritance has been turned over to aliens,
And our houses to foreigners.
3 We have become orphans and waifs,
Our mothers are like widows.

4 We pay for the water we drink,
And our wood comes at a price.
5 They pursue at our heels;
We labor and have no rest.
6 We have given our hand to the Egyptians
And the Assyrians, to be satisfied with bread.

7 Our fathers sinned and are no more,
But we bear their iniquities.
8 Servants rule over us;
There is none to deliver us from their hand.
9 We get our bread at the risk of our lives,
Because of the sword in the wilderness.

10 Our skin is hot as an oven,
Because of the fever of famine.
11 They ravished the women in Zion,
The maidens in the cities of Judah.
12 Princes were hung up by their hands,
And elders were not respected.
13 Young men ground at the millstones;
Boys staggered under loads of wood.
14 The elders have ceased gathering at the gate,
And the young men from their music.

15 The joy of our heart has ceased;
Our dance has turned into mourning.
16 The crown has fallen from our head.
Woe to us, for we have sinned!
17 Because of this our heart is faint;
Because of these things our eyes grow dim;
18 Because of Mount Zion which is desolate,
With foxes walking about on it.

19 You, O Lord, remain forever;
Your throne from generation to generation.
20 Why do You forget us forever,
And forsake us for so long a time?
21 Turn us back to You, O Lord, and we will be restored;
Renew our days as of old,
22 Unless You have utterly rejected us,
And are very angry with us!

"Is this really it?"
"It is up to you—Mankind."
"What do we do, My Lord?"
"Let us search out and examine our ways,
And turn back to the Lord; Let us lift our hearts and hands

To God in heaven" (Lamentations 3:40, 41).

"That's it?"

"For the Lord will not cast off forever.

Though He causes grief,

Yet He will show compassion

According to the multitude of His mercies.

For He does not afflict willingly,

Nor grieve the children of men"

(Lamentations 3: 31-33).


"And this can happen to America and the whole world?"

"If a kingdom is divided against itself, that kingdom cannot stand" (Mark 3:24).

"And how are we divided?"

"And how is the world not divided?"

"Please save us now, My Lord?"

"My servants, O ye wake up! Pick up your trumpets! Blow to the four corners of the Earth!"

"The trumpets?"

"Each has a gift for this final hour; for millions of lives are at stake."

"Please, not now?"

"For now is the time to leave all fears behind, and to walk in boldness with My Spirit."

"But no one will believe me?"

"But those that do, and react, shall receive their reward soon."

"Are you really coming after this whole thing is over?"

"I'm at the door!"

"You have to have another method besides just using us—your powerless servants."

"Powerless are those failing to see the truth."

"Which truth?"

"The truth I'm pouring out through you."

"But you are The Savior of the world, The One, who knows all things including the fact that most will not listen."

"For I have made all with free will, in My image, and all have the option of coming to Me or running away from Me—a choice."

"But You should have had created us to follow You only so that these horrible things would not exist."

"Then you would not be human; you'll be a robot."

"I give up."

"You must finish the mission, My son."

"Thank God, I'll be raptured!"

"Raptured!?"

"Yes. When those that are faithful will be lifted up into the heavens to dwell with You in a safe and wonderful place."

"My son, allow Me to guide you in truth."

"And 2016?"

"Follow Me and you'll see."

# Chapter 55

# The Rapture:
# Fact or Fiction?

"Go to 1 Thessalonians 4:17."

"Then we which are alive and remain shall be caught up together with them in the clouds, to meet the Lord in the air: and so shall we ever be with the Lord" (1 Thessalonians 4:17).

"This is the reason for your belief in the rapture."

"Correct."

"And unless those days were shortened, no flesh would be saved; but for the elect's sake those days will be shortened" (Matthew 24:22).

"So if the days are shortened for the elect's sake then the elect will be here, on earth, while a massacre occurs?"

"Very clear; isn't it?"

"I need more evidence, please."

"But the woman was given two wings of a great eagle, that she might fly into the wilderness to her place, where she is nourished for a time and times and half a time, from the presence of the serpent" (Revelation 12:14).

"The woman?"

"Yes, My True Church."

"The wilderness?"

"Yes, the wilderness on Earth, and not in Heaven."

"For a time and times and half a time?"

"Three and one-half years, My son."

"So we, your faithful servants, will be led to a safety place on Earth?"

"On Earth, My son."

"But what happened with the Rapture?"

"Will I return twice at the end of the age?"

"Yeah."

"How's that?"

"First to gather the saints, and then, to return with the saints."

"And where did you read that from?"

"I don't know, I remember I heard about this somewhere."

"Don't be deceived, My son; read from My Word."

"Where?"

"Watch therefore, and pray always that you may be counted worthy to escape all these things that will come to pass, and to stand before the Son of Man" (Luke 21:36).

"Watch and pray—to escape?"

"From the soon-to-come three and one-half final years of the Great Tribulation."

"How is this?"

"If the famous Rapture is true then why did I ask My faithful servants to watch and pray countless times throughout My word?"

"I see. And where will You be; where will You stand? I'd like to be there."

"And in that day His feet will stand on the Mount of Olives..." (Zechariah 14:4).

"On Earth?"

"And the Lord shall be King over all the earth.

In that day it shall be—

"The Lord is one,"

And His name one" (Zechariah 14:9).

"Not in Heaven or in the clouds somewhere, but on Earth?"

"One generation passes away, and another generation comes; But the earth abides forever" (Ecclesiastes 1:4).

"And will You truly rule over all the Earth?"

"I am the King of kings."

"And how about these scriptures?

"Then two men will be in the field: one will be taken and the other left. Two women will be grinding at the mill: one will be taken and the other left. Watch therefore, for you do not know what hour your Lord is coming. But know this, that if the master of the house had known what hour the thief would come, he would have watched and not allowed his house to be broken into" (Matthew 24:40-43).

"To where are they taken? To heaven?"

"The word 'heaven' is nowhere to be found from the 40th verse to the 43rd."

"So where will we be taken?"

"No, son, you are not in darkness. A better question could be: Where will the evil one take those living in darkness?"

"But I thought that your servants were the ones you would soon take away?"

"Wherever the ·dead body [carcass] is, there the vultures will gather" (Matthew 24:28, EXB).

"The dead bodies due to the massacre?"

"For as in the days before the flood, they were eating and drinking, marrying and giving in marriage, until the day that Noah entered the ark, and did not know until the flood came and took them all away, so also will the coming of the Son of Man be" (Matthew 24:38, 39).

"And what's this?"

"The flood came and took them all, the whole corrupted world, those living in darkness, but not Noah and his family. So then also shall the coming of the Son of Man be."

"Another flood?"

"You will see everything, but this time, humanity will truly see fire— lots of it!"

"Fire?"

"Fire will soon find its residence on Earth."

"And how about the Rapture?"

"Are you not paying attention?"

"I just need all the evidence, please?"

"The Fifth Seal."

"The fifth?"

"When He opened the fifth seal, I saw under the altar the souls of those who had been slain for the word of God and for the testimony which they held. And they cried with a loud voice, saying, "How long, O Lord, holy and true, until You judge and avenge our blood on those who dwell on the earth?" Then a white robe was given to each of them; and it was said to them that they should rest a little while longer, until both the number of their fellow servants and their brethren, who would be killed as they were, was completed (Revelation 6:9-11).

"Who were slain?"
"Those who held on to Your Word and Your testimony."
"And who else will be slain in this final hour?"
"Their fellow servants and their brethren.  But where is Your protection?"
"Remember, My sheep will not deny My Word nor My testimony, and for some, this act of valor will cost them their temporary and physical lives on Earth."
"How can this be, My Lord?"
"Remember?
'And I saw thrones, and they sat on them, and judgment was committed to them. Then I saw the souls of those who had been beheaded for their witness to Jesus and for the word of God, who had not worshiped the beast or his image, and had not received his mark on their foreheads or on their hands. And they lived and reigned with Christ for a thousand years" (Revelation 20:4).

"I'm lost."
"Will a fair God rapture some of his servants to Heaven, and leave his other servants on Earth to be beheaded?"
"I don't think so.  But a fair God wouldn't allow some of his servants to be beheaded and others to just hide in the wilderness."
"Remember, My son, some will choose to give their lives for the lost until the very end, and this act of courage and love will cost them their

earthly lives. But some will choose to flee to the wilderness wherever My Spirit leads them—a place of escape."

"And what should I do?"

"You will listen to Me as you are listening to Me now, My son."

"So Your faithful servants will be here on Earth during the soon-to-come final 42 months of tribulation?"

"Then they will deliver you up to tribulation and kill you, and you will be hated by all nations for My name's sake" (Matthew 24:9).

"But you said this to your disciples, does this apply to your modern day followers?"

"Is My Word used for true direction and perfection by My followers today?"

"For this load is heavy."

"But he who endures to the end shall be saved" (Matthew 24:13).

"And what's this all about?"

"Why will I ask My faithful servants to endure to the end?"

"To make it; I guess."

"Through what?"

"I don't know."

"The tribulation in the beginning and the Great Tribulation in the end, My son. I would not have asked my servants to 'endure to the end' if I had had a 'rapture plan' in place. My plan is much greater than that."

"So 1 Thessalonians 4:17 is not true, this scripture?

"Then we which are alive and remain shall be caught up together with them in the clouds, to meet the Lord in the air: and so shall we ever be with the Lord" (1 Thessalonians 4:17).

"My son, this will happen in the end, and not at the beginning or the midpoint of the tribulation."

"And Why not in the beginning or somewhere in the middle?"

"My son, we are in the Tribulation period already. Can't you see it clearly?"

"I'm not so bright, You know."

"Can't you see the events mentioned in Matthew 24 literally unfolding before your eyes?"

"I do. But how do we know for sure?"

"If you are watching the events, submerged in My Word, and listening to My Voice of Truth, day by day, then, you shall know when I'm at the door—some will know even the hour."

"Your hour?"

"Yes, My hour, when I shall return to establish My Kingdom on Earth."

"I need the evidence for this one."

"Remember:

'So remember what you have received and heard; and keep it, and repent. Therefore if you do not wake up, I will come like a thief, and you will not know at what hour I will come to you" (Revelation 3:3, NASB).

"So if I wake up I will know the hour as Your hour draws near, or perhaps you have revealed it to some of your faithful servants as the Book of Daniel has been reopened?"

"Keep listening, My son."

"So Your sheep will not be raptured into heaven before the tribulation or in the middle of this Great Tribulation?"

"Behold, I tell you a mystery: We shall not all sleep, but we shall all be changed—in a moment, in the twinkling of an eye, at the last trumpet. For the trumpet will sound, and the dead will be raised incorruptible, and we shall be changed" (1 Corinthians 15:51-52).

"At the last trumpet the dead will be raised incorruptible, and we shall be changed?"

"Exactly."

"But what trumpet are You referring to?"

"Which Book describes the sequences of trumpets with much detail?"

"The Book of Revelation?"

"Here:

"Then the seventh angel sounded: And there were loud voices in heaven, saying, "The kingdoms of this world have become the kingdoms of our Lord and of His Christ, and He shall reign forever and ever!" (Revelation 11:15).

"And this is?"

"The last trumpet, My son."

"So this is why in 1 Corinthians 15:51-52 it states that, '...*at the last trumpet*. For the trumpet will sound, and the dead will be raised incorruptible, and we shall be changed?'"

"Yes."

"But are not the saints raptured prior to this final trumpet?"

"Read all the events in the Book of Revelations, specifically the trumpet sounds, and see if you find a rapture plan in place before the Great Tribulation ends?"

"But how can this be, almost all Christians believe that we will be raptured in to the heavens right before a hell breaks loose?"

"I have revealed to you the truth as the Book of Daniel unseals."

"Can we talk about your love and perhaps something like peace and joy?"

"There is a time for everything, My son."

"And what time is it now?"

"It's time to blow the trumpets! It's time to rise! It's time to shout Hallelujah from the roof tops!"

"Hallelujah! Glory to God! Wait. Wait. Why I'm I shouting if evil is coming?"

"Remember this?

'THIS IS YESHUA—THE KING OF THE JEWS.'"

"My Savior and The Savior of all!"

"I'm at the door, My son."

"I didn't hear the bell ring."

"But you will soon hear the sound of the trumpets—from heaven."

"Soon?"

"Unless I see a worldwide act of repentance soon, then, a worldwide collapse will reveal their nakedness."

# Chapter 56

# The Collapse

"The Collapse? How's this?"

"I will break the pride of your power..." (Leviticus 26:19).

"And what have I done?"

"What is the pride of humanity's power?"

"Money?"

"Everything attached to it shall fall."

"But isn't everything, the good and the evil, attached to it?"

"Everything attached to it will fall, My son."

"Please explain this to me."

"I shared it with you in the Rebirth of Lamentations."

"More thoroughly please?"

"Nehemiah 5:4, 5."

"I'm here."

"Read it out loud."

"There were also those who said, "We have borrowed money for the king's tax on our lands and vineyards. Yet now our flesh is as the flesh of our brethren, our children as their children; and indeed we are forcing our sons and our daughters to be slaves, and some of our daughters have been brought into slavery. It is not in our power to redeem them, for other men have our lands and vineyards" (Nehemiah 5: 4, 5).

"And this means today?"

"You have enslaved your children's children into your passion."

"Our passion?"

"Yes. Your greed and the idolatry of materialism."

"Idolatry of materialism?"

"With its headquarters established in America."

"America?"

"What do you think of this: 'The U.S National Debt is currently; $18,094,552,000,000+-, as of January, 21, 2015?"

"What are those: millions, billions, trillions?"

"A lot, My son.

"And how about this: The Debt per taxpayer is currently; $154,000?"

"A lot more manageable."

"To count, but not to repay. Can you repay your portion now?"

"Can I borrow a loan from the heavenly banks?"

"My son, for I give, and not lend, and in due season, your debt shall be wiped clean."

"Clean. Clean?"

"Yes. For you shall enter into My soon-to-come Kingdom of Heaven, on Earth."

"Soon. Soon! Really?"

"Yes, but prior to this unimaginable Kingdom, the most courageous men of might shall flee naked in that day" (Amos 2:16).

"In that day?"

"When I will break the pride of their power" (Leviticus 26:19).

"But most people, particularly, Americans, believe that they will never fall?"

"Remember?

"Behold, I will make you small among the nations;

You shall be greatly despised.

The pride of your heart has deceived you,

You who dwell in the clefts of the rock,

Whose habitation is high;

You who say in your heart, 'Who will bring me down to the ground?'

Though you ascend as high as the eagle,

And though you set your nest among the stars,

From there I will bring you down," says the Lord" (Obadiah 1: 2-4).

"America shall fall?"

"And the world shall follow in this domino effect."

"How precisely?"

"Remember Zephaniah?

"Zephaniah?"

"He was one of the eleventh-hour prophets to Judah?"

"Oh, Judah?"

"And now, his words shout to the world—through My eleventh-hour prophets of this Era."

"This generation?"

"This hour, My son.

"*Tsephan-yah* means 'YHWH hides' or 'YHWH has hidden.'"

"Will You hide?"

"The great day of the Lord is near;
It is near and hastens quickly.
The noise of the day of the Lord is bitter;
There the mighty men shall cry out.
That day is a day of wrath,
A day of trouble and distress,
A day of devastation and desolation,
A day of darkness and gloominess,
A day of clouds and thick darkness,
A day of trumpet and alarm
Against the fortified cities
And against the high towers.
"I will bring distress upon men,
And they shall walk like blind men,
Because they have sinned against the Lord;
Their blood shall be poured out like dust,
And their flesh like refuse" (Zephaniah 1:14-17).

"Please, My Lord, forgive us."

"I have offered life everlasting, and My goodness, but only a remnant desire to taste and see."

"Can we talk about Your goodness and everlasting life instead?"

"Soon, but first recognize the seriousness of this life-saving message."

"I'm trying here."

"Wail, you inhabitants of Maktesh!
For all the merchant people are cut down;
All those who handle money are cut off" (Zephaniah 1:11).
"Of Maktesh?"
"Replace Maktesh for the world."
"The whole world!"
"You have sown much, and bring in little;
You eat, but do not have enough;
You drink, but you are not filled with drink;
You clothe yourselves, but no one is warm;
And he who earns wages,
Earns wages to put into a bag with holes" (Haggai 1:6).
"What's this all about?"
"Go! Isaiah 24."
"Wait. Wait. Here it is:

## Isaiah 24: Impending Judgment on the Earth

Behold, the Lord makes the earth empty and makes it waste,
Distorts its surface
And scatters abroad its inhabitants.
2 And it shall be:
As with the people, so with the priest;
As with the servant, so with his master;
As with the maid, so with her mistress;
As with the buyer, so with the seller;
As with the lender, so with the borrower;
As with the creditor, so with the debtor.
3 The land shall be entirely emptied and utterly plundered,
For the Lord has spoken this word.

4 The earth mourns and fades away,
The world languishes and fades away;
The haughty people of the earth languish.
5 The earth is also defiled under its inhabitants,

Because they have transgressed the laws,
Changed the ordinance,
Broken the everlasting covenant.
6 Therefore the curse has devoured the earth,
And those who dwell in it are desolate.
Therefore the inhabitants of the earth are burned,
And few men are left.

7 The new wine fails, the vine languishes,
All the merry-hearted sigh.
8 The mirth of the tambourine ceases,
The noise of the jubilant ends,
The joy of the harp ceases.
9 They shall not drink wine with a song;
Strong drink is bitter to those who drink it.
10 The city of confusion is broken down;
Every house is shut up, so that none may go in.
11 There is a cry for wine in the streets,
All joy is darkened,
The mirth of the land is gone.
12 In the city desolation is left,
And the gate is stricken with destruction.
13 When it shall be thus in the midst of the land among the people,
It shall be like the shaking of an olive tree,
Like the gleaning of grapes when the vintage is done.

14 They shall lift up their voice, they shall sing;
For the majesty of the Lord
They shall cry aloud from the sea.
15 Therefore glorify the Lord in the dawning light,
The name of the Lord God of Israel in the coastlands of the sea.
16 From the ends of the earth we have heard songs:
"Glory to the righteous!"
But I said, "I am ruined, ruined!

Woe to me!
The treacherous dealers have dealt treacherously,
Indeed, the treacherous dealers have dealt very treacherously."


17 Fear and the pit and the snare
Are upon you, O inhabitant of the earth.
18 And it shall be
That he who flees from the noise of the fear
Shall fall into the pit,
And he who comes up from the midst of the pit
Shall be caught in the snare;
For the windows from on high are open,
And the foundations of the earth are shaken.


19 The earth is violently broken,
The earth is split open,
The earth is shaken exceedingly.
20 The earth shall reel to and fro like a drunkard,
And shall totter like a hut;
Its transgression shall be heavy upon it,
And it will fall, and not rise again.


21 It shall come to pass in that day
That the Lord will punish on high the host of exalted ones,
And on the earth the kings of the earth.
22 They will be gathered together,
As prisoners are gathered in the pit,
And will be shut up in the prison;
After many days they will be punished.
23 Then the moon will be disgraced
And the sun ashamed;
For the Lord of hosts will reign
On Mount Zion and in Jerusalem
And before His elders, gloriously.

"Too many questions?"

"I'm listening."

"The inhabitants have transgressed the laws, changed the ordinances, and broken the everlasting covenant?"

"My Word and My Commandments have been replaced by the commandments of men, My son."

"How's this?"

"I'll show you later."

"Verses 7, 8, and 9?"

"What do you see?"

"The congregation is without the assembly; the parties have ended."

"And the Assembly without worship or wine."

"And the windows from on high are opened?"

"The windows of heaven, and the windows of the buildings of pride."

"From heaven?"

"For judgment."

"And the buildings of pride?"

"For the penthouses shall become basements."

"When, My Lord?"

"Soon, when the foundations of the Earth are shaken."

"And You will punish the host of exalted ones?"

"In the spiritual realm, and in the political fields."

"Political?"

"Those who have dealt treacherously with the nations; those who stand prideful behind their corrupted Armies."

"America?"

"Repentance!"

"To turn back?"

"Before it's too late."

"But almost the whole world has abandoned Your Commandments and Your Word?"

"And almost the whole world shall suffer due to this devastating collapse."

"Why now in my generation?"

"Assuredly, I say to you, this generation will by no means pass away till all these things take place" (Matthew 24:34).

"And will most be thrown into prison?"

"Remember the FEMA concentration camps?"

"Yes, Lord."

"The prisons of the world will turn into assassination sites."

"The prisons!"

"And many other locations, My son."

"Please stop this My Lord; I beg you."

"Repentance can stop it."

"But then the scriptures won't be fulfilled?"

"Remember The Book of Jonah?"

"Jonah?"

"Then God saw their works, that they turned from their evil way; and God relented from the disaster that He had said He would bring upon them, and He did not do it" (Jonah 3:10).

"And what if not all repent?"

"Not all will."

"So what's the point?"

"Repentance calls the individual and the individual accepts or denies."

"Accepts or denies? Is this some kind of game?"

"No, My son, this is true life."

"True life?"

"Then what's written shall live."

"This isn't fair."

"True fairness is coming soon through My Kingdom, My son."

"But what about for now?"

"Repentance from the heart is the way."

"The way?"

"The escape."

"And how are we supposed to buy or sell; to eat, or to visit a hospital; to simply provide for our families as the heads of our household?"

"Here is the patience and the faith of the saints."

"The saints of the Vatican?"

"No, most of those are devils; remember?"

"Really?"

"Yes. They are the modern Scribes and Pharisees of Matthew the 23$^{rd}$ chapter."

"But many good hearted people follow Pope Francis and the Roman Catholic Church, including, most who label themselves, *Christians*?"

"Yes, you are correct, but, 'come out of her, my people, lest you share in her sins, and lest you receive of her plagues" (Revelation 18:4).

"Come out of her?"

"The Roman Catholic Church and its daughters."

"Really?"

"Now is the time!"

"Its daughters?"

"Come out of New York and the United States of America."

"All people?"

"Some will be called to lead the lost, but most shall flee to their hiding place."

"And how do we know?"

"How are you listening to Me?"

"Why all this?"

"Certain prophesies have broad meanings, and only a remnant shall comprehend."

"And for now?"

"Know that Satan entered Her ages ago, and the Antichrist will soon be revealed..."

"Through The Roman Catholic Church?"

"And through the United States of America."

"And America!?"

"The daughter and partner in crime of the Vatican and of the Jesuit Order."

"Why?"

"Just open your eyes."

"Will The false messiah/false god/Antichrist truly be revealed?"

"Sound the Trumpets."

"But the whole world needs The True Messiah, and not more pain."

"And you will see Me face-to-face after the final age of cannibalism."

"Cannibalism?"

"Yes. When no one could buy or sell unless they receive *The Mark*."

"The mark?

"It's much more than a mark; go to Revelation 13:16-17."

"Now?"

"My clock is running out of sand, My son."

Chapter 57

# *The Mark*

"**H**e causes all, both small and great, rich and poor, free and slave, to receive a mark on their right hand or on their foreheads, and that no one may buy or sell except one who has the mark or the name of the beast, or the number of his name (Revelation 13:16-17).

"So no one will be able to buy or sell?"

"Except one who has 'the mark', or 'the name of the beast', or 'the number of his name.'"

"The mark?"

"The RFID chip and computerized tattoos being used by many currently—is just part of it."

"Really?"

"Just search throughout the internet."

"Ok."

"Have you heard of the RFID chip in The OBAMACARE Bill?"

"In Obamacare?"

"Yes."

"No! Where?"

"In the, '*H.R. 3200 IH section 2521, Pg. 1001 & 1002.*'"

"This can't be true?"

"Read:

*The Secretary shall establish a national medical device registry (in this subsection referred to as the 'registry') to facilitate analysis of postmarket safety and outcomes data on each device that— "is or has been used in or on a patient; "and is— "<u>a class III device; or "a class II device that is implantable, life-supporting, or life-sustaining.</u>*"

"And this is *the mark*?"

"This is just the beginning of the mark—part of the mark."

"And the end?"

"A mark and Antichrist/false god/false messiah worship will be enforced throughout the four corners of the earth, by the Antichrist system."

"How?"

"When the collapse of the U.S. dollar occurs, which will lead to the collapse of all currencies, then, the president of the Broken States will immediately sign all essential 'executive orders' according to his 'false god/antichrist' plan."

"But this is in the Obamacare; are you telling me he is the Antichrist?"

"My son, if I tell you he is; some will stop reading this book at this very moment because of fear..."

"And how about the Pope—Francis?"

"...and if I tell you Pope Francis is the Antichrist then some will do the same."

"Is it an extraterrestrial invasion?

"My son, just keep listening."

"Then what do I tell the people? What is the truth?"

"The president of the United States of America and the leader of Roman Empire will both play a major role in the destruction of Mystery Babylon and the world."

"By 2016?"

"Before that year ends horror shall initiate a journey through the land."

"And Mystery Babylon?"

"From which city in the U.S do the world bankers play evil games?"

"New York?"

"And which monetary currency holds the world's currencies?"

"The U.S dollar."

"And from which city states is the whole world deceived?"

"Vatican City, City of London, and Washington, D.C."

"Correct.

"And what's this all about?"

"Destruction is coming upon all."

"In 2016?"

"2016 is just the beginning of an era of destruction led by these criminals, My son. Tell all My little children to 'come out of her' now, and return to Me—for I long to save them."

"The Jews and Christians?"

"Those who consider themselves children of The God of Abraham, Isaac, and Jacob."

"Come out of her?"

"Yes, as in Revelation 18:4."

"But I thought this referred to the Roman Catholic Church system?"

"Yes, and all the churches influenced by her system, and the United States of America, also."

"So the pope is also an antichrist?"

"The Jesuits believe in ruling the entire world through one man alone."

"Ok?"

"And Pope Francis is the first pope in power—groomed from *The Society of Jesus,* and he's a Jesuit."

"And that's a great thing isn't it?"

"They are the society of Satan—a false god/false savior society."

"An Antichrist system?"

"Using the U.S president, and other secret societies as string-puppets."

"But I thought the Islamic Caliphate were the group behind all this beheading going on."

"My son, they are united; they are a team."

"A team?"

"Working united for the achievement of a mutual goal."

"But how is this possible?"

"The evidence is overwhelming, and if I share it with you; you'll have to write another book."

"But I need something."

"Just look at the infrastructures in Capitol Hill and at the Vatican City. Do they have anything in common?"

"Yes, much."

"Just tell the people to do their personal research for we have a much more vital topic to cover."

"So the Jesuits and the Islamic Caliphate remain steady on the same agenda."

"There is much more than that, but let's remain in pre-school."

"And what do I tell the people?"

"Who was the one who said: 'We are no longer a Christian Nation'?"

"Barack Hussein Obama."

"He is being led to secretly organize all things according to the Jesuit Order and its branches, and simultaneously, as a secret leader of the Muslims."

"But not all Muslims are evil?"

"Correct, but soon the whole world will see the devil in Barack Hussein Obama, and in the 'false messiah organizations' working behind scenes."

"The devil?"

"Clearly. Armageddon is at hand."

"World War III?"

"World War Z."

"In 2016?"

"The noticeable beginning of the 'End of this Age,' My son."

"Mentioned in the Book of Daniel? The last three and one-half years of this Sinful Era?"

"Mentioned through my servants John and Daniel."

"Why, My Lord?"

"...O My people! Those who lead you cause you to err,
  And destroy the way of your paths" (Isaiah 3:12).

"Our leaders?"

"I have raised the wicked ones for the wicked nations."

"You?"

"The Lord has made all for Himself,
Yes, even the wicked for the day of doom" (Proverbs 16:4).
"And what about the number '666' written in the 13<sup>th</sup> chapter of the Book of Revelation?"
"Before 2016 ends; the world will see."
"666?"
"The worst delusion of all times."
"A delusion?"

"The coming of the lawless one is according to the working of Satan, with all power, signs, and lying wonders, and with all unrighteous deception among those who perish, because they did not receive the love of the truth, that they might be saved.  And for this reason God will send them strong delusion, that they should believe the lie, that they all may be condemned who did not believe the truth but had pleasure in unrighteousness" (2 Thessalonians 2:9-12).

"So those who have turned away from the truth will recognize *the evil one* for righteous?"
"It's coming."
"And the so-called 'National Sunday Law' enforcement by the Catholic Church? And the Islamic Caliphate Friday Worship?"
"My son, it is not just 'National Sunday Law', or 'Islamic Caliphate Friday's.' But all My Laws, he and his system, the false messiah and his evil government, will attempt to abolish."
"How's this possible?"
"He shall speak pompous words against the Most High,
Shall persecute the saints of the Most High,
And shall intend to change times and law.
Then the saints shall be given into his hand
For a time and times and half a time" (Daniel 7:25).
"The time and the law?"
"Opposite of My Word."
"Opposite?"

"Those that live by My Word and honor My Sabbath—from sunset on Friday to sunset on Saturday will be forced to worship on a non-biblical day."

"And that's all?"

"It's just the beginning."

"Please deliver us."

"I am deliverance."

"But how, My Lord? How?"

"The name of the Lord is a strong tower: the righteous runneth into it, and is safe" (Proverbs 18:10, KJV).

"The name of the Lord?"

"YHWH"

"Y...H...?"

"My true name, My son."

"Are You going to save us?"

"I suggest a better question."

"Which is?"

"Am I running to the Tower of Strength?"

"And how do we get there?"

"It's in My Word, My son?"

"Where?"

"It's in the tablets, My son."

"The tablets?"

"Written by the Finger of My Father."

"The Ten Commandments?"

"The Ten Laws of Liberty."

"But weren't these abolish at the cross?"

"Follow Me and you'll see.

# Chapter 58

# The Law of Liberty

" **C** ompare the Old Testament with the New Testament."
"Yes, Lord."

|  | Old Testament | New Testament |
|---|---|---|
| **First Commandment** | Exodus 20:3; Deuteronomy 5:7 | Matthew 4:10; Luke 4:8; Revelation 14:7 |
| **Second Commandment** | Exodus 20:4-6; Deuteronomy 5:8-10 | Acts 15:20; 1 Corinthians 6:9-10; Galatians 5:19-20; Ephesians 5:5 |
| **Third Commandment** | Exodus 20:7; Deuteronomy 5:11 | Matthew 5:33-37; 1 Timothy 6:1; James 2:7 |
| **Fourth Commandment** | Exodus 20:8-11; Deuteronomy 5:12-15 | Luke 4:16; 23:55-56; Acts 17:1-2; 18:4; Hebrews 4:9; 1 John 2:6 |
| **Fifth Commandment** | Exodus 20:12; Deuteronomy 5:16 | Matthew 15:4-9; 19:19; Mark 10:19; Luke 18:20; Romans 1:29-30; Ephesians 6:1-3 |
| **Sixth Commandment** | Exodus 20:13; Deuteronomy 5:17 | Matthew 5:21-22; 19:18; Mark 10:19; Luke 18:20; Romans 1:29-30; 13:9 |
| **Seventh Commandment** | Exodus 20:14; Deuteronomy 5:18 | Matthew 5:27-28; 19:18; Mark 10:11-12, 19; Luke 16:18; 18:20; Romans 7:2-3; 13:9 |
| **Eighth Commandment** | Exodus 20:15; Deuteronomy 5:19 | Matthew 19:18; Mark 10:19; Luke 18:20; Romans 13:9; Ephesians 4:28; 1 Peter 4:15; Revelation 9:21 |

| Ninth Commandment | Exodus 20:16; Deuteronomy 5:20 | Matthew 19:18; Mark 10:19; Luke 18:20; Acts 5:3-4; Romans 13:9; Ephesians 4:25 |
|---|---|---|
| Tenth Commandment | Exodus 20:17; Deuteronomy 5:21 | Luke 12:15; Romans 1:29; 7:7; 13:9; 1 Corinthians 6:9-10; Galatians 5:19-21; Ephesians 5:3, 5 |

"Have I changed anything?"

"Not at all."

"For I am the Lord, I do not change;

Therefore you are not consumed, O sons of Jacob" (Malachi 3:6).

"May You explain this?"

"They worship Me in vain, My son?"

"How's this?"

"...Thus you have made the commandment of God of no effect by your tradition. Hypocrites! Well did Isaiah prophesy about you, saying:

'These people draw near to Me with their mouth,

And honor Me with their lips,

But their heart is far from Me.

And in vain they worship Me,

Teaching as doctrines the commandments of men'"

(Matthew 15:6-9).

"This can't be. How is this even possible?"

"Their hearts, when this was said; their hearts, when this was written, and their hearts, today—as history repeats itself—were frozen."

"But aren't many faithful servants worshiping You now?"

"Not everyone who says to Me, 'Lord, Lord,' shall enter the kingdom of heaven, but he who does the will of My Father in heaven. Many will say to Me in that day, 'Lord, Lord, have we not prophesied in Your name, cast out demons in Your name, and done many wonders in Your name?' And then I will declare to them, 'I never knew you; depart from Me, you who practice lawlessness!" (Matthew 7:21-23).

"Prophesying? Casting out demons in your name? And doing many wonders in your name?"
"Yes."
"Isn't this the church?"
"Practicing lawlessness by removing My Law of Liberty—My Ten Commandments."
"Who is doing this?"
"The Devil and Satan, who deceives the whole world" (Revelation 12:9).
"The Devil has entered the church?"
"I warned you all through my servant Paul also."
"Where?"
"But even if our gospel is veiled, it is veiled to those who are perishing, whose minds the god of this age has blinded, who do not believe, lest the light of the gospel of the glory of Christ, who is the image of God, should shine on them" (2 Corinthians 4:3-4).

"Have I been deceived?
"I believe you still reside in an earthly realm.
"My Law is life everlasting."
"Help me here."
"Search through the *Tomorrow's World Magazine*."
"Here? From *The Decline and Fall of the Roman Empire*?"
"Yes."
"The first fifteen bishops of Jerusalem were all circumcised Jews; and the congregation over which they presided united the laws of Moses with the doctrine of Christ" (Edward Gibbon, vol. 1, p.389).
"And this reveals?"
"The whole truth through a single piece of evidence."
"Which is?"
"My son, Christianity's beginnings reflect the whole truth."

"How so?"

"As you may read from its roots:

"...All authority has been given to Me in heaven and on earth" (Matthew 28:18).

"As The King of kings and The Lord of lords."

"And the King said,

"Go therefore and make disciples of all the nations, baptizing them in the name of the Father and of the Son and of the Holy Spirit, teaching them to observe all things that I have commanded you; and lo, I am with you always, even to the end of the age." Amen" (Matthew 28: 19, 20).

"I can clearly see now—in the proof above—how they wholeheartedly observed all things as 'THE KING OF KINGS' commanded from Christianity's birth."

"And why?"

"Why?"

"Why have they abolish My Law of Liberty?"

"Lord, please tell me; for I am only Your servant."

"The Nazarenes were faithful, but again came he—the Deceiver, through the Catholic Fathers during the Dark Ages—and deceived even My faithful servants."

"And why did you allow all this?"

"My son, the story isn't over."

"Really?"

"Those that consider themselves children of the God of Abraham, Isaac, and Jacob—living by My Word, and worshiping Me in spirit and truth and not in vain—will soon see their Lord and Savior as the trumpets  blow and the Resurrection becomes an illogical reality."

"I can't wait to see Your face."

"Live by the Law of Liberty, My son, and you will enter through the Gates."

"Guide me, please."

"Do not think that I came to destroy the Law or the Prophets. I did not come to destroy but to fulfill" (Matthew 5:17).

"To fulfill? And not abolished at the cross? The whole Law?"

"For truly I say to you, until heaven and earth pass away, not the smallest letter or stroke shall pass from the Law until all is accomplished" (Matthew 5:18, NASB).

"And when are Heaven and Earth passing away?"

"Then I saw a new heaven and a new earth; for the first heaven and the first earth passed away, and there is no longer any sea" (Revelation 21:1, NASB).

"How soon will I see this new Heaven and new Earth?"

"The second and final half of terror, on Earth—written by the prophets Daniel and John—shall commence before 2016 ends."

"So Your Law remains?"

"Look up!"

"I am."

"Do you still see a Heaven?"

"Yes, Lord."

"And the sun shining right through it?"

"Yes, Lord."

"Now bring your chin down before someone jabs you in the mouth."

"I'm ready."

"Do you still see the Earth?"

"Yes, Lord."

"With these two verses alone I've given you 100% proof of My current Law of Liberty—The Ten Commandments" (Matthew 5:18; Revelation 21:1).

"But some people still remain stupidly deceived by the Deceiver—the Devil and Satan. I need more."

"Is not this clear enough?"

"But how about those that say that You were not referring to the Ten Commandments in Matthew 5:18?"

"For I say to you, that unless your righteousness exceeds the righteousness of the scribes and Pharisees, you will by no means enter the kingdom of heaven" (Matthew 5:20).

"And this is?"

"The very next verse."

"Didn't these individuals live by the entire Law?"

"They sure tried, My son."

"And You are suggesting?"

"No, My son, for this is My Word to all My children, and not a suggestion: Keep My Commandments."

"Some still doubt."

"Many still doubt."

"So what do we do?"

"Which topics were covered immediately following these verses?"

"Murder, adultery, and..."

"Aren't these mentioned through the Ten Commandments?"

"Absolutely."

"Case solved."

"My Lord, please forgive me, but many still doubt."

"A higher Law was established, My son."

"Higher than something we couldn't keep to start with?"

"For God so loved the world that He gave His only begotten Son, that whoever believes in Him should not perish but have everlasting life" (John 3:16).

"My Lord, forgive me for my ignorance, but what does this verse has to do with the Ten Commandments?"

"For I am the only begotten Son, and through My death and resurrection I have given humanity all things necessary to overcome all evil."

"Really!"

"Through My unconditional love all humanity may choose to live through Me and My Spiritual Law—the Ten Commandments."

"Aren't we saved by grace?"

"Absolutely. Here:

'For by grace you have been saved through faith, and that not of yourselves; it is the gift of God, not of works, lest anyone should boast'" (Ephesians 2:8-9).

"And we are not supposed to do anything as it states in the 9th verse, right?"

"Incorrect, My son."

"How so?"

"Aren't you also saved by Me (Deut. 33:29; Rom 10:13; John 10:9; Acts 15:11); by hope (Rom. 8:24); by enduring unto the end...(Matt 24:13)?

"I agree."

"In which of these verses did you see the removal of My Law?"

"In Ephesians 2:9."

"The famous Ephesians 2:9, the verse behind lawlessness—this one: 'not of works, lest anyone should boast'" (Ephesians 2:9).

"Yes, Lord."

"It simply states that no one could have done anything through human effort to earn My death and resurrection—it was My gift, My son."

"O Lord, forgive us."

"You've been forgiven, My son.

"But why do you call Me 'Lord, Lord,' and not do the things which I say?" (Luke 6:46).

"Me!?"

"No, My son; those who worship Me in vain.

"Whoever comes to Me, and hears My sayings and does them, I will show you whom he is like: He is like a man building a house, who dug deep and laid the foundation on the rock. And when the flood arose, the stream beat vehemently against that house, and could not shake it, for it was founded on the rock. But he who heard and did nothing is like a man who built a house on the earth without a foundation, against which the stream beat vehemently; and immediately it fell. And the ruin of that house was great" (Luke 6:47-49).

"But how can we really keep it; it could be difficult at times?"

"I have been crucified with Christ; it is no longer I who live, but Christ lives in me; and the life which I now live in the flesh I live by faith in the Son of God, who loved me and gave Himself for me (Galatians 2:20).

"I am in you, and all who truly surrender may have the Son of the Living God, now on Earth, and in My soon-to-come Kingdom of Heaven on Earth (Revelation 21:2).

"So 'I can [truly] do all things through [The Messiah] who strengthens me? (Philippians 4:13).

"...The things which are impossible with men are possible with God" (Luke 18:27).

"Including—keeping Your Commandments?"

"If you love Me, keep My commandments" (John 14:15).

"How do we do this in such a time to soon come?"

"Never lose sight of your reward, My son."

"My reward?"

"Blessed is the one who perseveres under trial because, having stood the test, that person will receive the crown of life that the Lord has promised to those who love him" (James 1:12, NIV).

"The crown of life?"

"Overcome, all you My little children! And you shall inherit My kingdom!"

"Glory to God! Glory! Glory! Hallelujah!!!"

"My son, 'Jesus Christ is the same yesterday, today, and forever'" (Hebrews 13:8).

"Really?"

"Read, My son:

"Now it shall come to pass in the latter days

That the mountain of the Lord's house

Shall be established on the top of the mountains,

And shall be exalted above the hills;

And all nations shall flow to it.

Many people shall come and say,

"Come, and let us go up to the mountain of the Lord,

To the house of the God of Jacob;
He will teach us His ways,
And we shall walk in His paths."
For out of Zion shall go forth the law,
And the word of the Lord from Jerusalem.
He shall judge between the nations,
And rebuke many people;
They shall beat their swords into plowshares,
And their spears into pruning hooks;
Nation shall not lift up sword against nation,
Neither shall they learn war anymore" (Isaiah 2:2-4).

"My Lord, can we skip these soon-to-come three and one-half years of terror?"

"My son, judgment must come upon the Earth, but you:

'Watch therefore, and pray always that you may be counted worthy to escape all these things that will come to pass, and to stand before the Son of Man'" (Luke 21:36).

"I'm watching!"

"You lack one thing, My son."

"I do?"

"Blow the trumpets."

"How?"

"Read:

"Again the word of the Lord came to me, saying, "Son of man, speak to the children of your people, and say to them: 'When I bring the sword upon a land, and the people of the land take a man from their territory and make him their watchman, when he sees the sword coming upon the land, if he blows the trumpet and warns the people, then whoever hears the sound of the trumpet and does not take warning, if the sword comes and takes him away, his blood shall be on his own head. He heard the sound of the trumpet, but did not take warning; his blood shall be upon himself. But he who takes warning will save his life. But if the watchman sees the sword coming and does not blow the trumpet, and the people are not warned, and the sword comes and takes any person from among them, he is taken away in his iniquity; but his blood I will require at the watchman's hand.'

"So you, son of man: I have made you a watchman for the house of Israel; therefore you shall hear a word from My mouth and warn them for Me. When I say to the wicked, 'O wicked man, you shall surely die!' and you do not speak to warn the wicked from his way, that wicked man shall die in his iniquity; but his blood I will require at your hand. Nevertheless if you warn the wicked to turn from his way, and he does not turn from his way, he shall die in his iniquity; but you have delivered your soul.

"Therefore you, O son of man, say to the house of Israel: 'Thus you say, "If our transgressions and our sins lie upon us, and we pine away in them, how can we then live?"' Say to them: 'As I live,' says the Lord God, 'I have no pleasure in the death of the wicked, but that the wicked turn from his way and live. Turn, turn from your evil ways! For why should you die, O house of Israel?'" (Ezekiel 33:1-11).

"Can I borrow your trumpets from heaven?"
"Your request has been granted, My son: Blow the trumpets!"
"Now?"
"I'm coming quickly!"
"And the commandments?"
"For this is the love of God, that we keep His commandments. And His commandments are not burdensome" (1 John 5:3).
"This is Your love?
"My true love, My son:
'This is love, that we walk according to His commandments. This is the commandment, that as you have heard from the beginning, you should walk in it'" (2 John 1:6).

"As we have heard from the beginning?"

"Remember: 'In the beginning God created the heavens and the earth'" (Genesis 1:1).

"Ok?"

"I repeat: "For truly I say to you, until heaven and earth pass away, not the smallest letter or stroke shall pass from the Law until all is accomplished" (Matthew 5:18, NASB).

"In conclusion?"

"Let us hear the conclusion of the whole matter:

Fear God and keep His commandments,

For this is man's all.

For God will bring every work into judgment,

Including every secret thing,

Whether good or evil" (Ecclesiastes 12:13-14).

"Are You really coming quickly?"

"My sheep hear My voice, and I know them, and they follow Me" (John 10:27).

"How?"

"Listen! Listen!"

"Listen?"

"The Sabbath."

"What about it?"

# Chapter 59

# The Sabbath

"It's in the beginning."
"Where?"
"How you are fallen from heaven,
O Lucifer, son of the morning!
How you are cut down to the ground,
You who weakened the nations!" (Isaiah 14:12).
"Lucifer fell from Heaven?"
"And has weakened all Nations."
"How so, exactly?"
"Remember the 4th Commandment?"
"The fourth?"
"I asked you to remember it."
"When?"
"It is the only Commandment that begins with 'remember.'"
"Remember?"
"Remember the Sabbath day, to keep it holy. Six days you shall labor and do all your work, but the seventh day is the Sabbath of the Lord your God. In it you shall do no work: you, nor your son, nor your daughter, nor your male servant, nor your female servant, nor your cattle, nor your stranger who is within your gates. For in six days the Lord made the heavens and the earth, the sea, and all that is in them, and rested the seventh day. Therefore the Lord blessed the Sabbath day and hallowed it" (Exodus 20:8-11).

"Can I do a good deed on the Sabbath?"
"As long as the definition of 'good' is defined by My Word."
"By Your Word?"
"...What man is there among you who has one sheep, and if it falls into a pit on the Sabbath, will not lay hold of it and lift it out? Of how

much more value then is a man than a sheep? Therefore it is lawful to do good on the Sabbath" (Matthew 12: 11, 12).

"And what does the 4<sup>th</sup> Commandment have to do with Lucifer?"
"Remember?
"And they said, "Come, let us build ourselves a city, and a tower whose top is in the heavens; let us make a name for ourselves, lest we be scattered abroad over the face of the whole earth" (Genesis 11:4).
"And this?"
"It's the pride of men powered by Lucifer:
"For [he] have said in [his] heart:
'I will ascend into heaven,
I will exalt my throne above the stars of God;
I will also sit on the mount of the congregation
On the farthest sides of the north;
I will ascend above the heights of the clouds,
I will be like the Most High.'" (Isaiah 14:13-14).

"He wanted to be like the Most High?"
"What happens at My Father's Throne?"
"Never been there, My Lord."
"The four living creatures, each having six wings, were full of eyes around and within. And they do not rest day or night, saying:
"Holy, holy, holy,
Lord God Almighty,
Who was and is and is to come!"
Whenever the living creatures give glory and honor and thanks to Him who sits on the throne, who lives forever and ever, the twenty-four elders fall down before Him who sits on the throne and worship Him who lives forever and ever, and cast their crowns before the throne, saying:
"You are worthy, O Lord,
To receive glory and honor and power;
For You created all things,

And by Your will they exist and were created" (Revelation 4:8-11).

"Unceasing worship?"
"And not in vain."
"So we can worship our Father any time?"
"You can worship our Father in Heaven anytime, but remember the Sabbath day, to keep it holy."
"On Resurrection Sunday?"
"Resurrected by the Spiritually Dead Roman Catholic Church?
"The Dead Catholic Church!"
"Read, My son:
"The Catholic Church for over one thousand years before the existence of a Protestant, by virtue of her divine mission, changed the day from Saturday to Sunday" (Catholic Mirror, Sept., 1893).
"Tertullian (202ad) is the first writer who expressly mentions the Sunday rest: 'We, however (just as tradition has taught us), on the day of the Lord's Resurrection ought to guard not only against kneeling, but every posture and office of solicitude, deferring even our businesses lest we give any place to the devil'" (article: "Sunday," The Catholic Encyclopedia). [That was not until 202ad, more than 170 years after the death, burial, and resurrection of the Messiah, Jesus Christ!]

"Tradition?"
"Keep reading, My son:

"Later, in the fourth century AD, the Roman emperor Constantine enforced Sunday worship throughout his empire. Constantine had been a pagan sun-worshiper. He gave the following edict in 321AD: "On the venerable day of the Sun let all magistrates and people ... rest" (article: "Sunday Legislation," Schaff-Herzog Encyclopedia of Religious Knowledge).

"Did You honor the Sabbath?"

"So He came to Nazareth, where He had been brought up. And as His custom was, He went into the synagogue on the Sabbath day, and stood up to read. And He was handed the book of the prophet Isaiah. And when He had opened the book, He found the place where it was written:

"The Spirit of the Lord is upon Me,
Because He has anointed Me
To preach the gospel to the poor;
He has sent Me to heal the brokenhearted,
To proclaim liberty to the captives
And recovery of sight to the blind,
To set at liberty those who are oppressed;
To proclaim the acceptable year of the Lord."

Then He closed the book, and gave it back to the attendant and sat down. And the eyes of all who were in the synagogue were fixed on Him. And He began to say to them, "Today this Scripture is fulfilled in your hearing" (Luke 4:16-21).

"So not only did You honor the Sabbath, but You also fulfilled the scriptures?

"And the Word became flesh and dwelt among us, and we beheld His glory, the glory as of the only begotten of the Father, full of grace and truth" (John 1:14).

"How about the disciples; did they honor the Sabbath as You did, also?"

"Now when they had passed through Amphipolis and Apollonia, they came to Thessalonica, where there was a synagogue of the Jews. Then Paul, as his custom was, went in to them, and for three Sabbaths reasoned with them from the Scriptures, explaining and demonstrating that the Christ had to suffer and rise again from the dead, and saying, "This Jesus whom I preach to you is the Christ." And some of them were persuaded; and a great multitude of the devout Greeks, and not a few of the leading women, joined Paul and Silas" (Acts 17:1-4).

"Anything else?"

"Much more; take a look:

"Now when Paul and his party set sail from Paphos, they came to Perga in Pamphylia; and John, departing from them, returned to Jerusalem. But when they departed from Perga, they came to Antioch in Pisidia, and went into the synagogue on the Sabbath day and sat down. And after the reading of the Law and the Prophets, the rulers of the synagogue sent to them, saying, "Men and brethren, if you have any word of exhortation for the people, say on" (Acts 13:13-15).

"Why so much emphasis on the Sabbath day?"

"So when the Jews went out of the synagogue, the Gentiles begged that these words might be preached to them the next Sabbath. Now when the congregation had broken up, many of the Jews and devout proselytes followed Paul and Barnabas, who, speaking to them, persuaded them to continue in the grace of God. On the next Sabbath almost the whole city came together to hear the word of God" (Acts 13:42-44).

"They were true saints, weren't they?"

"...And they kept My Word" (John 17:6).

"So you did not resurrect on Sunday?"

"The false god/false messiah/Antichrist system resurrects on Sundays."

"But there are many Catholics that love you wholeheartedly."

"Unless they come out of her, Protestants and Catholics will remain wholeheartedly deceived."

"To come out of the Roman Catholic Church?"

"Not only, My son, but out of every 'Sunday Worship System' also."

"And what's so evil about Sundays?"

"Confusion."

"Confusion?"

"My little children remain confuse in every other aspect of life and of My Word due to this false worship system."

"How so?"

"If they cannot obey the only single commandment of the Ten Commandments designed for an appointed time, how can they discern even the times of My appointed return or the times of the arrival of the false god/false messiah?"

"But we've been deceived by the Roman Catholic Institution?"

"Satan has entered her."

"As he entered Judas?"

"But he is moving quicker now."

"Why?"

"His time is at hand. And he knows the truth."

"But he is not the Truth."

"Can't you see, My son?"

"In the couch?"

"No."

"Next to me?"

"No."

"Where?"

"He wanted to be worshiped from the beginning, but since this never became his reality in Heaven he accomplished it on Earth."

"He is truly the ruler of this world, and the prince of the power of the air" (John 12:31, Ephesians 2:2).

"Yet [he] shall be brought down to Sheol,

To the lowest depths of the Pit" (Isaiah 14:15).

"When O Lord? When?"

"You will see his true desires beginning in 2016, and soon after, he will surely receive his reward:

"Those who see you will gaze at you,

And consider you, saying:

'Is this the man who made the earth tremble,

Who shook kingdoms,

Who made the world as a wilderness

And destroyed its cities,
Who did not open the house of his prisoners?'" (Isaiah 14:16-17).

"Will You open the house of the prisoners?"

"From this very moment, let all those who are called by My Name; those who consider themselves children of the God of Abraham, Isaac, and Jacob lift up their hands and shout, "Hallelujah!"

"Hallelujah?"

"Hallelujah!"

"Hallelujah!! Wait. Wait. Why?"

"Because all prisoners, all people, can initiate the escape plan, now."

"Right now?"

"Right now. Just tell them to unite now more intensely than history has ever recalled."

"When?"

"On My true Sabbath, My son—from sundown on Friday to sundown on Saturday."

"On every Sabbath?"

"Until My Kingdom comes."

"And what do we do?"

"Just worship! Just sing beautifully!"

"But I can't sing?"

"O yes you can; just worship in Spirit and Truth!"

"No longer on Sundays?"

"By uniting to worship on Sundays you remain as a prisoner of Lucifer."

"But many good and faithful servants worship You sincerely on Sundays?"

"And they faithfully remain in bondage as they worship Me in vain."

"But you have healed me on Sunday worship gatherings."

"My grace has covered the ignorance of My little children."

"What's so evil about it, my Lord?"

"Bring no more futile sacrifices;
Incense is an abomination to Me.
The New Moons, the Sabbaths, and the calling of assemblies—

I cannot endure iniquity and the sacred meeting.
Your New Moons and your appointed feasts
My soul hates;
They are a trouble to Me,
I am weary of bearing them.
**When you spread out your hands,**
**I will hide My eyes from you;**
**Even though you make many prayers,**
**I will not hear.**
**Your hands are full of blood.**
"Wash yourselves, make yourselves clean;
Put away the evil of your doings from before My eyes.
Cease to do evil,
Learn to do good;
Seek justice,
Rebuke the oppressor;
Defend the fatherless,
Plead for the widow" (Isaiah 1:13-17).


"And You are referring to...?"
"Christmas, Easter, Halloween, Saint Valentin's Day, Saint Patrick's Day, Ash Wednesday...
"I hate, I despise your feast days,
And I do not savor your sacred assemblies" (Amos 5:21).
"Really?
"But these are innocent festivals and almost all children love Christmas. Right?"
"Who's leading My little children, My son?"
"I guess we are."
"And why are you writing this book, My son?"
"To sound the trumpets."
"And who will not listen?"
"I guess some deceived will and some deceived will not."
"My son, most just don't care."

"Why?"

"They imagine that all things will remain perfectly organized, according to their individually organized life, created by their selfishly tailored culture, no matter the circumstance hovering their environment.

"Most ignore their current reality in a perfectly deceived environment, but only a remnant escapes from an environment when reality is no longer perfect."

"A remnant escapes?"

"From the soon-to-come worldwide Great Tribulation."

"The Great Tribulation?"

"And pray that your flight may not be in winter or on the Sabbath" (Matthew 24:20).

"During Christmas season?"

"For then there will be great tribulation, such as has not been since the beginning of the world until this time, no, nor ever shall be. And unless those days were shortened, no flesh would be saved; but for the elect's sake those days will be shortened" (Matthew 24:21, 22).

"And how about the sharing of gifts and the joy of Christmas? Most Christians see it as the celebration of Your birth, right?"

"My son, Christmas was celebrated long before My coming to Earth. It is a pagan tradition; just search it. If it is not found in My Word, then I feel as in Isaiah 1:13-17, and Amos 5:21."

"But isn't this book about the rise of the false messiah/the false god in 2016?"

"Correct."

"And why are we having a dialog about Christmas and all sorts of things?"

"All connects in the end, My son—all."

"All?"

"Follow Me and you'll see."

"Where to; where's the truth?"

"Begin from the 23rd chapter of the Book of Leviticus."

"Isn't this the Old Testament, and, therefore, no longer valid?"

"Would you like a New Testament Scripture?"

"Sure!"

"All Scripture is given by inspiration of God, and is profitable for doctrine, for reproof, for correction, for instruction in righteousness, that the man of God may be complete, thoroughly equipped for every good work" (2 Timothy 3:16, 17).

"All Scripture?"

"All: New and Old Testament.

"Again, go to the 23rd chapter of the Book of Leviticus."

"The Weekly Sabbath? Passover? The Feast of Unleavened Bread? The Day of Pentecost? The Feast of Trumpets? The Day of Atonement? The Feast of Tabernacles? The Last Great Day? Aren't these to be honored by the Jewish people only?"

"These are God's Holy Days, My son, and not just Jewish Festivals. Those that honor YHWH, honor these, My son."

"I try to honor You daily, but I've never heard of these Biblical Holy Days."

"The prince of the power of the air has used well his devices, and most remain in a strong delusion, but you go now, and live by the Truth."

"What is the truth?"

"...I am the way, the truth, and the life. No one comes to the Father except through Me" (John 14:6).

"Through You?"

"Only through Me the whole truth can be found.

"Only My way leads to the Main Gate.

"And only through My Gate can you enter into everlasting life."

"How can I get there, My Lord?"

"My sheep hear My voice, and I know them, and they follow Me" (John 10:27).

"But I'm not a sheep."

"I am the good shepherd. The good shepherd gives His life for the sheep" (John 10:11).

"Can I be your sheep?"

"Keep listening, My son."

"Just like that; Your sheep hear Your voice, and keep listening?"

"And they follow Me also."

"And the eternal life part; is it truly eternal?"

"And I give them eternal life, and they shall never perish; neither shall anyone snatch them out of My hand. My Father, who has given them to Me, is greater than all; and no one is able to snatch them out of My Father's hand. I and My Father are one" (John 10:28-30).

"My Lord, why is honoring the Sabbath from sundown on Friday through sundown on Saturday so important?

"Because if you can honor a weekly seventh day Sabbath, then the Law of the Sabbath year will shine truth among My sheep..."

"The Law of the Sabbath year?"

"...and My sheep will seek for more wisdom."

"Wisdom?"

"And they shall find a portion of it in the Law of the year of Jubilee."

"The Law?"

"And if My sheep keep listening then they will comprehend the soon-to-come rise of the Antichrist before 2016 ends."

"In 2016?"

"My son, begin with the 4th."

"The 4th?"

"Truth shall spring out of the earth,
And righteousness shall look down from heaven" (Psalm 85:11).

"Truth? But how about the 4th?"

"...I tell you that if these should keep silent, the stones would immediately cry out" (Luke 19:40).

"The stones crying?"

"The tablets were the 4th remains written, also, are crying in this very moment to all humanity, My son."

"Now tablets, but what about the 4th?"

"It's in the tablets, My son..."

"I'm still asking for the meaning of the 4th."

"...written by My Father's finger."

"Ok, I'm lost."

"My son, the fourth is the honoring of the 4th Commandment, the Sabbath; the tablets are where My Father wrote the Ten Commandments, and the stones are crying to the whole world, at this very moment, through the Stone the builders rejected."

"The builders rejected?"

"The Chief Cornerstone."

"Now, The Chief Cornerstone?"

"Whoever falls on that stone will be broken; but on whomever it falls, it will grind him to powder" (Luke 20:18).

"And now it grinds to powder?"

"My son, choose to be broken and you'll never smell the powder."

"I give up."

"For I am the Chief Cornerstone:

"I am the bread of life. He who comes to Me shall never hunger, and he who believes in Me shall never thirst" (John 6:35).

"You give to all?"

"To the hungry and thirsty."

"And how about 2016 and the rising of the false messiah/false god system—the Antichrist?"

"Follow Me and you'll see."

## Chapter 60

# *Yeshua Ha Mashiach*

"**B**ut some, especially the Jewish people, don't even believe that You are the True Messiah. Why should they believe in the coming of an Antichrist—a false messiah?"

"Remember the Old Testament?"

"Yes."

"My Jewish people believe in it—some live by it."

"And?"

"Who did Moses and the Prophets say would be The Messiah?

"I don't know."

"Allow Me to demonstrate this truth minimally, My son.

### The Messiah's Lineage

- Would come from the seed of a woman and not a man (Genesis 3:15).
- Would be descended from the seed of Abraham (Genesis 12:3).
- Would be descended from the seed of Isaac (Genesis 17:19).
- Would be descended from the seed of Jacob (Genesis 28:14).
- Would be descended from the seed of Jesse (Isaiah 11:1).
- Would come from the Tribe of Judah (Genesis 49:10).

### The Messiah's Birth

- Would be heir to the Throne of David (Isaiah 9:7 & 2 Samuel 7:13).
- Would be born during a time of infant massacres (Jeremiah 31:15).
- Would be born in Bethlehem (Micah 5:2).
- Would be born of a virgin (Isaiah 7:14).

## The Messiah's Walk

- Would be declared the Son of God (Psalm 2:7).
- Would be a Prophet that preached in Galilee (Isaiah 9:1).
- Would be a Prophet as foretold of by Moses (Deuteronomy 18:15).
- Would be compassionate and heal the brokenhearted (Isaiah 61:1).
- Would be rejected by His own people (Isaiah 53:3).
- Would be hated without a cause (Psalm 69:4).
- Would be a Jewish Priest after The Order of Melchizedek (Psalm 110:4).
- Would enter Jerusalem on the colt of an ass (Zechariah 9:9).
- Would teach in parables (Psalm 8:2).
- Would not be understood (Isaiah 6:9).
- Would perform miracles (Isaiah 35:5).

## The Messiah's Rejection

- Would be betrayed by a friend (Psalm 41:9).
- Would be sold for Thirty Pieces of Silver (Zechariah 11:12).
- The money would be used for a Potter's Field (Zechariah 11:13).
- Would be abandoned by His disciples (Zechariah 13:7).
- Would be accused by false witnesses (Psalm 35:11).
- Would be smitten and spat upon (Isaiah 50:6).

"My son, all these I fulfilled and more."

"But not all believe?"

"You search the Scriptures, for in them you think you have eternal life; and these are they which testify of Me. But you are not willing to come to Me that you may have life.

"I do not receive honor from men. But I know you, that you do not have the love of God in you. I have come in My Father's name, and you do not receive Me; if another comes in his own name, him you will receive. How can you believe, who receive honor from one another, and do not seek the honor that *comes* from the only God? Do not think that I shall accuse you to the

Father; there is *one* who accuses you—Moses, in whom you trust. For if you believed Moses, you would believe Me; for he wrote about Me. But if you do not believe his writings, how will you believe My words?" (John 5:39-47).

"But still, not all believe?"

"It's ok; I'm not trying to save the whole world at this very moment."

"You're not?"

"If I wanted to save the whole world now, in this very moment, don't you think I would?"

"And why don't You? We desperately need a Savior to rescue us now."

"I am El Shaddai—The All-Sufficient One."

"But the world is insufficiently completed."

"My Word is perfect, My son."

"Your Word?"

"In it, you may allocate My perfect plan for Mankind."

"Can I search for it now?"

"Yes, but search also for the soon-to-come worldwide calamities prior to My Return..."

"Your return?"

"...And prior to the establishment of The Kingdom of Heaven soon coming to Earth."

"Where may I begin searching?"

# Chapter 61

# The End:
# Matthew 24

"**T**ake heed that no one deceives you" (Matthew
24:4).

• • • "Deception?"

"For many will come in My name, saying, 'I am the Christ,' and will
deceive many" (Matthew 24:5).

"Claiming to be You?"

"And claiming to be of My flock.

"And you will hear of wars and rumors of wars..." (Matthew 24:6).

"Wars?"

"Many wars."

"But we've had wars and rumors of wars since men received a spirit,
and everything remains the same?"

"Remember:

"But you, Daniel, shut up the words, and seal the book until the time
of the end; many shall run to and fro, and knowledge shall increase"
(Daniel 12:4).

"And this?"

"I'm unsealing the book through you and My true servants."

"And knowledge is increasing?"

"Because of the unsealing, because of technology, and because of
time—for now is the time!"

"Unsealing? Technology? Time?"

"The availability of these were an impossibility then, but today, they
have become mankind's reality."

"O Voice of Truth please help us?"

"...See that you are not troubled; for all these things must come to
pass, but the end is not yet" (Matthew 24:6).

"What else should I expect?"

"For nation will rise against nation, and kingdom against kingdom. And there will be famines, pestilences, and earthquakes in various places" (Matthew 24:7).

"But this is all I see in the news now?"

"This nation is greater than that one.

"This one has the better technology.

"This other one claims to be The Beast."

"All these are the beginning of sorrows" (Matthew 24:8).

"The beginning?"

"Remember: 'Then they will deliver you up to tribulation and kill you, and you will be hated by all nations for My name's sake'" (Matthew 24:9).

"Tribulation? Kill us? Hated by all nations for Your name's sake? What kind of security is this?"

"A prudent man foresees evil and hides himself,

But the simple pass on and are punished" (Proverbs 22:3).

"Hide from who? I'm not afraid."

"My son, judgment is coming upon the land very soon and if you consider yourself My servant, depart from it now."

"Now?"

"...Come out of her, my people, lest you share in her sins, and lest you receive of her plagues" (Revelation 18:4)

"Right now?"

"Go forth from Babylon!

Flee from the Chaldeans!

With a voice of singing,

Declare, proclaim this,

Utter it to the end of the earth;

Say, "The Lord has redeemed

His servant Jacob!"

And they did not thirst

When He led them through the deserts;

He caused the waters to flow from the rock for them;

He also split the rock, and the waters gushed out.

"There is no peace," says the Lord, "for the wicked" (Isaiah 48:20-22).

"Now?"

"It is the time of Jacob's trouble."

"Jacob's trouble?"

"Alas! For that day is great,

So that none is like it;

And it is the time of Jacob's trouble,

But he shall be saved out of it" (Jeremiah 30:7).

"Who is Jacob? And why is he in trouble?"

"This will take too long to explain, but know this: 'I am referring to the Collapse of the English-speaking nations—where most of Jacob's descendants reside.'"

"The United States of America?"

"The Destroyed States of the Great Tribulation."

"The Great Tribulation?"

"And then many will be offended, will betray one another, and will hate one another" (Matthew 24:10).

"Why?"

"...God will send them strong delusion, that they should believe the lie, that they all may be condemned who did not believe the truth but had pleasure in unrighteousness" (2 Thessalonians 2:11, 12).

"You! You will do this?"

"For I am holy—My judgment is at hand."

"Why now?"

"Judgment must come now, and the Kingdom of Heaven on Earth will soon follow."

"Can we skip the Judgment?"

"That will make me imperfect, My son."

"But You have done it before."

"Before, My little children repented, and before, My little children rebelled also."

"What if we all repent?"

"My son, unfortunately not all will..."

"Why?"

"...but soon, all nations will come to Me."

"And why don't you send countless prophets to sound the trumpets, now?"

"Instead, due to the soon-rising of the false messiah, in 2016, '...many false prophets will rise up and deceive many' (Matthew 24:11).

"False prophets?"

"False."

"But we don't even have a few real ones, how can we get many false ones?"

"This is the Great Tribulation:

"And because lawlessness will abound, the love of many will grow cold" (Matthew 24:12).

"Will most break the law?"

"Most are breaking My Law."

"Your Law?"

"My Law of Liberty, My son."

"Liberty?"

"And it will lead them to captivity through men's wicked laws."

"Captivity?

"Remember the FEMA concentration camps, and the countless already-prepared facilities?"

"Yes."

"Captivity and martyrdom is at hand."

"Why My Lord? Why? Why!?"

"My son..."

"But no one deserves this?"

"...For My thoughts are not your thoughts,

Nor are your ways My ways," says the Lord.

"For as the heavens are higher than the earth,

So are My ways higher than your ways,

And My thoughts than your thoughts" (Isaiah 55:8-9).

"Who can endure this?"

"Hold on to Me."

"Hold on? In this horrific environment? How?"

"...the truth shall make you free" (John 8:32).

"That's it? The truth?"

"It is, in this very moment, making free those who have eyes to read and ears to listen."

"To read? To listen?"

"My Word and the sound of the trumpets sounding through these pages."

"The Trumpets?"

"The alarm is sounding, but the sound is foreign."

"Foreign?"

"The sound-waves are stopped."

"Why?"

"Because the entertainment industry is paving the way for the strong delusion—through hip-hop beats and Hollywood scenes."

"But who can make it through in these times?"

"Watch therefore, and pray always that you may be counted worthy to escape all these things that will come to pass, and to stand before the Son of Man" (Luke 21:36).

"To escape?"

"To a place of safety."

"How's this possible?"

"Be part of the Philadelphian Church."

"But You know I'm not from Philadelphia?"

"It's in the Book of Revelation."

"Where?"

"Because you have kept My command to persevere, I also will keep you from the hour of trial which shall come upon the whole world, to test those who dwell on the earth" (Revelation 3:10).

"Keep the Commandments?"

"Every good gift and every perfect gift is from above, and comes down from the Father of lights, with whom there is no variation or shadow of turning" (James 1:17).

"Please help us all, now."

"But he who endures to the end shall be saved" (Matthew 24:13).

"Saved?"

"Physically and spiritually—the soul."

"Forever?"

"He who overcomes, I will make him a pillar in the temple of My God, and he shall go out no more. I will write on him the name of My God and the name of the city of My God, the New Jerusalem, which comes down out of heaven from My God. And I will write on him My new name.

"He who has an ear, let him hear what the Spirit says to the churches'" (Revelation 3:12, 13).

"The Spirit spoke to the churches?"

"And He is speaking to the True Church, now."

"Please guide me."

"Go back to Matthew 24."

"Where?"

"The 14th verse."

"And this gospel of the kingdom will be preached in all the world as a witness to all the nations, and then the end will come" (Matthew 24:14).

"How can this be made possible?"

"Remember: the Book of Daniel?"

"Where exactly?"

"But you, Daniel, shut up the words, and seal the book until the time of the end; many shall run to and fro, and knowledge shall increase" (Daniel 12:4).

"And what does this scripture have to do with the gospel of the kingdom being preached in all the world as a witness to the nations, and then, the end coming?"

"The words in Matthew 24:14 cannot come to life completely, unless the Book of Daniel is unsealed."

"Why not?"

"Because without the unsealing, one cannot receive My divine and complete wisdom."

"How so?"

"For the Lord gives wisdom;

From His mouth come knowledge and understanding" (Proverbs 2:6).

"Ok?"

"I give it freely."

"I comprehend, but...?"

"My son, preaching the gospel of My Kingdom 'in all the world,' before the rising of the false messiah and before My Return, cannot be made possible, unless, I unseal the words of the Book of Daniel."

"Really?"

"Humanity cannot operate all the weapons of mass destruction unless knowledge increases through all sorts of fields due to the unsealing of the Book of Daniel..."

"Why?"

"...and the necessary amount of wisdom I'm giving you and My other servants cannot be unless the seal of the Book of Daniel is broken."

"Really?"

"He stores up sound wisdom for the upright;

He is a shield to those who walk uprightly" (Proverbs 2:7).

"So You have kept this information till now?"

"Therefore when you see the 'abomination of desolation,' spoken of by Daniel the prophet, standing in the holy place" (whoever reads, let him understand), "then let those who are in Judea flee to the mountains" (Matthew 24:16).

"Daniel again?"

"It is unsealed."

"It sounds like fiction."

"Before 2016 ends, all the nations shall see 'The True Abomination of Desolation.'"

"The Antichrist beast power?"

"Clearly, My son."

"And how about those in Judea?"

"Most of My little children in Judea do not believe this false messiah/false god prophecy since most haven't received the True Messiah, but let them know this...."

"What is it, my Lord? What is it?"

"...for he will rise before 2016 ends."

"And what do I tell to the Lost Tribes of Israel residing throughout the whole world?

"...then let those who are in Judea flee to the mountains" (Matthew 24:16).

"Another dual-prophecy?"

"2016, My son."

"And how about Jerusalem?"

"O Jerusalem, Jerusalem, the one who kills the prophets and stones those who are sent to her! How often I wanted to gather your children together, as a hen gathers her chicks under her wings, but you were not willing! See! Your house is left to you desolate; for I say to you, you shall see Me no more till you say, 'Blessed is He who comes in the name of the Lord!' " (Matthew 23:37-39).

"Really?"

"My son:

"Blow the trumpet in Zion,
And sound an alarm in My holy mountain!
Let all the inhabitants of the land tremble;
For the day of the Lord is coming,
For it is at hand" (Joel 2:1).

"After the Antichrist?"

"Whom will claim to be Me."

"A false messiah?"

"Let him who is on the housetop not go down to take anything out of his house. And let him who is in the field not go back to get his clothes" (Matthew 24:17, 18).

"And what about the rest not living in Judea or of the Tribes of Israel?"

"Let him who is on the housetop not go down to take anything out of his house. And let him who is in the field not go back to get his clothes" (Matthew 24:17, 18).

"But this is worldwide persecution?"

"Can you imagine being a pregnant woman in the midst of this?"

"My Lord, You will not allow this to happen; will You?

"But woe to those who are pregnant and to those who are nursing babies in those days!" (Matthew 24:19).

"Why! Why! Why the pregnant and those nursing babies?"

"My son, are My true servants watching and blowing the trumpets throughout all four corners of the earth?"

"Only You know this, My Savior."

"The blood of the innocent is on their hands, My son."

"But aren't we all trying our best?"

"Make sure you blow the trumpets loudly, and truly, try your best."

"I'm trying, I'm trying; why loudly?"

"Remember, humanity will enter into the final three and one-half years of the soon-to-come Great Tribulation beginning before 2016 ends."

"Right."

"Therefore, let all My servants rise now at the sound of the trumpets."

"Now?"

"All My faithful servants must pray like Elijah and truly walk in My Words found specifically in the Book of James."

"Why Elijah...?"

"Elijah was a man with a nature like ours, and he prayed earnestly that it would not rain; and it did not rain on the land for three years and six months" (James 5:17).

"Three years and six months?"

"Pray for true peace and security in these final three and one-half years of the Great Tribulation mentioned in the last chapter of the Book Daniel."

"...And why Elijah and the Book of James?"

"Faith."

"Faith?"

"Read the Book of James and you'll comprehend."

"And what about Matthew?"

"And pray that your flight may not be in winter or on the Sabbath" (Matthew 24:20).

"Why specifically the winter?"

"Can you imagine fleeing from persecution during the coldest season of the year with your pregnant wife as you carry your two-year-old son, Jonah, and drag your eight-year-old son, Brandon?

"But my wife isn't pregnant?"

"Just imagine, My son."

"It's too horrific to imagine."

"But woe to those who are pregnant and to those who are nursing babies in those days!' (Matthew 24:19).

"I get it! I get it! And why the Sabbath?"

"Remember, My son?"

"Remember?"

"Remember the Sabbath day, to keep it holy" (Exodus 20:8).

"The fourth Commandment, right?"

"Expand your horizons, My son."

"Expand? The Sabbath? Holiness? Your Law? I don't know."

"Think."

"Nothing enters."

"Here:

"We have the weekly Sabbath.

"We have the Law of the Sabbath Year in Leviticus the 25th chapter.

"We have the Law of the Year of Jubilee in the Leviticus as well."

"It sounds like the book: *The Mystery of the Shemitah* written by Jonathan Cahn."

"And it is also connected with: *The Harbinger: The Ancient Mystery that holds the Secret of America's Future*, also written by Jonathan Cahn.

"Remember how Jonathan connects the dots and finds divine evidence pointing to the events of 9/11, the collapse soon after 9/11, the economic collapse of 2008, and the potential collapse in late 2015?"

"I do."

"Now these events coming in the soon-to-come Great Tribulation will be somewhat similar, but with much more intensity."

"Intensity?"

"For then there will be great tribulation, such as has not been since the beginning of the world until this time, no, nor ever shall be" (Matthew 24:21).

"The Great Tribulation!"

"And unless those days were shortened, no flesh would be saved; but for the elect's sake those days will be shortened" (Matthew 24:22).

"How can the days be shorten?"

"I will intervene Mankind to save My little children."

"How?"

"For as the lightning comes from the east and flashes to the west, so also will the coming of the Son of Man be" (Matthew 24:27).

"And You will do this?"

"Then if anyone says to you, 'Look, here is the Christ!' or 'There!' do not believe it. For false christs and false prophets will rise and show great signs and wonders to deceive, if possible, even the elect" (Matthew 24:23, 24).

"I'm starting to believe this is important—kind of like: life or death."

"See, I have told you beforehand.

"Therefore if they say to you, 'Look, He is in the desert!' do not go out; or 'Look, He is in the inner rooms!' do not believe it" (Matthew 24:25, 26).

# Chapter 62
## *What to Do*

"What can we do O Voice of Truth?"
"...Whom shall I send,
And who will go for Us?" (Isaiah 6:8).
"Send?"
"Go!"
"Where to?"
"Go, and tell this people:
'Keep on hearing, but do not understand;
Keep on seeing, but do not perceive'" (Isaiah 6:9).
"But most won't care?"
"But My chosen ones will listen and act according to My will."
"And what's 'Your will' in times as such for your chosen flock?"
"Woe to those who call evil good, and good evil;
Who put darkness for light, and light for darkness;
Who put bitter for sweet, and sweet for bitter!
Woe to those who are wise in their own eyes,
And prudent in their own sight!
Woe to men mighty at drinking wine,
Woe to men valiant for mixing intoxicating drink,
Who justify the wicked for a bribe,
And take away justice from the righteous man!
Therefore, as the fire devours the stubble,
And the flame consumes the chaff,
So their root will be as rottenness,
And their blossom will ascend like dust;
Because they have rejected the law of the Lord of hosts,
And despised the word of the Holy One of Israel" (Isaiah 5:20-24).

"I comprehend that Your Law has been rejected and that most have despised Your Word, but may You please give us a chance, My Lord?"

"Fight!"

"Fight? Aren't we supposed to flee, and escape, and watch?"

"You referred to a chosen flock in your question, correct?"

"You know all things, My Lord."

"Children ·treat my people cruelly [oppress my people],

and ·women [or creditors; usurers] rule over them.

My people, your guides lead you ·in the wrong way [astray]

and ·turn you away [mislead you; or confuse you] from ·what is right [the right road; your paths]" (Isaiah 3:12, EXB).

"Children?"

"These are aged men with evil knowledge, but with minds of children according to My Word."

"And the women?"

"Remember the first fall of men?"

"In Genesis?"

"Men still fall today because they have forgotten to use their hearts, their minds, and My infinite wisdom."

"Why?"

"...each one is tempted when he is drawn away by his own desires and enticed. Then, when desire has conceived, it gives birth to sin; and sin, when it is full-grown, brings forth death" (James 1:14, 15).

"The desire to chase women? But are not women the glory of men?"

"But men and women have exchanged marriage and true glory for corruption and death."

"This is horrible, isn't it?"

"Just read King Solomon's story, My son."

"And our guides lead us also?"

"Those who lead you: from a single community leader to the kings of the earth."

"But how are we supposed to fight our leaders if You have raised them to their positions?"

"Correct:

"For exaltation comes neither from the east
Nor from the west nor from the south.
But God is the Judge:
He puts down one,
And exalts another" (Psalm 75:6, 7).
  "Again! How?"
  "With My Word."
  "Your Word; that's it?"
  "He has put down the mighty from their thrones,
And exalted the lowly" (Luke 1:52).
  "But how, My Lord? How do we warn the leaders? How?"
  "For we do not wrestle against flesh and blood, but against principalities, against powers, against the rulers of the darkness of this age, against spiritual hosts of wickedness in the heavenly places" (Ephesians 6:12).
  "And this?"
  "Remember when you practiced sports?"
  "Isn't that a dumb question?"
  "No such thing, My son; I had to ask you now to hand you over my wisdom."
  "Wisdom?"
  "You ran, punched, jumped, swam, pushed, pulled, tackled, hit and got hit...and you mostly saw the physical part."
  "Right."
  "But then through My freely given wisdom you began to perceive the connection between the physical and the spiritual."
  "I guess."
  "As you trained harder you no longer just counted on your nutrition, or sleeping time, but you began to rely on Me.
  "As you saw your next step through your visions and dreams; your hunger increased toward My will.
  "As you tasted true hunger you no longer walked, but you ran toward the Promised Land..."
  "The Promised Land?"

"...You no longer desired to swim in the lukewarm waters, but you chose to fly through the Spirit of Truth's atmosphere."

"The Spirit of Truth?"

"I long to give it to all, but only a remnant choose this atmosphere. I desire to bring all to The Promise Land, but only a remnant run with The Promise Land in their hearts. I promised to all that 'I'm coming quickly,' but most flee from the promise of My Second Coming. My coming is inevitable, unbreakable, supernatural, and sealed. And unsealed now, as the Book of Daniel reveals and unseals. Do you believe, My son?"

"Yes, my Lord."

"Most flee from this truth."

"Then how do we fight and lead them to You?"

"Go to the top."

"The top?"

"The presidents, the kings, the leaders of each nation and warn them face to face—now!"

"They are not going to listen."

"Now!"

"How?"

"How did you get from Miami, FL to Bottineau, ND?"

"You know the answer, my Lord."

"Use the technology while you still have it, My son."

"Now?"

"And the blood of the innocent I have entrusted you shall no longer be on your hands."

"That's all?"

"No. Just the beginning."

"What else?"

"Use all your gifts relentlessly—the internet, writing, speech, action...to deliver My inspired message, now."

"What else?"

"Fear not, for I am with you;
Be not dismayed, for I am your God.

I will strengthen you,
Yes, I will help you,
I will uphold you with My righteous right hand'" (Isaiah 41:10).

"I'm listening."

"It is 11:59pm on My watch, and in a minute all will see the day of the false messiah."

"And then?"

"The Day of Yeshua, The Messiah."

"I'm still here."

"Don't just watch, but also act according to My will."

"Why?"

"What does it profit, my brethren, if someone says he has faith but does not have works? Can faith save him? If a brother or sister is naked and destitute of daily food, and one of you says to them, "Depart in peace, be warmed and filled," but you do not give them the things which are needed for the body, what does it profit? Thus also faith by itself, if it does not have works, is dead.

But someone will say, "You have faith, and I have works." Show me your faith without your works, and I will show you my faith by my works. You believe that there is one God. You do well. Even the demons believe—and tremble! But do you want to know, O foolish man, that faith without works is dead? Was not Abraham our father justified by works when he offered Isaac his son on the altar? Do you see that faith was working together with his works, and by works faith was made perfect? And the Scripture was fulfilled which says, "Abraham believed God, and it was accounted to him for righteousness." And he was called the friend of God. You see then that a man is justified by works, and not by faith only.

Likewise, was not Rahab the harlot also justified by works when she received the messengers and sent them out another way?

For as the body without the spirit is dead, so faith without works is dead also" (James 2:14-26).

"Why all this?"
"Are you alive?"
"Yes."
"Would you like to perfect your faith?"
"Yes."
"Do you still have My Spirit within you?"
"Yes."
"Would you like to be called: the friend of God?"
"It will be an honor."
"Now go! And put your faith to work."
"How, My Lord? How?"
"Therefore take up the whole armor of God, that you may be able to withstand in the evil day, and having done all, to stand" (Ephesians 6:13).
"The whole armor of God?"
"Stand therefore, having girded your waist with truth, having put on the breastplate of righteousness, and having shod your feet with the preparation of the gospel of peace" (Ephesians 6:14, 15).
"My waist with truth? The breastplate of righteousness? The gospel of peace?"
"Above all, taking the shield of faith with which you will be able to quench all the fiery darts of the wicked one" (Ephesians 6:16).
"Now the shield of faith, and above all?"
"Keep listening."
"I'm still here, my Lord."
"And take the helmet of salvation, and the sword of the Spirit, which is the word of God; praying always with all prayer and supplication in the Spirit, being watchful to this end with all perseverance and supplication for all the saints." (Ephesians 6: 17, 18).
"A helmet for salvation? The sword of the Spirit? Praying and supplicating in the Spirit? Watching? It sounds like a lot."

"A lot more may be written about worldly things that amount to death, but the dead may be born again and find everlasting life through My Word."

"Like the leaders, the presidents, the kings...?"

"If My faithful servants would just stop playing *Call of Duty*, and instead, answer 'The Call' to honor their duty, then My people will know what to do as I lead them directly."

"That sounds like Andy Mineo, the Christian, hip-hop artist?"

"I'm using all in this final hour, My son:

"The harvest truly is great, but the laborers are few; therefore pray the Lord of the harvest to send out laborers into His harvest" (Luke 10:2).

"How can we really warn the people and prepare ourselves for the soon-to-come rise of the Antichrist?"

"Actions speak louder than words, but:
'Death and life are in the power of the tongue,
And those who love it will eat its fruit'" (Proverbs 18:21).

"I'm lost here."

"My Word must be delivered to the highest rulers, now!—through My faithful servants."

"Your Word?"

"As The Spirit of Truth delivers to each one according to My perfect will."

"Now?"

"Today—as you write—is the 1st day of June, 2015, and it is 2:16pm in Florida."

"Ok?"

"How much time you think it will take to warn millions prior to the soon-to-come collapse of the U.S dollar, and prior to the rising of the Antichrist in 2016 soon after?"

"Not much."

"Remember this:

"A prudent man foresees evil and hides himself;
The simple pass on and are punished" (Proverbs 27:12).

"Hide or be punished?"

"The prudent will choose wisely."

"Now?"

"Wouldn't it be wise to hide and find true peace and security before horror is poured out through the four corners of the Earth?"

"But where can we hide if horror will cover all four corners?"

"Because you have kept My command to persevere, I also will keep you from the hour of trial which shall come upon the whole world, to test those who dwell on the earth" (Revelation 3:10).

"But how can your servants and the wise hide when we must go to the leaders and sound the trumpets?"

"The days are counted, My son, so sound the trumpets as I lead you, and quickly go to your place of safety."

"But how?"

"Follow Me and you will see."

"But how? How?"

"You know."

"I don't think I'll be asking if I knew."

"My sheep hear My voice, and I know them, and they follow Me" (John 10:27).

"How is this really possible?"

# Chapter 63
## *Diversity of the Gifts*

"**T**here are diversities of gifts, but the same Spirit. There are differences of ministries, but the same Lord. And there are diversities of activities, but it is the same God who works all in all. But the manifestation of the Spirit is given to each one for the profit of all: for to one is given the word of wisdom through the Spirit, to another the word of knowledge through the same Spirit, to another faith by the same Spirit, to another gifts of healings by the same Spirit, to another the working of miracles, to another prophecy, to another discerning of spirits, to another different kinds of tongues, to another the interpretation of tongues. But one and the same Spirit works all these things, distributing to each one individually as He wills" (1 Corinthians 12:4-11).

"And what's so important about this?"
"Each member has a gift."
"Each member?"
"Read, My son:

"For as the body is one and has many members, but all the members of that one body, being many, are one body, so also is Christ. For by one Spirit we were all baptized into one body—whether Jews or Greeks, whether slaves or free—and have all been made to drink into one Spirit. For in fact the body is not one member but many.

If the foot should say, "Because I am not a hand, I am not of the body," is it therefore not of the body? And if the ear should say, "Because I am not an eye, I am not of the body," is it therefore not of the body? If the whole body were an eye, where would be the hearing? If the whole were hearing, where

397

would be the smelling?  But now God has set the members, each one of them, in the body just as He pleased.  And if they were all one member, where would the body be?

But now indeed there are many members, yet one body.  And the eye cannot say to the hand, "I have no need of you"; nor again the head to the feet, "I have no need of you."  No, much rather, those members of the body which seem to be weaker are necessary.  And those members of the body which we think to be less honorable, on these we bestow greater honor; and our unpresentable parts have greater modesty, but our presentable parts have no need. But God composed the body, having given greater honor to that part which lacks it, that there should be no schism in the body, but that the members should have the same care for one another.  And if one member suffers, all the members suffer with it; or if one member is honored, all the members rejoice with it.

Now you are the body of Christ, and members individually. And God has appointed these in the church: first apostles, second prophets, third teachers, after that miracles, then gifts of healings, helps, administrations, varieties of tongues. Are all apostles? Are all prophets? Are all teachers? Are all workers of miracles?  Do all have gifts of healings? Do all speak with tongues? Do all interpret?  But earnestly desire the best gifts. And yet I show you a more excellent way" (1 Corinthians 12:12-31).

"Who wrote this?"

"A member of My Body, My son."

"And how is this interrelated to the soon-to-come rising of the Antichrist in 2016?"

"Each member must fully comprehend where each stand."

"Why?"

"To initiate and finish their work according to their gift."

"In the midst of this soon-to-come Great Tribulation?"

"Is it better to receive the warning before or after a disaster?"

"Before sounds better."

"It isn't pleasant when the warning is delivered in the midst of an all-out entertained world. Right?"

"And why does it have to be this way?"

"Do you have another method?"

"I don't know, but You are my Lord, and perhaps you have a perfect plan."

"I do."

"Which is?"

"Just listen, My son; just listen."

"I'm trying."

"Pursue love, and desire spiritual gifts, but especially that you may prophesy" (1 Corinthians 14:1).

"But especially that you may prophesy?"

"Yes."

"Why?"

"Because prophecy saves countless lives."

"What is love?"

"He who does not love does not know God, for God is love" (1 John 4:8).

"How can I prophecy if I'm not a prophet?"

"And He Himself gave some to be apostles, some prophets, some evangelists, and some pastors and teachers, for the equipping of the saints for the work of ministry, for the edifying of the body of Christ" (Ephesians 4:11, 12).

"And what's this?"

"My son, if you say you are a prophet, publicly, then you shall be judged by most men, especially within 'the church,' as a 'false prophet.'"

"Then I should say that I'm not, and deny it, and remain silent regarding this—right?"

"No!"

"Why?"

"Because you are My servant, a messenger, a vessel, a prophet."

"A prophet?"

"One of the many for this final hour."

"Really!"

"What's the difference between the prophets of the Bible and the prophets delivering My message today?"

"I don't know?"

"Are not all inspired by the same Spirit of Truth?"

"Right."

"And are not all directed by the Voice of Truth?"

"And when asked about this, what do I say then?"

"Speak boldly in truth, My son—no matter what this wicked generation believes. And it truly doesn't matter what you are called or not called; what matters is that you know what your job is, and most importantly, who you are in My Body."

"But I don't want to be labeled a prophet."

"Because the 'church' says that if anyone claims to be a prophet chances are he's a false one, right?"

"Right."

"And do you know how many of My faithful servants have retained vital information due to this deception?"

"They have been silenced?"

"By the same church that's supposed to encourage them."

"How?"

"When was the last time you saw a teacher allow one of My servants to stand and edify My Body in a congregation or outside?"

"I don't remember. Oh, wait! They are some sounding the trumpets: Jonathan Cahn, David Montaigne, Thomas Horn, the people from *Tomorrowsworld.org*..."

"For I have chosen you for this final hour, also."

"But how do I do this?"

"Abide in Me, and I in you. As the branch cannot bear fruit of itself, unless it abides in the vine, neither can you, unless you abide in Me" (John 15:4).

"How can I do this?"

"I am the vine, you are the branches. He who abides in Me, and I in him, bears much fruit; for without Me you can do nothing. If anyone does not abide in Me, he is cast out as a branch and is withered; and they gather them and throw them into the fire, and they are burned. If you abide in Me, and My words abide in you, you will ask what you desire, and it shall be done for you. By this My Father is glorified, that you bear much fruit; so you will be My disciples" (John 15:5-8).

"Please help us all in these times to come. Please guide us all, in all Your ways."

"As the Father loved Me, I also have loved you; abide in My love. If you keep My commandments, you will abide in My love, just as I have kept My Father's commandments and abide in His love.

"These things I have spoken to you, that My joy may remain in you, and that your joy may be full" (John 15:9-11).

"Joy in the midst of the soon-to-come Great Tribulation?"

"...With men this is impossible, but with God all things are possible" (Matthew 19:26).

"Is it possible to prevent this soon-to-come judgment and the rising of the Antichrist?"

"It is."

"Really? How?

"My son, unfortunately, due to the sinful nature of Humanity this will all unfold soon."

"So it isn't possible."

"Repent! And the soon-to-come judgement and the rising of the Antichrist shall not find you in My wilderness."

"But only a remnant will do this, right?"

"Right."

And I began to shout:

"So what's the point of taking all kinds of trips to work on this book?

"Why have you dragged me out of jobs to focus completely on this book?

"Why have you allowed me to argue with my wife countlessly over Your will throughout all these years?

"Why so much pain and sorrow for nothing?

"Why can't I even satisfy my wife whom You gave me divinely?

"Why did I have to drop out of college three times?

"Why did I have to hang my football cleats and showcase my boxing gloves?

"Why can't I even get a job and at least support my family financially when Your Own Word declares I must?

"Why am I selling coconuts one day and then You ask me to leave it?

"I can be making a six or seven figure income. Why all this?

"Why have I had to fast and pray endlessly?

"Why is even my penis quitting on me?

"Why me?

"Why now?

"Why not anyone else?

"Why not my neighbor?

"Why not the well-known pastor down the street?

"Why do I even exist in these times?

"Why must I just write and nothing else is permitted outside of this task?

"Why am I sleeping in a 5x5 storage room when I can be at home with my family?

"Why am I sleeping on the beach and watching these stars move while most sleep or dance?

"Why has my wife become my enemy?

"Why? Why? Why...?"

"My son, I feel the load of your burden, but please, also feel the load of this truth."

"Which truth!?"

"The Great Tribulation will soon entrap the whole Earth."

"Who wants this truth!?"

"Many lives, My son...many lives."

"I get it! But for what reason am I writing all these words?"

"My obedient children deserve to know where they stand."

"Your obedient children?"

"Those who live by My Word."

"By Your Word?"

"And those who are willing to accept this message of warning."

"How can they?"

"By turning back from their wicked ways?"

"How?"

"Repentance."

"To repent from what?"

"Again: 'If My people who are called by My name will humble themselves, and pray and seek My face, and turn from their wicked ways, then I will hear from heaven, and will forgive their sin and heal their land'" (2 Chronicles 7:14).

"Humble themselves? Praying and seeking and turning?

"But You have been telling me that the Antichrist will rise in 2016. And that after this, horror will cover the earth?"

"Not all will receive this message of warning, My son. And you will not save the world, but you can warn My people, and they may seek for salvation on Earth, and then soon enter into My Kingdom."

"Then what's the real purpose of writing another word?"

"Not all shall find true peace and security in these times to come, but:

"My sheep hear My voice, and I know them, and they follow Me. And I give them eternal life, and they shall never perish; neither shall anyone snatch them out of My hand. My Father, who has given them to Me, is greater than all; and no one is able to snatch them out of My Father's hand" (John 10:27-29).

"Then this is for Your sheep?"

"The invitation remains for all mankind, but only a few will accept it."

"Why?"

"My little children have the freedom to choose good or evil."

"Free will again?"

"And My perfect will is free to those who chose to accept it."

"But it can get really tough to follow You in this world."

"Can you imagine how much tougher it can get without My hand?"

"But then again, lots of people have fun and enjoy life without You."

"Exchanging truth for deception can equate to a delusional state of mind—resulting in an inevitable, unpredictable, undesirable death."

"Death?"

"Choose eternal life instead!"

"Eternal?"

"Forever."

"But most don't believe."

"Because they need evidence."

"And aren't we supposed to walk by faith?"

"How is your faith developed?"

"I guess by believing, working toward the finish line, and then receiving."

"Do you sometimes have to experience a revelation to believe? Do you sometimes have to have a moment to trust? Don't you sometimes have to find evidence to find strength?"

"Yes. Yes."

"Didn't you find evidence as you opened the door of your heart?"

"I believe I did."

"For I am the evidence; My Word is truth. And through Me all can be set free."

"O how, my Lord? How?"

"For I have chosen you to blow the trumpets."

"But my name is nowhere to be found in the Holy Bible?"

"Aren't you a member?"

"Of which club?"

"We just covered this."

"Oh...I just remembered."

"And remember this also: 'The Antichrist will rise before the year 2016 ends.'"

"I'm listening."

"Prior to this the world will be in the beginning stages of horror.

"He who rises in 2016 will not be God or the True Messiah..."

"I'm still here."

"...and he will not be the True Savior of the World."

"And what must I do?"

"Just listen:

"Behold, I am coming quickly! Blessed is he who keeps the words of the prophecy of this book" (Revelation 22:7).

"But not in 2016?"

"Just remember that the final tribulation period in Daniel's prophecy is only three and one-half years."

"Beginning soon?"

"Sixteen."

"Sixteen?"

"Before 2016 ends."

"This is really it?"

"This is reality; this is it."

"But most of us will not have time to find a shelter, or the funds for many necessities, or even know where to go and hide?"

"And which of you by worrying can add one cubit to his stature?" (Luke 12:25).

"Forgive me O Lord, but I'm just trying to prepare for what's about to unfold."

"Then just prepare, My son."

"I'm lost here."

"If you then are not able to do the least, why are you anxious for the rest?" (Luke 12:26).

"The least?"

"The least that My people can do is to repent, and all things shall fall into place."

"Repentance?"

"Freely offered, My son."

"And what about the necessities like a safe and self-sustainable shelter, long-lasting canned foods, rice, beans, grains, water, antibacterial and medical supplies... for this soon-to-come three and one-half years of terror?

"My sheep shall eat."

"But some will also be beheaded right?"

"These are from My other flock."

"Another flock?"

"These will share My testimony in the midst of the fire."

"Fire?"

"Coming from all four corners of the Earth."

"Why?"

"And they will lead countless lives in the midst of persecution."

"O my Lord, why don't You just come now?"

"And behold, I am coming quickly, and My reward is with Me, to give to every one according to his work" (Revelation 22:12).

"Right now?"

"Watch the rise of the false god/the false messiah as countdown began, 'Blessed is he who waits, and comes to the one thousand three hundred and thirty-five days'" (Daniel 12:12).

"And the countdown begins in 2016?"

"Before 2016 ends."

"Just months away?"

"Be ready!"

"But most won't believe?"

"My son, remember this..."

"What is it?"

"...You are not the only one sounding the trumpets."

"I'll remember."

"And I have raised many of My faithful servants in this final hour."

"Like?"

"Like, Jonathan Cahn, who wrote: *The Harbinger: The Ancient Mystery That Holds the Secret of America's Future,* and *The Mystery of the Shemitah: The 3,000-Year-Old Mystery That Holds the Secret of America's Future, the World's Future, and Your Future!*

"And like, Thomas R. Horn, who wrote: *Zenith 2016: Did Something Begin In The Year 2012 That Will Reach Its Apex In 2016?* And *Petrus Romanus: The Final Pope Is Here.* And wrote together with, Cris Putnam: *Exo-Vaticana: Petrus Romanus, Project L.U.C.I.F.E.R. And the Vatican's Astonishing Plan for the Arrival of an Alien Savior.*

"And how about David Montaigne, who just recently published: *Antichrist 2016-2019: Mystery Babylon, Barack Obama & the Islamic Caliphate.* Just to name a few."

"Why is this important?"

"Because My people need to flee from the houses of corruption and cling to the Truth."

"The houses of corruption?"

"Where the false prophets prophesy about mansions, cars, yachts... and everything else but the truth."

"Now?"

"Repentance remains as the only true escape."

"But You have blessed many financially."

"But most remain blind because their cash has covered their eyes."

"And what can we do to help?"

"Blow the trumpets throughout all four corners of the Earth quickly, prepare yourself and your family, and listen to Me as I direct your path.

"For My people are foolish,

They have not known Me.

They are silly children,

And they have no understanding.

They are wise to do evil,

But to do good they have no knowledge." (Jeremiah 4:22).

"O Lord forgive us!"

"And when you are plundered,

What will you do?

Though you clothe yourself with crimson,

Though you adorn yourself with ornaments of gold,

**407**

Though you enlarge your eyes with paint,
In vain you will make yourself fair;
Your lovers will despise you;
They will seek your life" (Jeremiah 4:30).

"And why is the church falling apart?"
"My son, above all know that I have it all under control.
"And know this:
'Her heads judge for a bribe,
Her priests teach for pay,
And her prophets divine for money.
Yet they lean on the Lord, and say,
"Is not the Lord among us?
No harm can come upon us'" (Micah 3:11).
"And what else?"

"But know this, that in the last days perilous times will come: For men will be lovers of themselves, lovers of money, boasters, proud, blasphemers, disobedient to parents, unthankful, unholy, unloving, unforgiving, slanderers, without self-control, brutal, despisers of good, traitors, headstrong, haughty, lovers of pleasure rather than lovers of God, having a form of godliness but denying its power. And from such people turn away! For of this sort are those who creep into households and make captives of gullible women loaded down with sins, led away by various lusts, always learning and never able to come to the knowledge of the truth" (2 Timothy 3:1-7).

"But this is happening today?"
"You've seen nothing yet."
"But My Lord, the churches remain packed, people worship You, and everyone says they believe!"
"And in vain they worship Me,
Teaching as doctrines the commandments of men.'

For laying aside the commandment of God, you hold the tradition of men—the washing of pitchers and cups, and many other such things you do."

He said to them, "All too well you reject the commandment of God, that you may keep your tradition" (Mark 7:7-9).

"O Lord help us."

"Shout!"

"Shout?"

"With joy!"

"With joy?"

"Yes, these Words, My son:

"Blessed are the poor in spirit,
    For theirs is the kingdom of heaven.
 Blessed are those who mourn,
    For they shall be comforted.
 Blessed are the meek,
    For they shall inherit the earth.
 Blessed are those who hunger and thirst for righteousness,
    For they shall be filled.
 Blessed are the merciful,
    For they shall obtain mercy.
 Blessed are the pure in heart,
    For they shall see God.
 Blessed are the peacemakers,
    For they shall be called sons of God.
 Blessed are those who are persecuted for righteousness' sake,
    For theirs is the kingdom of heaven.

"Blessed are you when they revile and persecute you, and say all kinds of evil against you falsely for My sake. Rejoice and be exceedingly glad, for great is your reward in heaven, for so they persecuted the prophets who were before you" (Matthew 5:3-12).

"For they shall inherit the Earth?"

"The soon-to-come Kingdom of Heaven on Earth."

"And are we truly blessed?"

"My sheep hear My voice, and I know them, and they follow Me" (John 10:27).

"And if I had to choose one single scripture out of your Word to prove that Your message to Mankind is true: which one may I choose?"

"My sheep hear My voice, and I know them, and they follow Me" (John 10:27).

"Just like that—My sheep hear My voice?"

"Surely the Lord God does nothing,

Unless He reveals His secret to His servants the prophets"

(Amos 3:7).

"Before 2016 ends?"

"The false god temporary reign begins."

"For how long again?"

"Three and a half years of horror, I repeat, once more."

"And then—the end?"

"And behold, I am coming quickly, and My reward is with Me, to give to every one according to his work" (Revelation 22:12).

"Really. Is it really the end?"

"The End of this Age."

"And The Kingdom of Heaven?"

"Coming to Earth soon after."

"Right after?"

"I AM THE VOICE OF TRUTH."

# Chapter 64
## *I Heard The Voice*

"**A**re you truly The Voice of Truth?"
"Remember the voice?"
"Which voice?"
"When you were 12 years young, and you lived with your father."
"What happened then?"
"Remember: 'You'll never die.'"
"I'll never die?"
"The voice that said: 'You'll never die.'"
"I do; I do."
"It was I."
"You! The Voice of Truth?"
"The same Voice leading you in this very moment."
"But how did I not comprehend, then?"
"You weren't supposed to, My son."
"But, I will die."
"My son..."
"Yes, Lord."
"Where are you from?"
"You know the answer, my Lord."
"Where are you from?"
"My Lord, You know I was born in The Dominican Republic and have traveled all over."
"My son, when you fall asleep tonight I will show you a mystery."
"A mystery?"
"Be ready!"

I woke up because of the revelation, and suddenly, He said, "Pick up your Bible now!"

"I'm going, I'm going...where?"

"Here:

"Then it happened, as he drew back his hand, that his brother came out unexpectedly; and she said, "How did you break through? This breach be upon you!" Therefore his name was called Perez" (Genesis 38:29).

"And what's this?"

"Go to Genesis 46:12."

"Wait, wait; here it is:

"The sons of Judah were Er, Onan, Shelah, Perez, and Zerah (but Er and Onan died in the land of Canaan). The sons of Perez were Hezron and Hamul."

"I'm still lost."

"Now go to the Book of Ruth."

"Where to?"

"There:

"Then Naomi took the child and laid him on her bosom, and became a nurse to him. Also the neighbor women gave him a name, saying, "There is a son born to Naomi." And they called his name Obed. He is the father of Jesse, the father of David.

Now this is the genealogy of Perez: Perez begot Hezron; Hezron begot Ram, and Ram begot Amminadab; Amminadab begot Nahshon, and Nahshon begot Salmon; Salmon begot Boaz, and Boaz begot Obed; Obed begot Jesse, and Jesse begot David" (Ruth 4:16-22).

"Would you please tell me what this is all about?"

"Patience My son... Patience."

"But I don't comprehend?"

"Go to the first chapter of Matthew."

"I'm here."

"Begin."

"The book of the genealogy of Jesus Christ, the Son of David, the Son of Abraham:

Abraham begot Isaac, Isaac begot Jacob, and Jacob begot Judah and his brothers. Judah begot Perez...And Jacob begot Joseph the husband of Mary, of whom was born Jesus who is called Christ.  So all the generations from Abraham to David are fourteen generations, from David until the captivity in Babylon are fourteen generations, and from the captivity in Babylon until the Christ are fourteen generations"

"Please tell me already what this is all about."

"Seek me throughout the day and tonight you shall receive an answer."

### 5am the Following Morning

"The same dream again! What is it? What is it? Is this what it seems like?"

"My son, you are of the descendants of Pharez."

"Pharez?"

"Perez."

"Of Perez?"

"Of the sons of Judah."

"The lost tribes?"

"Yes, of the descendants of Perez."

"But I wasn't born in Israel, and..."

"My son, what is your mother's last name?"

"Peña."

"Perez."

"Perez?"

"Yes, this is her second last name."

"Really?"

"Call her and ask her."

"When?"

"Later on."

"But it goes by the father: right?"

"Call your mother."

## Speaking to my mother

"Mother, what is your last name?"

"You forgot my last name!"

"Maybe."

"Maybe!"

"I just need to know for sure."

"You know is Peña."

"I see, but do you have any other?"

"And Perez, my second last name."

"Perez!"

"Yeah.  Didn't you know?"

"Oh, ok mother; I'll call you later."

## Again with The Voice of Truth

"But this doesn't mean anything, there are thousands of Perez all around the world."

"You are correct; there are many, but I have revealed this to you through a dream, then I promised you to show you something, and I did, when I blessed you with the same dream, then I revealed it to you in My Word, then I asked you to receive it from your mother, and finally, I AM is telling you through The Voice of Truth."

"But how about my father?"

"Your father was Cuban, your grandmother Puerto Rican, and you and your mother were born in The Dominican Republic."

"And this means?"

"My son, this isn't about you, instead, about what is about to unfold."

"But my father was not of Perez?"

"I am the Spirit of Truth."

"But this cannot be."

"I am the Voice of Truth."

"Is this You?"

"You are My law giver."

"Your law giver?"

"...Judah is My lawgiver" (Psalm 108:8).

"Ok?"

"This is why you thirst for truth."

"But how can this be?"

"My sheep hear My voice, and I know them, and they follow Me" (John 10:27).

"And where do they go?"

"As they hear, they move."

"Truly, my Lord; truly?"

"I will instruct you and teach you in the way you should go; I will guide you with My eye" (Psalm 32:8).

"With Your eye?"

"Many sorrows shall be to the wicked; But he who trusts in the Lord, mercy shall surround him" (Psalm 32:10).

"And what do I do? Where do I go now?"

"Follow Me and you shall see."

"Where to, My Lord; where to? Why all this?"

"And He is before all things, and in Him all things consist" (Colossians 1:17).

"All things in You?"

"For unto us a Child is born,
Unto us a Son is given;
And the government will be upon His shoulder.
And His name will be called
Wonderful, Counselor, Mighty God,
Everlasting Father, Prince of Peace.

"Who was inspired to state these words, My son?"

"Isaiah, right?"

"And why will I hide My servants of what's coming to this era, when I have always revealed through the prophets in previous eras?"

"I don't know?"

"Before 2016 ends, the Antichrist/false messiah, the new world order, the one world religion, and the mark of the beast will all cover the face of the Earth."

"And what about in late 2015 and the beginning of 2016?"

"Watch for the largest collapse of mankind."

"The largest...?"

"Watch for CERN; it is the new Tower of Babel that could open the door for the real demons."

"The demons!"

"My little children! Who shall I send? Who shall go?"

"Send me! Send me!"

"My little children! Who shall I send? Who shall go?"

"I'm here."

"Stand now all My people, and demand a shutdown at CERN's headquarters."

"But are not You allowing this?"

"Yes."

"What's the point?"

"Judgment is here, but still, warn all My little children."

"For what? It's coming regardless."

"My son, I know all things and you and the whole world still lacks."

"So help us! Help us all now! Please!"

"JADE HELM 15."

"JADE HELM what?"

"It is one of the many psychological wars attempting to prepare the minds of the innocent for what's really coming."

"For what's really coming?"

"Originating from American soil, My son."

"America again?"

"My son, the judgment."

"What do we do? What do I tell the people?"

"Watch therefore, and pray always that you may be counted worthy to escape all these things that will come to pass, and to stand before the Son of Man" (Luke 21:36).

"But I've been watching and watching and watching!"

"That's the problem."

"Now this is the problem? I thought this was the solution."

"My son, if you see the sword coming, wouldn't you blow the trumpets?"

"I'm trying here."

"Wouldn't you blow with all your strength, with all your heart, and with My help."

"Sure."

"My son I asked all to watch and pray so that all move instead of watching till they fall asleep."

"So many are watching, but not reacting?"

"Exactly."

"Now what?"

"Now Walmart."

"Walmart?"

"Can't you see how the official partners of Homeland Security just shut down all those Walmart stores and simply laid off my little children?"

"Yes! Yes! Why is this happening?"

"Can't you see how JADE HELM 15, the Walmart closings, the soon-to-come Blood Moon, and many other major events are happening almost simultaneously?"

"Other events?"

"133 Target stores just closed in Canada."

"Ok, what's the big deal?"

"Much room for preparation."

"They need space?"

"To hide and prepare in darkness until they are ready to strike."

"What do we do?"

"Prepare."

"But how?"

"Keep listening."

"I'm trying."

"International Day of Peace (United Nations) happening on Monday, September 21, 2015."

"And this?"

"Just wait and see.

"Yom Kippur/The Day of Atonement/The Day of Judgment begins in the evening of Tuesday, September 22, 2015."

"The day of judgment!"

"Pope Francis will visit the Black House September 23, 2015."

"The Black House?"

"Much darkness has entered her, My son.

"Remember French Foreign Minister Laurent Fabius?"

"Laurent?"

"He said, 'we have 500 days—not a day more—to avert a climate disaster.'"

"When?"

"On Tuesday, May 13, 2014."

"Ok?"

"Just count My son and you'll see where you end up in September."

"What do we do?"

"And September 28, 2015."

"What about it?"

"Sukkot."

"Sukkot?"

"And the last Red Blood Moon shining through darkness on this same date."

"In September 2015?"

"The 28th, My son."

"All this in September, 2015?"

"Are you starting to get the big picture?"

"I don't want the camera."

"And the signs are everywhere."

"Where can I find them?"

"No more time for searching; go where The Spirit of Truth tells you, and follow His commands."

"And where's that? How's that?"

"My sheep hear My voice."

"And those not of Your flock?"

"Behold, I stand at the door and knock. If anyone hears my voice and opens the door, I will come in to him and eat with him, and he with me" (Revelation 3:20).

"But how can they hear You if they're not Your sheep?"

"They hear the knocks."

"How?"

"I'm knocking right now."

"Standing at the door?"

"And I long to eat with all."

"Now?"

"Who will serve Me, My son?"

"Can I?"

"All ye that thirst and want to be filled come and serve Me."

"And what about the events You just mentioned?"

"These events will prepare the way for the introduction of a false god/ a false savior/ a false messiah—he is mostly known as the Antichrist."

"The Antichrist!"

"Don't be afraid and move as wild fire toward My perfect will."

"How? What do we do?"

"Start by standing at CERN's headquarters and demand a shutdown, those of you that want to serve.   Stand in all evil places; stand and demand righteousness and truth—stand now!"

"Right now? But I can't even afford to buy the airplane ticket to get there?"

"You must go to Jerusalem."

"Now Jerusalem?"

"And speak with Benjamin Netanyahu, for he longs for righteousness and My little children also"

"Now Benjamin?"

"For I will pour out My Spirit of Truth through you when you see him face to face."

"But we have no more time?"

"You must speak face to face to Barack Hussein Obama II, also."

"Barack Obama?"

"Let Pope Francis—he who claims to be God on Earth—and the Jesuits and their branches grow in humility before you as I will warn them through you."

"Through me?"

"Remember how the prophet Nathan spoke to King David?"

"Yes."

"All these men and more will be warned through you, My son."

"But most of these individuals and organizations are my enemies—they desire to kill me."

"Love your enemies."

"How?"

"Stand with boldness and declare to them truth."

"You—the way, the truth, and the life?"

"Me—The way, the truth, the life, and the judgment."

"But haven't You raised these men for the coming judgment?"

"Yes, I have allowed it. And I am raising an Army to warn My little children."

"But wouldn't this make You evil?"

"No, but evil shall cover the Earth very soon. And remember, prophecy is fulfilling, and soon, after three and one half years of the Great Tribulation, all will stand and face The True Judge."

"You?"

"Warn the people of the already here judgment before the soon-to-come Day of Judgment arrives."

"Judgment Day?"

"Focus on the Final and Great Tribulation, and warn all people— 'He who has an ear, let him hear what the Spirit says to the churches'" (Revelation 3:13).

"How?"

"Unite with Jonathan Cahn, Thomas Horn, David Montaigne, Cris D. Putnam, John Shorey ... and all those willing to blow."

"To blow?"

"Yes, the trumpets—louder than ever!"

"But I have nothing. What do I do?"

"Some will contact you."

"Me?"

"Remember I will raise an Army, and they will help you."

"Me?"

"In this way they will serve Me."

"How?"

"Some will listen to you as I speak through you, some will listen to Me directly, and they will move and help My people. Blow the trumpets!"

"But it's too late."

"Yes it is late, but you all still have seconds before reality strikes."

"So we can avoid this?"

"You will not change The Word, but many shall open their hearts and live."

"I'm lost here."

"Fifteen and sixteen, My son."

"Now I'm truly lost."

"2015 is the warm up and 2016 is the reality."

"Can I have a solution?"

"I've given you many, and soon, you'll receive many more."

"Please do not leave us or forsake us."

"In this very moment, finish the book and move!"

"This is risky."

"You shall receive your crown."

"But how?"

"The days are counting down, My son."

"And after all this?"

"After three and one-half years of Great Tribulation, I'm coming, My little children!"

"You're coming?"

"The Three and one half years of The Great Tribulation prophesied in the Holy Bible will commence before the year 2016 ends."

"And then You are coming?"

"The Book of Daniel has been unsealed, My son."

"Unsealed?"

"Literally."

"I don't know, but this can't be."

"Literally, My son."

"Am I a false prophet?"

"I am The Spirit of Truth declaring all things to come, My son."

"This can't be it."

"This is it, My son."

"But all have failed to predict Your coming, and the coming of the false Messiah also. Why are you revealing to me these things? How do I know I'm not just another one in line about to make a fool of myself?"

"The Book of Daniel has been unsealed, My son."

"Alright fine, but that's it?"

"My sheep hear My voice, and I know them, and they follow Me" (John 10:27).

"Again with the sheep."

"My sheep receive from Me and declare all things boldly."

"Most wont handle all this: what do I tell them?"

"And you shall know the truth, and the truth shall make you free" (John 8:32).

"Is this truly You? Are You really talking to me? Are You really coming after this to establish Your Kingdom? Is this why You said,

"In this manner, therefore, pray:

Our Father in heaven,
Hallowed be Your name.
Your kingdom come.
Your will be done
On earth as *it is* in heaven.

Give us this day our daily bread.
And forgive us our debts,
As we forgive our debtors.
And do not lead us into temptation,
But deliver us from the evil one.
For Yours is the kingdom and the power and the glory forever.
Amen?" (Matthew 6:9-13).

"My Kingdom is at the door, My son."
"When?"
"Right after the end of the Great Tribulation."
"And the beginning again?"
"16."
"2016?"
"Yes, the beginning."
"And the end?"
"Just add three and one half years before 2016 ends."
"Why 2016 and not 2080, or 2038, or just...?"
"John 16, My son."
"Now?"
"Flip the pages. Hurry!"

# Chapter 65

# *John 16:*
# *The Alpha And The Omega*

## John 16, NKJV

T hese things I have spoken to you, that you should not be made to stumble. [2] They will put you out of the synagogues; yes, the time is coming that whoever kills you will think that he offers God service. [3] And these things they will do to you because they have not known the Father nor Me. [4] But these things I have told you, that when the time comes, you may remember that I told you of them.
And these things I did not say to you at the beginning, because I was with you.

## The Work of the Holy Spirit

[5] "But now I go away to Him who sent Me, and none of you asks Me, 'Where are You going?' [6] But because I have said these things to you, sorrow has filled your heart. [7] Nevertheless I tell you the truth. It is to your advantage that I go away; for if I do not go away, **the Helper** will not come to you; but if I depart, **I will send Him to you.** [8] **And when He has come, He will convict the world of sin, and of righteousness, and of judgment:** [9] of sin, because they do not believe in Me; [10] of righteousness, because I go to My Father and you see Me no more; [11] of judgment, because the ruler of this world is judged.
[12] "I still have many things to say to you, but you cannot bear *them* now. [13] However, **when He, the Spirit of truth, has come, He will guide you into all truth; for He will not speak on His own *authority,* but whatever He hears He will speak; and He will tell you things to come. [14] He will glorify Me, for He will take of what is Mine and declare *it* to you. [15] All things that the Father**

has are Mine. Therefore I said that He will take of Mine and declare *it* to you.

## Sorrow Will Turn to Joy

¹⁶ "A little while, and you will not see Me; and again a little while, and you will see Me, because I go to the Father."

¹⁷ Then *some* of His disciples said among themselves, "What is this that He says to us, 'A little while, and you will not see Me; and again a little while, and you will see Me'; and, 'because I go to the Father'?" ¹⁸ They said therefore, "What is this that He says, 'A little while'? We do not know what He is saying."

¹⁹ Now Jesus knew that they desired to ask Him, and He said to them, "Are you inquiring among yourselves about what I said, 'A little while, and you will not see Me; and again a little while, and you will see Me'? ²⁰ Most assuredly, I say to you that you will weep and lament, but the world will rejoice; and you will be sorrowful, but your sorrow will be turned into joy. ²¹ A woman, when she is in labor, has sorrow because her hour has come; but as soon as she has given birth to the child, she no longer remembers the anguish, for joy that a human being has been born into the world. ²² Therefore you now have sorrow; **but I will see you again and your heart will rejoice, and your joy no one will take from you.**

²³ "And in that day you will ask Me nothing. Most assuredly, I say to you, whatever you ask the Father in My name He will give you. ²⁴ Until now you have asked nothing in My name. Ask, and you will receive, that your joy may be full.

## Jesus Christ Has Overcome the World

²⁵ "These things I have spoken to you in figurative language; but the time is coming when I will no longer speak to you in figurative language, but I will tell you plainly about the Father. ²⁶ In that day you will ask in My name, and I do not say to you that I shall pray the Father for you; ²⁷ for the Father Himself loves you, because you have loved Me, and have believed that I came forth from God. ²⁸ I came forth from the

Father and have come into the world. Again, I leave the world and go to the Father."

²⁹ His disciples said to Him, "See, now You are speaking plainly, and using no figure of speech! ³⁰ Now we are sure that You know all things, and have no need that anyone should question You. By this we believe that You came forth from God."

³¹ Jesus answered them, "Do you now believe? ³² Indeed the hour is coming, yes, has now come, that you will be scattered, each to his own, and will leave Me alone. And yet I am not alone, because the Father is with Me.³³ These things I have spoken to you, that in Me you may have peace. **In the world you will have tribulation; but be of good cheer, I have overcome the world."**

## Speaking with The Voice of Truth Again

"My son!"

"Yes, Lord"

"Open your mouth for the speechless,

In the cause of all who are appointed to die" (Proverbs 31:8).

"O Lord, how?"

"My son."

"Yes, Lord."

"Open your mouth, judge righteously,

And plead the cause of the poor and needy" (Proverbs 31:9).

"But I'm not The Judge, my Lord. How? How?"

"My son!"

"Yes, Lord."

"I'm coming quickly!"

"Is it You? Are You...? Really?"

"My son."

"Yes, Lord."

"Rejoice always" (1 Thessalonians 5:16).

"Always?"

"Pray without ceasing" (1 Thessalonians 5:17).

"Without ceasing?"

"In everything give thanks; for this is the will of God in Christ Jesus for you" (1 Thessalonians 5:18).

"In Spirit and Truth?"

"Do not quench the Spirit" (1 Thessalonians 5:19).

"The Spirit of Truth?"

"Do not despise prophecies" (1 Thessalonians 5:20).

"Is this a prophecy?"

"Test all things; hold fast what is good" (1 Thessalonians 5:21).

"Should I hold on to this?"

"Whatever I tell you in the dark, speak in the light; and what you hear in the ear, preach on the housetops" (Matthew 10:27).

"Now?"

"Abstain from every form of evil" (1 Thessalonians 5:22).

"How?"

"Brethren, pray for us" (1 Thessalonians 5:25).

"Should I continue to write this epistle?"

"I charge you by the Lord that this epistle be read to all the holy brethren" (1 Thessalonians 5:27).

"You mean to the Thessalonian church?"

"I mean to the church in Philadelphia also" (Revelation 3:7).

"And only these two?"

"No, to all My little children—all people!"

"O Spirit of Truth, thank you!"

"In the past God overlooked such ignorance, but now he commands all people everywhere to repent" (Acts 17:30, NIV).

"And now we know the truth?"

"The Book of Daniel unsealed, My son."

"For me?"

"For all My little children!"

"O Voice of Truth!

"O Yeshua!

"Hallelujah!

"Praise JHWH all creation!

"Praise Him with all you got!

"Praise Him you sheep!

"Praise Him all you little children! Oh wait, wait; why am I praising You?"

"Because The Kingdom of Heaven is coming to Earth soon after."

"Your Kingdom? Our Kingdom!"

"I'm at the door!"

"Praise Him O Jerusalem! O Israel!

"Praise Him all tribes!

"Hallelujah! Hallelujah!

"Your Kingdom come!

"Your will be done!"

"I am the Alpha and the Omega, the Beginning and the End, the First and the Last" (Revelation 22:13).

"Hallelujah!!"

"I, *Yeshua*, have sent My angel to testify to you these things in the churches. I am the Root and the Offspring of David, the Bright and Morning Star" (Revelation 22:16).

"To testify to me?"

"To all!"

"To all?"

"I AM THE SPIRIT OF TRUTH."

"The Truth?"

"I AM THE VOICE OF TRUTH."

# *For More Information...*

To learn how to prepare for the times ahead; to learn about true salvation; to become part of the one man team and help spread righteousness, truth, love, and the warning of the soon to come judgment throughout the whole world; or to contact Marcial J. Ferreira, please write to:

Marcial J. Ferreira
P.O. Box 565218
Pinecrest, Florida 33256
USA

You can also communicate through the internet at contact@marcialferreira.org or visit Marcial's *Facebook* page (Marcial Ferreira) or visit the under construction website at www.marcialferreira.org.

# About the Author

No, Marcial is not a well-known pastor; he is not on TV; he is not preaching the message that tickles people's ears ("fabricated grace"), and he doesn't have money because he chose not to work for pay since April, 2014 to allow himself to write this book according to God's will. In fact, to publish this book, he had to sell the diamonds he gave to his wife—and many other things—for Mother's Day (mentioned in the book), which were supposed to be for a wedding ring. And he also received money from his brother-in-law, Dodanin, for the book cover.

The amazing news is that he is married to an spectacular woman that goes by the name of Bianka Ferreira, and he also has two loving sons, Brandon and Jonah. He loves them both equally even though Brandon came from another mother when Marcial was in the world and knew not his Savior—Yeshua Ha Mashiach. In fact, Marcial is a quitter. Yes, he had to quit from everything most people call success, and fight against his personal desires daily, to isolate himself and write this life saving book. The great news is that he is also a champion because some will comprehend *the big picture*, and take this message to heart and act, hopefully. He is one man attempting to do all he can to warn as many as possible from the soon to come judgment. And he believes that all must prepare for the near future, individually and united, especially those held responsible for their loved ones, as Yeshua said,

"Who then is a faithful and wise servant, whom his master made ruler over his household, to give them food in due season?  Blessed *is* that servant whom his master, when he comes, will find so doing.  Assuredly, I say to you that he will make him ruler over all his goods" (Matthew 24:45-47).

"By this all will know that you are My disciples, if you have love for one another" (John 13:35).

"Greater love has no one than this, than to lay down one's life for his friends" (John 15:13).

# References

Ames, Richard F. 2008. "Should Christians Keep the Sabbath?" *Tomorrow's World*. January-February . Accessed July 9, 2015. http://www.tomorrowsworld.org/magazines/2008/january-february/should-christians-keep-the-sabbath.

Cahn, Jonathan. 2012. *The Harbinger: The Ancient Mystery holds the Secret of America's Future.* Frontline Publishing Inc.

Horn, Thomas R. 2013. *Zenith 2106: Did Something Begin in the Year 2102 that will reach its Apex in 2016?* Defender .

Meredith, Roderick C. 2014. "Which Jesus Do You Worship." *Tomorrows World Magazine*, September-October: 7. Accessed November 10, 2014.

Montaigne, David. 2014. *Antichrist 2016-2019: Mystery Babylon, Barack Obama & the Islamic Caliphate* . CreateSpace Independent Publishing Platform.

*The Holy Bible: New King James Version.* 2006. Thomas Nelson.

—. 2014. *The Mystery of the Shemitah: The 3,000-Year-Old Mystery That Holds the Secret of America's Future, the World's Future, and Your Future!* Frontline Publishing Inc.

# Recommended Reading

Horn, Thomas and Cris D. Putnam. 2012. *Petrus Romanus: The Final Pope Is Here*. Defender.

Horn, Thomas. 2013. *Exo-Vaticana : Petrus Romanus, Project L.U.C.I.F.E.R. And the Vatican's Astonishing Plan for the Arrival of an Alien Savior* . Defender.

Shorey, John. 2013. *The Window of the Lord's Return: Are We the Tribulation Generation?* . HigherLife Publishing.

*The Holy Bible: New King James Version*. Thomas Nelson.

www.ingramcontent.com/pod-product-compliance
Lightning Source LLC
Chambersburg PA
CBHW032051090426
42744CB00005B/170